INTENTIONAL
Devotion

*A daily devotional plan for pursuing
God and praying for those you love*

HEATHER MCCASKILL

Contact information: intentionaldevotion@gmail.com

Additional copies of *Intentional Devotion* may be purchased at:
- www.amazon.com
- www.createspace.com/3912819
- other online retailers

"We may have as much of God as we will. Christ puts the key of the treasure-chamber into our hand, and bids us take all that we want. If a man is admitted into the bullion vault of a bank, and told to help himself, and comes out with one cent, whose fault is it that he is poor? Whose fault is it that Christian people generally have such scanty portions of the free riches of God?"[1]

–McLaren

Note from the author

I am an ordinary woman, perhaps just like you. I am the shopper who passes you in the aisle at the grocery store, the patient who sits beside you in the doctor's waiting room, or the stranger who reads the magazine you left behind after getting your hair cut. I could be your neighbor, your sister, your co-worker, or your friend. I am just an ordinary woman making her way through life, doing the best she can as a wife and mother to three boys. But this ordinary, middle-aged woman serves a very extraordinary God Who loves me, Who has a plan for my life that can be trusted, and Who delights when I come to Him. And this extraordinary God has taught me that even though I am just an ordinary woman, a closer walk with Him is not beyond my reach. And it's not beyond your reach either.

When I was in my early thirties, I began a quest to experience God personally and develop an intimacy with Him that went far beyond Sunday morning church attendance. Since that time, the Lord has taught me that a closer relationship with Him does not happen overnight. It comes day by day, month by month, year by year, as I intentionally seek His face and ask Him for more. It comes by consistently reading His Word every day and making it the standard for how I live my life. It comes by hiding His Word in my heart and learning to pray His very words back to Him. It comes through a willingness to obey His Word, no matter how humbling or difficult, if it brings me one step closer to Him. It comes – slowly but certainly – and definitely contingent on how much of my time and energy I put into it.

God is always there. He is always ready to speak. He is always ready to work on my behalf. And He is always ready to take me to the next level of intimacy with Him. Some days I make the time to receive what God has for me, but very honestly, some days I miss it. I oversleep, I over-schedule, or I simply just do not make room for Him in my day.

And when that happens, I get up the next morning, brush myself off, and "press on" - determined not to miss Him again.

So, this is a book of intention, written by an ordinary woman who daily strives to seek an extraordinary God and delights when she finds Him. It is my prayer that as you consistently seek the Lord, you will find Him too. He is there…ready and willing. So what are you waiting for?

Heather

How to use this book

This book is a daily devotional plan that incorporates all of the spiritual disciplines that have led me to a closer walk with the Lord:

- Reading God's Word every day, allowing Him time to speak.
- Receiving His Words as being spoken directly to me, in need of a response.
- Spending time in praise, confession and thanksgiving.
- Memorizing and meditating on a verse of Scripture every week.
- Making prayer a priority and learning to pray God's Word back to Him.
- Applying God's Word to my life as an act of obedience.

If I am not intentional about doing these things, they will not get done. If you are not intentional about doing these things, you will not achieve them either. Just as we need a calendar to keep up with all the events that fill our busy lives, so we need a schedule to help us stay on track with spiritual discipline. It is my desire that by using this book as a guide and determining to grow a little closer to the Lord every day, you will begin to experience Him in ways you never thought possible.

While planning this book, I asked the Lord to show me different areas where I needed to be spending time in prayer. I was amazed when I had more than 50 topics written down, and I am adding to the list all the time! Topics like freedom from worry, spiritual growth, wisdom in making decisions, protection for loved ones, self-control, and forgiveness. In using this book, one such topic will be the focus each week. At the beginning of each week, there will be a short story dealing with the week's topic. Every day you will be asked to read a short passage of Scripture, meditate on God's Word, and listen to what He has to say to you. Using the text as a guide, you will be prompted to spend time praising the Lord, confessing your sins before Him, and thanking Him for all His blessings. Then you will experience the joy of praying Scripture: Mondays – for yourself; Tuesdays – for your husband; Wednesdays – for your marriage or household; Thursdays – for your children; and Fridays – for your pastor, church, president or country. Saturdays will be days of application, and Sundays will be days of praise.

After each day's prayer there will be a few empty lines for you to use as a journal. This practice of journaling has become a habit that I highly value. It gives me a place to write down my own prayers to the Lord, to copy a verse of Scripture that I want to memorize, and to write out words of praise or thanksgiving. The very act of writing also keeps me from becoming distracted while I pray! It is always a joy to read back through my journals later on and see the very handprint of God across the pages.

Every week, you will be encouraged to memorize a verse or two of Scripture. Please don't skip this part! Yes, it will take a little extra time and discipline, but I have found that it dramatically transforms my prayer life. When I have God's Word hidden my heart, the Holy Spirit can bring it back to my mind when I need it most. For example, if my child wakes up afraid in the middle of the night, I can reassure him by praying II Timothy 1:7. "Lord, Your Word tells me that You do not give us a spirit of fear. Please remove any fear from my child and replace it with a spirit of power and of love and of sound mind." In learning to "plead the promises of God" our prayers take on power because we are praying His words, not our own.

So don't let one more day pass you by. Start being intentional with God and you will discover for yourself the truth of I Chronicles 28:9... if you seek Him, you will find Him!

Acknowlegments

To my husband Greg…Without your initial encouragement to write this book I never would have started. You believed in me when I didn't believe in myself, and for that, I am grateful. Thank you for the many pep talks along the way and for never letting me give up.

To my mother, Tanya Groves…Only a mother never tires of endless talk about a project! Thank you for your steadfast encouragement, for your enthusiasm in reading each completed lesson, for being willing to help in any way I asked, and for always being there for me.

To my dear friend, Kelly Ohlsson…Thank you for being that "intentional friend" – the one who has made the time and effort to maintain our close friendship for the past 30 years. Thank you for continually cheering me on in this endeavor and asking about my progress along the way.

To my cousin, Sheila Everett…Thank you for all your time and effort in the editing process. I truly appreciate your willingness to proof-read every single word of the original manuscript (and for all the lessons in rules of grammar and sentence structure!)

To my sister, Janna Vaughan, and each of you dear friends – Landis Melicks, Karen Woelke, Millie Gillis, Amy Barron, Cheri Holcomb, Angela Hynds, Deana Newbill, and Laurie Hendricks…Thank you for your prayers, encouragement and support!

To my three sons – Ian, Mitchell and Alec…Thank you for allowing me to share stories from each of your lives. I am so proud of each one of you, and I am grateful that God chose me to be your mother. "I have no greater joy than to hear that my children are walking in the truth" (III John 4).

And to my Lord and Savior Jesus Christ…I am continually amazed at Your faithfulness to me! From the moment You put the idea for this book on my heart, You have been faithful to reveal the next step at just the right time. You reminded me over and over again: "Now what I am commanding you today is not too difficult for you or beyond your reach" (Deuteronomy 30:11). Thank You for being faithful to see me through to the end. It is my prayer that You will be honored and glorified by every single word. I love You, Lord Jesus.

Order of Lessons

Week 1   Seeking God 13

Week 2   Inner Peace and Rest. 20

Week 3   Freedom from Worry 27

Week 4   Having a Servant's Heart 34

Week 5   The Power of our Words. 41

Week 6   Accepting Yourself as God Created You. 48

Week 7   Spiritual Growth 55

Week 8   Making Prayer a Priority. 62

Week 9   Waiting on God and Expecting Him to Work. 69

Week 10   Memorizing and Meditating on God's Word 76

Week 11   Patience. 83

Week 12   Being a Godly Example 90

Week 13   Cultivating Relationships 97

Week 14   Listening to God 104

Week 15   Protection 111

Week 16   Forgiveness. 118

Week 17   Developing a Craving for God 125

Week 18   Thought Life 132

Week 19   Trusting God. 139

Week 20   Rejoicing in the Lord 146

Week 21   Salvation 153

Week 22   Love for Others. 160

Week 23   Wisdom and Discernment. 167

Week 24   Self-Control. 174

Week 25   Confession and Cleansing from Sin 181

Week 26   Relying on God's Power for Strength. 188

Week 27   Purity and Holiness........................ 195
Week 28   Compassion and Mercy...................... 202
Week 29   Whatever You Do, Do It Well............... 209
Week 30   Contentment 216
Week 31   Kindness and Hospitality 223
Week 32   Obedience................................. 230
Week 33   Humility 237
Week 34   Turning Your Back on Sin.................. 244
Week 35   Unity, Not Division....................... 251
Week 36   Being Thankful 258
Week 37   Faith 265
Week 38   Yielding to God's Plan 272
Week 39   Doing the Right Thing 279
Week 40   Anger..................................... 286
Week 41   Being Honest and Trustworthy 293
Week 42   Wholehearted Love and Devotion to God 300
Week 43   Standing Up to Satan 307
Week 44   Generosity................................ 314
Week 45   Respect for Authority 321
Week 46   Transformed, Not Conformed................ 328
Week 47   Freedom from Fear 335
Week 48   Good Works 342
Week 49   Witnessing................................ 349
Week 50   Accepting Correction & Discipline 357
Week 51   Seeking God's Blessing 364
Week 52   Continuing in Him 371

Seeking God

"And you, my son Solomon, acknowledge the God of your father, and serve Him with wholehearted devotion and with a willing mind, for the Lord searches every heart and understands every motive behind the thoughts. If you seek Him, He will be found by you; but if you forsake Him, He will reject you forever"
(I Chronicles 28:9).

A DETERMINED WOMAN

When I was thirty years old I attended a Beth Moore Conference at the Pyramid in Memphis, TN. I had participated in several of Beth Moore's Bible studies through my church, and every time I heard her speak I was jealous of the relationship she had with the Lord. As I left the last session of that conference, my jealousy reached an all-time high. I knew the Lord as my personal Savior, but I wanted more...I wanted to know Him more intimately. The next morning I woke up early, a determined woman. I remember sitting on the floor in my den, with my hand on my unopened Bible repeatedly saying, "Lord, I want more of You... show me how to get it. Lord, I want more of You... show me how to get it." I began writing prayers in my journal for several weeks after that, focusing on the fact that I knew He alone was worthy of my time and confessing that I had not made Him my priority, had not given Him much of my time.

After a month of rising early, reading God's Word, and asking Him to show me how I could have a closer relationship with Him, I came across this verse in I Chronicles 28:9: "And you, my son Solomon, acknowledge the God of your father, and serve Him with wholehearted devotion and with a willing mind, for the Lord searches every heart and understands every motive behind the thoughts. If you seek Him,

He will be found by you; but if you forsake Him, He will reject you forever." God spoke these words directly to my heart, showing me that it was His will for me to know Him more intimately, but it was up to me to seek Him more fully. He wanted me to acknowledge Him as the One True God, Who alone deserved my wholehearted devotion. He didn't want access to just part of my life, or to the parts with which I was comfortable…He wanted all of my life! And that meant having a mind that was willing for Him to teach, rebuke, correct and train, even when it was uncomfortable and painful.

A similar passage in Deuteronomy 4:29 says, "But if from there you seek the Lord your God, you will find Him if you look for Him with all your heart and with all your soul." In that passage of Scripture, "from there" was a life of sin – disobedience to God's command and even worshiping idols. Even "from there" God will hear us if we return to Him and seek Him wholeheartedly. I started praying these verses daily, clinging to the promise that if I seek Him I WILL find Him. He is true to His Word. God began to allow me glimpses of Him and His hand on my life. As I sought Him wholeheartedly with a willing mind, He did indeed search my heart and my motives, revealing sin in my life that needed to be confessed and repented of. As I began to allow Him full access to my life, He could then begin to reveal Himself to me in new and wonderful ways.

A closer walk with God is not beyond your reach. No matter where you are, "from there" God is ready and waiting for you to take the first step toward intimacy with Him. Start seeking Him today.

Memory Verse:
"If you seek Him, He will be found by you; but if you forsake Him, He will reject you forever" (I Chronicles 28:9b).

MONDAY: Read I Chronicles 28:1-10. Meditate on God's Word and listen to what He has to say to you. Using the text as a guide, spend time in praise, confession and thanksgiving.

Pray for yourself, asking God for a closer walk with Him: Oh how I praise You, Oh God! How amazing that You, the Lord God Almighty, would not only allow me to have a personal relationship with You, **but that You would desire it!** Forgive me for neglecting You.... forgive me for my tendency to place other things ahead of You. You alone are worthy of my time and my devotion. I truly want to serve You "with wholehearted devotion and with a willing mind" (I Chronicles 28:9a). So I open my heart to Your examination, asking You to search my heart and reveal the true motive behind my thoughts (I Chronicles 28:9b). Show me areas of my life that are not pleasing to You, or that hinder my relationship with You, so that those barriers to intimacy with You can be destroyed. Oh, how I long for a closer walk with You! I cling to Your promise that if I seek You, I will find You (I Chronicles 28:9c). Thank You that I can trust You to do what You say You will do. Now, as "I have sought Your face with all my heart; be gracious to me according to Your promise" (Psalm 119:58).

JOURNAL: _____

_____

_____

TUESDAY: Read Psalm 105:1-7. Meditate on God's Word and listen to what He has to say to you. Using the text as a guide, spend time in praise, confession and thanksgiving.

Pray for your husband, that he will have a desire to seek God: Oh Father, I thank You for my dear husband, the partner You have given me on this earth. As much as I long for a closer walk with You for myself, I long for it for my husband as well. So I pray that he would have the desire to seek You in every aspect of his life...in his personal Christian walk, in his work, and in his role as husband and father. Your Word teaches that he is to be the spiritual leader of our home, and in order to do that he must seek Your face daily. Please give my husband a burden to pursue the spiritual disciplines of reading Your Word, making application of it, hiding it in his heart, and searching it for wisdom in every decision he must make. May he look to You and Your strength, seeking

Your face always (Psalm 105:4). And as You reveal Yourself to him, I pray that he would respond in obedience. Your blessings await… May he seek You and delight himself in You, so that You will give him the desires of his heart (Psalm 37:4).

JOURNAL: _____

_____

_____

—————◦◦◦◦◦—————

WEDNESDAY: Read Jeremiah 29:4-14. Meditate on God's Word and listen to what He has to say to you. Using the text as a guide, spend time in praise, confession and thanksgiving.

Pray for those in your household, that you would seek the Lord together and experience all the wonderful plans He has for your family: Oh Lord, I praise You as the Lord Almighty, the One Who created us, Who knows us inside and out, and Who can be trusted. What wonderful promises are contained in this passage of Scripture! Thank You, Lord Jesus, that You have plans to prosper our family, and not to harm us, plans to give us hope and a future. Thank You that when we call upon You and come and pray to You, You promise to listen to us. And thank You that when we seek You with all our hearts, we will find You (Jeremiah 29:11-13). As my husband and I make a life for ourselves, settle down, have children, and increase in number (Jeremiah 29:5-6), may we not miss out on a single thing You have planned for us because we were too busy to make time for You. I pray that we would make our family devotions and prayer times together a priority, continually leading our family to seek Your face and Your Presence. Finally, may we be content to seek peace in our marriage and prosperity for our family in the exact place You have planted us (Jeremiah 29:7).

JOURNAL: _____

_____

_____

—————◦◦◦◦◦—————

THURSDAY: Read Matthew 7:7-12. Meditate on God's Word and listen to what He has to say to you. Using the text as a guide, spend time in praise, confession and thanksgiving.

Pray for your children, that they would seek God, not the things of this world: Lord, our culture today entices the flesh to seek after worldly things… things like fame, fortune, and self-focus. But this is a direct contradiction to what You said about seeking first the kingdom of God and His righteousness (Matthew 6:33). Oh, how I pray that my children would listen to You and not to this world! Your Word says, "Ask and it will be given to you; seek and you will find; knock and the door will be opened to you. For everyone who asks receives; he who seeks finds; and to him who knocks, the door will be opened" (Matthew 7:7-8). May my children learn to seek Your face and experience the thrill of finding God Himself! Even when the path is dark and the way before them is uncertain, may they search hard for You, not giving up until they find You (II Timothy 1:17). I rest in Your Word that reminds me: "If you, then, though you are evil, know how to give good gifts to your children, how much more will your Father in heaven give good gifts to those who ask Him!" (Matthew 7:11). Please Lord, give them the gift of intimacy with You!

JOURNAL: _____

_____

_____

FRIDAY: Read II Chronicles 7:11-22. Meditate on God's Word and listen to what He has to say to you. Using the text as a guide, spend time in praise, confession and thanksgiving.

Pray for your country, to be humble and seek God: Heavenly Father, I thank You for this country – the land of the free and the home of the brave. I thank You that this nation was founded on You and Your principles, and that You have blessed us in so many ways. But Lord we know we have failed You… we have turned away and forsaken the decrees and commands You have given us. We have served other gods and worshipped them (II Chronicles 7:19). Please forgive us, dear Lord, and turn our hearts back to You. I claim Your Word in II Chronicles 7:14 that says,

"If my people, who are called by my name, will humble themselves and pray and seek my face and turn from their wicked ways, then will I hear from heaven and will forgive their sin and will heal their land." So I pray that we would humble ourselves and seek Your face, turning from sin, so that You will hear, forgive, and bring healing. Your Word tells us that, "The Lord is good to those whose hope is in Him, to the one who seeks Him" (Lamentations 3:25). May we not wait another day, but seek You while You may be found; call on You while You are near (Isaiah 55:6).

JOURNAL: _____

_____

_____

SATURDAY: A Day of Application

Read Deuteronomy 4:25-31.

Deuteronomy 4:29 says, "But if <u>from there</u> you seek the Lord you God, you will find Him if you look for Him with all your heart and with all your soul." "From there" is anywhere you find yourself... It can be a life of sin, a life of complacency about your relationship with God, a life of disobedience, etc. Where do you find yourself today?

_____

_____

Thank the Lord for His promise that "if you seek Him, you will find Him!"

II Chronicles 15:12 says, "They entered into a covenant to seek the Lord, the God of their fathers, with all their heart and soul." Determine to start seeking the Lord for yourself. Write out your prayer of commitment here:

_____

_____

SUNDAY: A Day of Praise

Read Psalm 139:7-12.

Praise God that He is Jehovah Shammah - The Lord is There. This name promises His Presence...He will meet us where we are.

WRITE OUT YOUR PRAYER OF PRAISE :

_____

_____

CHECK YOURSELF! WRITE YOUR MEMORY VERSE HERE:

_____

_____

Inner Peace and Rest

"Come to Me, all you who are weary and burdened, and I will give you rest. Take My yoke upon you and learn from Me, for I am gentle and humble in heart, and you will find rest for your souls. For My yoke is easy and my burden is light" (Matthew 11:28-30).

IDENTITY CRISIS!

The year 2009 was somewhat of a turning point for me. I celebrated my 40th birthday and joined the ranks of the "middle-aged." My oldest son Ian turned eleven, entering middle school and the second decade of his life. And my youngest son Alec started kindergarten, leaving me at home alone with an empty nest and a sad heart. Where had the toddler and preschool days gone? Instead of my usual excitement on the first day of school, I found myself in tears. My baby no longer needed me, and after being home for 11 years, I found myself wondering, "Now what? What am I supposed to do now, God?"

After crying on my husband's shoulder, I tried to get busy. Busy at home, busy at school, and busy at church. But in all my "busy-ness" I couldn't seem to get away from an unsettled feeling that I needed to be doing something else. My uneasiness doubled when several well meaning people asked what I was going to do now that all my kids were in school. I took each question as a personal affront that I wasn't already doing enough. So I started looking into going back to school to get another degree or finding a job outside the home. But each option had its drawbacks...going back to school would cost money...finding a full time job would be overwhelming in addition to the responsibilities I already had at home, church and school.

After weeks of restlessness I finally got still enough to allow the Lord to speak to me. I opened my favorite devotional book <u>Jesus Calling</u> where the author, Sarah Young, shares the way the Lord has spoken to her through His Word. The words washed over me: *"Wait with Me for awhile. I have much to tell you. You are walking along the path I have chosen for you...Do not worry about what other people think of you. The work I am doing in you is hidden at first. But eventually blossoms will burst forth and abundant fruit will be borne. Stay on the path of Life with Me. Trust me wholeheartedly, letting My Spirit fill you with Joy and Peace."*[2] The Lord used those words to speak directly to my soul, reminding me of His very real Presence, of His control of every day of my life, that His plan for me would bring forth fruit, and that I could simply rest in the present. Such clarity, acceptance, relief and peace washed over me!

Jesus said, "Come to Me, all you who are weary and burdened, and I will give you rest. Take My yoke upon you and learn from Me, for I am gentle and humble in heart, and you will find rest for your souls. For My yoke is easy and my burden is light" (Matthew 11:28-30). I had been spending way too much time wondering what other people might think of me, and not nearly enough time asking God what He already had planned for me! I was allowing myself to be burdened with uncertainty and robbed of the peace that God promises in spite of circumstances. I was trying to hurry things along, instead of allowing God the time to reveal His "easy" plan one step at a time in a way that I could handle.

When I rose from my "quiet time chair" that morning, I had no more certainty of the future than I did before I sat down. But I was completely at peace just knowing that God did!

Memory Verse:

"Come to Me, all you who are weary and burdened, and I will give you rest" (Matthew 11:28).

MONDAY: Read Matthew 11:28-30 first, then read Jeremiah 6:16. Meditate on God's Word and listen to what He has to say to you. Using the text as a guide, spend time in praise, confession and thanksgiving.

Pray for yourself, to turn to God for rest and peace: Lord Jesus, in reading these two passages it is clear that I have a choice to make when I feel weary and burdened. I can come to You, choosing to walk in the good way and find rest for my soul; or, I can stubbornly refuse the peace You freely offer, pridefully declaring I "will not walk in it" (Jeremiah 6:16)! Forgive me, Father, when I determine to cling to anxiety, fear, self-pity or hopelessness rather than take hold of the rest that is right before me. I am fully aware that it is a control issue, and as an act of my will I submit it to You, asking You to help me release my tight grip. May I throw off the unnecessary burdens in my life that either I have placed on myself or allowed others to place on me. You say that Your "yoke is easy and [Your] burden is light" (Matthew 11:30) – and that is all that I want to carry! Please help me keep my eyes fixed on You, so as not to pick up these burdens again. And thank you for the standing offer to come to You with the promise of rest.

JOURNAL: _____

_____

_____

———————

TUESDAY: Read Psalm 62:1-8. Meditate on God's Word and listen to what He has to say to you. Using the text as a guide, spend time in praise, confession and thanksgiving.

Pray for your husband, to look to God for rest: Father, I praise You today as my Rock, my Fortress, my Salvation, and my Rest! It is such a comfort to know that just as You gave rest to King David when faced with difficulty, so You promise Your rest to my husband when he turns to You in times of trouble. May he learn to say as David did, "My soul finds rest in God alone; my salvation comes from Him" (Psalm 62:1).

When my husband is overwhelmed by his responsibilities, I pray that You would step in to carry his burdens for him. When he feels alone or uncertain, please turn his thoughts toward You and fill him with Your Presence. When his mind is swirling with a multitude of things to do, please bring clarity and focus to his schedule, proving that You are not "a God of disorder but of peace" (I Corinthians 14:33). And when my husband feels like Job who said: "I have no peace, no quietness; I have no rest, but only turmoil" (Job 3:26), please prompt me to intercede on his behalf. I pray that he would learn to trust in You at all times; pour out his heart to You, for You are his refuge (Psalm 62:8).

JOURNAL: _____

_____

_____

⎯⎯⎯⎯⎯⎯

WEDNESDAY: Read Hebrews 4:1-11. Meditate on God's Word and listen to what He has to say to you. Using the text as a guide, spend time in praise, confession and thanksgiving.

Pray for those in your household, to enter into God's rest: Father God, thank You that we do not have to wait until we get to heaven to enjoy Your rest and peace…You offer it to all today through faith in Christ Jesus Your Son! I pray that not a single person in my home would miss this privilege because of disobedience or a lack of faith. May my husband and I be living examples before our children of lives lived in rest and dependence on You. Please remind us to carefully observe the Sabbath-rest You instituted, "for anyone who enters God's rest also rests from his own work, just as God did from His" (Hebrews 4:10). May we be careful to "make every effort to enter that rest" on a daily basis, knowing that as believers, our eternity with You is secure. I pray that Your peace "which transcends all understanding" (Philippians 4:7) would pervade our home and be felt by the entire family. Thank You for the perfect home of peace You are preparing for us in heaven! And may we "live in peaceful dwelling places, in secure homes, in undisturbed places of rest" (Isaiah 32:18) for the remainder of our days on this earth.

JOURNAL: _____

_____

_____

———⊰⊷⊰⊷———

THURSDAY: Read Isaiah 54:10-13. Meditate on God's Word and listen to what He has to say to you. Using the text as a guide, spend time in praise, confession and thanksgiving.

Pray for your children, to experience God's rest as they walk through the storms of life: Lord Jesus, what comfort Your Words bring to me as a parent! "Though the mountains be shaken and the hills be removed, yet My unfailing love for you will not be shaken nor My covenant of peace be removed" (Isaiah 54:10). May I constantly remind my children that no matter what happens in this life, You promise Your love and peace to them! When they are lashed by storms and feel no comfort, You are in the process of building beautiful character in them that will shine like sparkling jewels and precious stones. I cling to Your Word that says, "All your sons will be taught by the Lord, and great will be your children's peace" (Isaiah 54:13). May my children submit to Your teaching and be blessed with the rest You offer. Please keep me sensitive to what is going on in each of their lives, taking the time to ask questions when I sense that something is bothering them. I pray that You would fill my children with "all joy and peace" as they trust in You, so that they will "overflow with hope by the power of the Holy Spirit" (Romans 15:13).

JOURNAL: _____

_____

_____

———⊰⊷⊰⊷———

FRIDAY: Read John 14:26-31. Meditate on God's Word and listen to what He has to say to you. Using the text as a guide, spend time in praise, confession and thanksgiving.

Pray for your church, to listen to the Holy Spirit Who reminds us that we can have God's peace: Lord Jesus, what a scary time it must have been for the disciples when You told them that You were going away. They thought that they would be left all alone, not yet understanding the precious gift of the indwelling Holy Spirit. Thank You so much that as believers today, we are not alone! May Your precious Holy Spirit be as real in my church as You were to the disciples, constantly teaching us all things and reminding us of everything You said (John 14:26). Thank You, Lord Jesus, that before You returned to the Father You left a wonderful gift: "Peace I leave with you; my peace I give you. I do not give as the world gives. Do not let your hearts be troubled and do not be afraid" (John 14:27). The gift of peace truly is priceless... it cannot be purchased, only received. And without it, we have only unrest, uncertainty, and fear. So I claim Your Word for my church: "The Lord gives strength to His people; the Lord blesses His people with peace" (Psalm 29:11). May the peace You grant us turn a lost world to seek You.

JOURNAL: _____

_____

_____

SATURDAY: A Day of Application

Read Isaiah 26:1-4.

Name one area where you lack peace/rest:

_____

Ask the Lord to forgive you for refusing to trust Him in this area:

_____

_____

Give this matter to the Lord and receive His perfect peace! "You will keep in perfect peace him whose mind is steadfast, because he trusts in You" (Isaiah 26:3).

Write out your prayer here:

_____

_____

SUNDAY: A Day of Praise

Read Isaiah 9:6-7, 53:5

Praise God that He is the Prince of Peace!

WRITE OUT YOUR PRAYER OF PRAISE HERE:

_____

_____

_____

CHECK YOURSELF! WRITE YOUR MEMORY VERSE HERE:

_____

_____

Freedom from Worry

"Therefore I tell you, do not worry about your life, what you will eat or drink; or about your body, what you will wear. Who of you by worrying can add a single hour to his life? But seek first His kingdom and His righteousness, and all these things will be given to you as well. Therefore do not worry about tomorrow, for tomorrow will worry about itself. Each day has enough trouble of its own" (Matthew 6:25, 27, 33-34).

WHAT A WASTE OF TIME!

One of the necessities in life that I sometimes see as a total waste of time is getting myself ready for the day... "You mean I have to shower again, wash my hair again, put on makeup again, decide what to wear again?" The nun's habit is quite appealing on some days...just throw it on without another thought. George Jetson's wife Jane had a mask she could grab when someone called before she had her hair and makeup done...where can I get one of those? The ponytail is an easy hair option when I am short on time, or the baseball cap when I'm desperate! I'm sure my family is glad that I haven't abandoned personal hygiene yet, but it is most appealing on busy days when I have seemingly more important things to do. You might see another one of your daily tasks as a waste of time, things like cleaning up the kitchen when it is just going to be dirty again, or making up your bed when you are just going to get back in it.

But a big way that we all waste time at some point or another is through worry. Scripture says: "Who of you by worrying can add a single hour to his life?" (Matthew 6:27). And it is so true... All the days ordained for us were written in God's book before a single one of them came to pass

(Psalm 139:16). Each one of us only has a predetermined number of days on this earth, and no amount of worry will change that! We were meant to spend each of our days fulfilling the purposes God has for us, not worrying about things that may never come to pass. We cannot allow worry, stress, or uncertainty to rob us of valuable time we should be using in other ways. When we allow our minds to go over and over a troubling or difficult situation instead of lifting the issue up in prayer, we are wasting our time. When we rehearse in our minds a criticism or unkind word spoken to us, instead of claiming the truth, we are wasting our time. When we fret and stew about an unknown future event that might not even happen, we are wasting our time!

Every once in a while I'll start worrying, usually about my kids, and say something to my husband like, "What will we do if our boys grow up and _____ (do drugs/never come see us/turn their backs on God?) My husband's gentle rebuke is always the same: "So you think we should go ahead and start worrying about it now?" Not only are thoughts like these a waste of time, they are sin and can easily become a stronghold in our lives.

"Therefore, do not worry about tomorrow, for tomorrow will worry about itself. Each day has enough trouble of its own" (Matthew 6:34). So quit wasting time with worry! Put on your ball cap and get on your knees, committing your concerns to the only One Who can do anything about them.

Memory Verse:

"Therefore do not worry about tomorrow, for tomorrow will worry about itself. Each day has enough trouble of its own" (Matthew 6:34).

MONDAY: Read Matthew 6:25-34. Meditate on God's Word and listen to what He has to say to you. Using the text as a guide, spend time in praise, confession and thanksgiving.

Pray for yourself, asking God for freedom from worry: Oh Lord, I praise You today, acknowledging that You are Sovereign and in control of everything that will cross my path today, tomorrow, and every day in the future. Thank You that Your Word assures me that I am valuable to You and that I do not need to worry about my life or my body (Matthew 6:25). Just as You feed the birds of the air and dress the flowers in the field, You will supply all my needs according to Your glorious riches in Christ Jesus (Philippians 4:19). I ask You to "search me, O God, and know my heart; test me and know my anxious thoughts. See if there is any offensive way in me, and lead me in the way everlasting" (Psalm 139:23-24). Please help me to "take captive every thought to make it obedient to Christ" (II Corinthians 10:5), turning my back on the sin of worry. Thank You God, that Your Word promises me Your peace that passes all understanding when I turn my concerns over to You through prayer, supplication and thanksgiving (Philippians 4:6-7).

JOURNAL: _____

_____

_____

TUESDAY: Read Colossians 3:1-4. Meditate on God's Word and listen to what He has to say to you. Using the text as a guide, spend time in praise, confession and thanksgiving.

Pray for your husband, to turn his back on worry and turn his heart toward Christ: Oh Father, Your Word says that "an anxious heart weighs a man down" (Proverbs 12:25). When my husband begins to worry about earthly things like problems at work, mounting bills, uncertainty about the future, or even just the day's irritations, I pray that You would prompt him to fill his thoughts with Christ instead. I know it is not Your will for his life to be full of stress, but to be filled with Your peace, so remind my husband to purposely set his "mind on things above, not on earthly things" (Colossians 3:2). May You even give him the vision of being seated with Christ at Your right hand, experiencing the support and companionship that You offer. Remind him that You are in control, and that You are with him always (Matthew 28:20), every minute of every day. How wonderful to know that nothing is too big or too little for You to handle! Thank You that we can cast our cares on You and You will sustain us; You will never let the righteous fall (Psalm 55:22).

JOURNAL: _____

_____

_____

WEDNESDAY: Read Hebrews 12:1-3. Meditate on God's Word and listen to what He has to say to you. Using the text as a guide, spend time in praise, confession and thanksgiving.

Pray for those in your household, to remind each other to trust in the Lord and commit all things to Him: Thank you Lord that my husband and I do not have to worry about our family. We do not have to spend our days worrying about how to make ends meet, or our nights sleeplessly wondering how to raise our children. You are the head of this household, and You will take care of us! Please help us keep our eyes fixed and focused on You (Hebrews 12:2) day by day, refusing to become entangled in the cares of this world. When troubles come across our path, and fear threatens to overwhelm us, remind us to consider Him (Jesus Christ) who endured opposition from this world, so that we will not grow weary and lose heart (Hebrews 12:3). Prepare us now so that when disaster strikes, we would not turn our backs on You, but turn our faces toward You in search of Your very sure strength and help. May we experience Your comfort like the psalmist did who said, "When anxiety was great within me, Your consolation brought joy to my soul" (Psalm 94:19).

JOURNAL: _____

_____

_____

THURSDAY: Read Psalm 23. Meditate on God's Word and listen to what He has to say to you. Using the text as a guide, spend time in praise, confession and thanksgiving.

Pray for your children, to look to the Lord when they are worried: I praise You, Lord Jesus, that with You as our Shepherd we will not want for anything (Psalm 23:1)! Your Word says that You are able to make us lie down in green pastures and lead us beside quiet waters (Psalm 23:2). Thank You that it is not Your plan for my children to be full of worry and the cares of this world, but for them to experience Your rest and tranquility in every situation. If anything is worrisome for them today, I pray that they would feel comfortable discussing it with me so that I can pray for them. May I take the time to ask about their concerns and to show them that I care. It is reassuring to me as a parent to read the words of the psalmist who proclaimed: "I will fear no evil, for you are with me" (Psalm 23:4). How I pray that my children would grasp that You are with them at every moment of their day. In fact, there is nowhere they can go that You will not be present! No matter where they are, "even there Your hand will guide [them], Your right hand hold [them] fast" (Psalm 139:10). And may that knowledge alleviate any worries they might have.

JOURNAL: _____

_____

_____

FRIDAY: Read Psalm 8:3-9. Meditate on God's Word and listen to what He has to say to you. Using the text as a guide, spend time in praise, confession and thanksgiving.

Pray for the President of your country, to understand that God is waiting to help him with every concern: "O Lord, our Lord, how majestic is Your name in all the earth!" (Psalm 8:1). I praise You today that You, the very One Who created the heavens, the moon and the stars is mindful of each one of us and that You care for us (Psalm 8:4). How I pray for our President, the one You have placed in a position of authority to rule over our country. May he know this wonderful truth from Your Word, that You are "mindful of him," always ready and waiting to help in his time of need. What an important role he has, heavy with responsibility. Unemployment, national debt, foreign relations, homeland security and the stability of the economy...I pray that he would not drown under the weight of these issues, but turn to You for guidance in each one of them. May he recognize Your lordship and acknowledge Your sovereignty over this land. And please Lord, surround him with godly men and women who will remind him to cast all his anxiety on You because You care for him (I Peter 5:7).

JOURNAL: _____

_____

_____

SATURDAY: A Day of Application

Read Philippians 4:4-9.

Write down your biggest problem or cause for concern this week:

_____

_____

Are you trusting the Lord with this situation or are you worrying about it endlessly?

_____

_____

Claim Philippians 4:6-7 over this situation: Lord, Your Word says that I do not need to be anxious about _____ _____, but in everything, by prayer and petition, with thanksgiving, to present it to You. So I give this issue to You, asking You to work, and thanking You in advance for what You are going to do. I claim this verse as Your Word to me, exchanging my worry for Your peace.

"Rejoice in the Lord always. I will say it again: Rejoice!" (Philippians 4:4). Take a moment to rejoice that God loves you and is there for you anytime you need Him:

_____

_____

SUNDAY: A Day of Praise

Read Psalm 47:1-9.

Praise God that He is Sovereign: holding the position of ruler, royal, reigning; independent of all others; above or superior to all others; controlling everything, able to do anything.

WRITE OUT YOUR PRAYER OF PRAISE HERE:

_____

_____

CHECK YOURSELF! WRITE YOUR MEMORY VERSE HERE:

_____

_____

Having a Servant's Heart

"Serve wholeheartedly, as if you were serving the Lord, not men, because you know that the Lord will reward everyone for whatever good he does, whether he is slave or free"
(Ephesians 6:7-8).

MAKING TEA IS SUCH A SMALL THING

One of my heroes in the faith is Corrie Ten Boom. Many are familiar with her book The Hiding Place, in which she chronicles her life in Holland during Nazi occupation. Her family made it their mission to hide Jews who were in danger of losing their lives, and as a result, she was imprisoned and put in a concentration camp. For the latter part of her life, Ms. Ten Boom traveled the world, serving the Lord and telling others about Him. She finished her life in Haarlem, Holland, where a woman named Pamela Rosewell was her companion. After Ms. Ten Boom's death, Mrs. Rosewell wrote a book in her honor called The Five Silent Years of Corrie Ten Boom. Even during the difficult years at the end of her life when she could no longer speak, Ms. Ten Boom continued with her work for the Lord and acts of service for others.

In her book, Mrs. Rosewell recounts her own struggle of living a life of continual service. One of her many duties included receiving all the visitors who came to Ms. Ten Boom's home every day. With each visit, Mrs. Rosewell was responsible for acting as "hostess".... greeting the visitor at the door, making sure he was comfortably seated, and serving tea to Ms. Ten Boom and her guest. Finally one day, Mrs. Rosewell confessed that she was not entirely happy in her role and asked Ms. Ten Boom to stop accepting so many visitors. When Ms. Ten Boom asked the reason why, Mrs. Rosewell gave an honest reply: "I feel overwhelmed by all these people. We never have any private life. I don't love them the way you do…and I spend half my life making tea." I have never forgotten Ms. Ten Boom's quiet response: "Pam, making tea is such a small thing."[3]

I can so relate to the frustration that Mrs. Rosewell was experiencing, can't you? The chores of daily life for women in their service to others sometimes seem to never end...making beds, preparing meals, cleaning up after meals, packing lunches, cleaning the house, doing laundry, ironing clothes, shopping for groceries, and on and on and on. Making sure everybody has what they need and when they need it is exhausting work! I love being a wife and mother and want to serve my family well, but when the duties pile up and the service seems endless, it is easy to feel overwhelmed and allow a negative attitude to fill my heart. Add just one more thing, "a small thing" like making tea, and I am ready to throw in the towel. (Maybe if I went ahead and threw the towel in the washing machine that would be one less thing to do later!)

Ephesians 6:7 is a gentle reminder for us: "Serve wholeheartedly, as if you were serving the Lord, not men." I have this verse written on a sticky note on my refrigerator where I will see it often. Long ago memorized, these words of the Lord speak gently to my heart whenever my frustration begins to build and my service to others is performed out of resentment instead of love. When I look at the task ahead of me, envisioning that I am doing it for the Lord Himself, the Ultimate Servant, it always changes my motivation and my attitude.

———

Memory Verse:
"Serve wholeheartedly, as if you were serving the Lord, not men"
(Ephesians 6:7).

———

MONDAY: Read John 13:1-16. Meditate on God's Word and listen to what He has to say to you. Using the text as a guide, spend time in praise, confession and thanksgiving.

Pray for yourself, that you would willingly serve others as Jesus did: You really do amaze me, Lord Jesus. You, Who "knew that the Father had put all things under [Your] power…poured water into a basin and began to wash [Your] disciples' feet" (John 13:3&5). Wow, what an example of a servant! If I knew that God Himself had put all things under my power, I think it would have fed my pride, not motivated me to an act of service. But in order to reveal the full extent of Your love for Your children, You humbly performed one of the most menial tasks of all time. Please forgive me Lord when I go about my tasks begrudgingly rather than lovingly. You ask nothing of me that You were not willing to do Yourself. Show me where I need to improve in this matter. Lay a task on my heart that I can do for someone else today. And even if it is to wash his feet, may I do it as if I were serving You, and not man (Ephesians 6:7). You promise that we will be blessed if we do for others the things You have done for us (John 13:17). May I not miss out on Your blessing because of my own pride or selfishness.

JOURNAL: _____

_____

_____

TUESDAY: Read Matthew 20:20-28. Meditate on God's Word and listen to what He has to say to you. Using the text as a guide, spend time in praise, confession and thanksgiving.

Pray for your husband, asking God to help him be servant minded: Oh Father, it is incredible to think that You sent Your Son to this earth not just to rule, but to serve: "the Son of Man did not come to be served, but to serve" (Matthew 20:28). And as You have placed my husband in the position of leading our household, may he follow Your example of service to others too. I pray that he would find great joy in serving and that in fact, it would bring him even more satisfaction than having others wait on him! Thank you for the ways I already see him serving, and may he be motivated to continue…helping out at home by pitching in with daily chores, doing more at work than is even required, and going the extra mile to serve where needed at church. Your Word says that "whoever wants to become great among you must be your servant, and whoever wants to be first must be your slave" (Matthew 20:26-27). At the end of each day, I pray that my husband will be able to stand as one who has served well, gaining an excellent standing and great assurance in his faith in Christ Jesus (I Timothy 3:13).

JOURNAL: _____

_____

_____

WEDNESDAY: Read Joshua 24:1-15. Meditate on God's Word and listen to what He has to say to you. Using the text as a guide, spend time in praise, confession and thanksgiving.

Pray for your household, that all those within will serve the Lord willingly: Father God, I thank you for this reminder from history of why we should serve You and You alone...because You have proven Your worthiness and faithfulness to Your people time after time. Just as You commanded the Israelites to throw away any other gods and serve only You, so You command every household today to do the same. Whether we are aware of it consciously or not, we do in fact make a choice either for You, or against You. As Joshua declared before the tribes of Israel, so may my husband and I firmly declare, "But as for me and my household, we will serve the Lord" (Joshua 24:15b). We must not just say it with our lips, but demonstrate by our actions that we are willing to serve You and others in any way that You ask. May we prove that we serve You by serving one another in our marriage, always putting the needs of the other before our own. And I pray that each member of our family would be willing to "use whatever gift he has received to serve others, faithfully administering God's grace in its various forms" (I Peter 4:10).

JOURNAL: _____

_____

_____

THURSDAY: Read Matthew 25:14-30. Meditate on God's Word and listen to what He has to say to you. Using the text as a guide, spend time in praise, confession and thanksgiving.

Pray for your children, that they would learn to be good and faithful servants: Father, I understand that this parable describes two differing attitudes toward Christ's return. We can use the time, gifts and resources that You have given us to invest them in serving You, or we can make excuses and avoid doing what You ask of us. How I pray that my children would have the desire to use whatever You give them in service toward others! I know that even serving is a learned quality... so the more my children see me doing it, the more likely they will learn by my example. Remind me to take the time to include them when I serve, and please give me the patience to let them help. Show me an act of service that we can do together this week. And when I see them "serve one another in love" (Galatians 5:13b), may I be the first one to compliment them. I pray that they would receive joy from serving and be motivated to do even more as the day of Your return approaches. May they hear Your words of encouragement whispered to their hearts, "Well done, good and faithful servant" (Matthew 25:21)!

JOURNAL: _____

_____

_____

———

FRIDAY: Read Deuteronomy 10:12-22. Meditate on God's Word and listen to what He has to say to you. Using the text as a guide, spend time in praise, confession and thanksgiving.

Pray for your pastor, not to falter in his service but to depend on God's strength: Lord Jesus, I am sure that my pastor feels overwhelmed at times with all of the needs of his congregation. When he feels tired and weak, may he remember that You are there, ready and waiting to help! Then he can serve with the strength that You provide, so that in all things You may be praised (I Peter 4:11b). Remind him that You are not unjust; You will not forget his work and the love he has shown You as he has helped Your people and continues to help them (Hebrews 6:10). Please bless him today as he gives of himself in service to those in our church. I pray that my pastor would fear You, the Lord his God, walk in all Your ways, love You, serve You with all his heart and with all his soul, and observe Your commands (Deuteronomy 10:12-13). May he earn a reputation like that of Hezekiah in the Old Testament: "In everything that he undertook in the service of God's temple and in obedience to the law and the commands, he sought his God and worked wholeheartedly. And so he prospered." (II Chronicles 31:21).

JOURNAL: _____

_____

_____

SATURDAY: A Day of Application

Read Genesis 24:10-19.

Confess to the Lord your own tendency to serve out of duty instead of love:

_____

_____

Ask God to change the motive of your heart. Pray that He would give you the desire to go the extra mile in serving as Rebekah did, bringing water not only for Abraham's servant, but for his camels also (Genesis 24:17-19).

_____

_____

Perform an act of service for someone today, expecting nothing in return. Suggestions:
- serve your husband breakfast in bed.
- bake a pie for a neighbor; take the time to visit when you deliver it.
- send a card to someone, including a bible verse of encouragement.

Record what you did here:

_____

_____

SUNDAY: A Day of Praise

Read Isaiah 53:1-12.

Praise the Lord as the Suffering Servant, Who served unto death.

WRITE OUT YOUR PRAYER OF PRAISE HERE:

_____

_____

CHECK YOURSELF! WRITE YOUR MEMORY VERSE HERE:

_____

_____

The Power of Our Words

"May the words of my mouth and the meditation of my heart be pleasing in Your sight, O Lord, my Rock and my Redeemer"
(Psalm 19:14).

YOU CAN DO IT!

Three mornings a week I go upstairs to my boys' playroom to work-out using a pre-recorded exercise program on DVD. I must admit that there are many days when I am less than enthusiastic about getting started. God's words from I Timothy 4:8 come quickly to mind when I want to talk myself out of exercising: "For bodily exercise profiteth little; but godliness is profitable unto all things" (KJV). It is tempting to sit back down with my Bible and another cup of coffee to work on my "godliness" instead of my physical fitness! But I know that neglecting exercise is not the point of this verse, so I try to persevere in taking care of this body God has given me.

One of the best things about using these exercise DVDs is the moti-vating words of the instructor: "I know you can do it!" "Good job!" "You did great today!" Just when I'm tempted to give up, the instructor with the fit and toned body yells out, "You're looking awesome!", moti-vating me to do just one more push-up, or one more lunge. Her words have the power to boost me up and encourage me to do my best. And who doesn't thrive on words of praise and encouragement, especially in the day-to-day tasks that are less than rewarding? When my son Ian was just three years old, he watched me set the table one night before dinner. As I placed the last set of napkins and utensils on the table, he clapped his hands and exclaimed, "Good job, Mommy!" That little boy put a smile on my face and made my day!

We should never underestimate the impact of our words, both to pull up and to pull down. With a single phrase we have the power to make another person feel good about himself, or to feel bad....the power to motivate, or the power to intimidate.... the power to bless, or the power to curse. The Bible says, "Pleasant words are like a honeycomb...sweet to the soul and health to the bones" (Proverbs 16:24 KJV). Do the words that come out of our mouths sound sweet to the hearers and promote health, or are they like gravel even in our own mouths as they come forth critically, negatively, and harshly? And while we are on the subject of our words, how about the constant temptation to gossip and spread either unflattering facts or unsubstantiated rumors? "The words of a gossip are like choice morsels; they go down to a man's inmost parts" (Proverbs 18:8). Because of our sinful nature and twisted sense of self-elevation by putting others down, we sometimes gobble up those "choice morsels," anxious to feed them to the next person we see. Not only does "gossip separate close friends" (Proverbs 16:28), a few careless words have the power to bring utter despair and destruction to their victim for years to come.

I do want my conversation to be acceptable to my Lord and Savior and to be pleasant to those around me. With God's help, may I think before I speak, so that both the words of my mouth and the meditation of my heart will be pleasing in God's sight (Psalm 19:14). Scripture reminds us that it is "better to live on a corner of the roof than share a house with a quarrelsome wife" (Proverbs 21:9). May my husband and sons never wish to escape to the rooftop to get away from me and my less than encouraging words.

Memory Verse:

"May the words of my mouth and the meditation of my heart be pleasing in Your sight, O Lord, my Rock and my Redeemer" (Psalm 19:14).

MONDAY: Read Matthew 12:33-37. Meditate on God's Word and listen to what He has to say to you. Using the text as a guide, spend time in praise, confession and thanksgiving.

Pray for yourself, asking the Holy Spirit to convict you of your sinfulness and fill you up with His Presence, so that His Words will pour forth from your lips: Heavenly Father, I know that "nothing good lives in me, that is, in my sinful nature" (Romans 7:18). Without the power of the Holy Spirit working in me, I will never be able to speak and use my words to please You. Your Word says that "out of the overflow of the heart the mouth speaks" (Matthew 12:34). So I commit myself afresh to You this morning, asking You to overflow my heart with Your goodness, Your love, Your mercy and Your peace. Please place a guard on my lips, because I know that I will have to give account on the day of judgment for every careless word I have spoken. For by my words I will be acquitted, and by my words I will be condemned (Matthew 12:36-37). When I am on the receiving end of gossip, may I be the one to put an end to it. When I am tempted to ridicule or nag, remind me to look for a reason to compliment instead. May all those I come in contact with today leave my presence feeling encouraged, accepted and loved.

JOURNAL: _____

_____

—————◦◦◦◦◦—————

TUESDAY: Read Ephesians 4:29-5:7. Meditate on God's Word and listen to what He has to say to you. Using the text as a guide, spend time in praise, confession and thanksgiving.

Pray for your husband, that his conversation would be pleasing to God: Lord Jesus, I lift my husband up to You in this area of his words. May he strive to imitate You in his speech, living a life of love that is evident to those around him (Ephesians 5:1-2). As he interacts with friends, coworkers, and even strangers, please protect my husband from hearing "obscenity, foolish talk or coarse joking" (Ephesians 5:4). Help him turn his back on such talk, refusing to listen to it, speak it, or participate in it in any way. For Your Word says that "what goes into a man's mouth does not make him 'unclean,' but what comes out of his mouth, that is what makes him 'unclean' " (Matthew 15:11). May he stand 'clean' before You, choosing to speak words of kindness, compassion and love. Help him to see the good in every situation rather than the bad, to focus on the positive qualities in others instead of the negative ones, and to maintain an attitude of thanksgiving at all times. Remind my husband to say only "what is helpful for building others up according to their needs, that it may benefit those who listen" (Ephesians 4:29).

JOURNAL: _____

_____

―――――○●●○――――――

WEDNESDAY: Read Proverbs 10:11-21. Meditate on God's Word and listen to what He has to say to you. Using the text as a guide, spend time in praise, confession and thanksgiving.

Pray for your household, that it would be filled with words of love and encouragement: Oh Father, how I want my home to be a place of peace.... where everyone gets along, where Your Presence is palpable, and where pleasant words continually pour forth. Your Word teaches that love is the key to such harmony: "Hatred stirs up dissension, but love covers over all wrongs" (Proverbs 10:12). I pray that each one of us would choose to overlook offenses out of love, rather than responding with ugly or hurtful words. The Bible says that "when words are many, sin is not absent, but he who holds his tongue is wise" (Proverbs 10:19). Help us keep a tight rein on our lips so that demeaning or critical words don't slip out, and may we refuse to even allow our minds to dwell on them. After all, "before a word is on my tongue you know it completely, O Lord" (Psalm 139:4). May my husband and I use our words to bless one another, modeling before our children a loving relationship that they would desire to emulate. Please sweeten our words so that all who live under this roof will "encourage one another and build each other up" (I Thessalonians 5:11).

JOURNAL: _____

_____

―――――○●●○――――――

THURSDAY: Read Psalm 141:1-10. Meditate on God's Word and listen to what He has to say to you. Using the text as a guide, spend time in praise, confession and thanksgiving.

Pray for your children, that they would hear and speak only words that God would approve of: Lord Jesus, in a world that has grown increasingly desensitized to cursing and immoral jokes, I often cringe at the words I hear on television, at the movies, and just out at the shopping mall. How I pray that You would protect my children from hearing such obscenities! At home may my husband and I be very careful in speaking to our children, only breathing words of life into them, never speaking words which kill or destroy. You say in Proverbs 13:3 that "he who guards his lips guards his life, but he who speaks rashly will come to ruin." I would never want my children to come to ruin, so I ask You to "set a guard" over the mouths of my children, O Lord; "keep watch over the door of [their] lips" (Psalm 141:3). Let not their hearts be drawn to what is evil (Psalm 141:4); rather, may they be respectful in speaking to us and kind when speaking to their siblings. May they "do everything without complaining or arguing, so that [they] may become blameless and pure, children of God without fault in a crooked and depraved generation" (Philippians 2:14).

JOURNAL: _____

_____

———•———

FRIDAY: Read James 3:1-11. Meditate on God's Word and listen to what He has to say to you. Using the text as a guide, spend time in praise, confession and thanksgiving.

Pray for the members of your church, that you would honor God and each other with your words: Father, we know that our church is made up of many members, but we also recognize that we make up one body, the body of Christ. Therefore it is so important that our words build up the body and bring honor to You. Your Word warns us that "the tongue also is a fire, a world of evil among the parts of the body" (James 3:6). I would never want my church to be corrupted or split apart by careless, unloving or divisive words. I know it would take only a small spark of discontentment or hurt feelings for the whole congregation to be set afire with dissatisfaction and resentment. So I ask that You convict and turn any member from sinful speech that would tear the church body apart. We fully recognize that "no man can tame the tongue. It is a restless evil, full of deadly poison" (James 3:8), so we depend on Your Holy Spirit to do the work within us. Please protect our church from those who have "an unhealthy interest in controversies and quarrels about words that result in envy, strife, malicious talk, evil suspicions and constant friction between men" (I Timothy 6:4).

JOURNAL: _____

_____

SATURDAY: A Day of Application

Read Psalm 17:1-6.

Ask God to "probe your heart and examine" your words, revealing anything about your speech that needs to change. Write what He tells you here:

_____

_____

Make this verse your commitment to God: "I have resolved that my mouth will not sin" (Psalm 17:3). Write out your prayer of commitment here:

_____

_____

Ask God who He would have you encourage with your words. Write his/her name here:

_____

Now make a point to call that person, send him a note, or spend some time with him today.

SUNDAY: A Day of Praise

Read I Thessalonians 5:23-24.

Praise God that He is Jehovah M'Kaddesh - The Lord Who Sanctifies.

Definition of sanctify - to cleanse or set apart for sacred use; to declare or make holy.

Praise God that His Holy Spirit in us can "sanctify us through and through" (v.23)... He can make us blameless in our spirit, soul, body and speech.

WRITE OUT YOUR PRAYER OF PRAISE HERE:

_____

_____

_____

CHECK YOURSELF! WRITE YOUR MEMORY VERSE HERE:

_____

_____

Accepting Yourself as God Created You

"For You created my inmost being; You knit me together in my mother's womb. I praise You because I am fearfully and wonderfully made; Your works are wonderful, I know that full well" (Psalm 139:13-14).

I'M NOT REALLY 6' TALL....MORE LIKE 5'12"

I am a tall person. From childhood, my height has been one of my defining characteristics. I towered over my brownie troop in the first grade, was forced to stand on the back row of the bleachers in school pictures, and was always taller than all the boys at school. When my best friend Kelly, who at 5'2", started dating the one boy in youth group who was actually taller than I was, my hopes of finding a suitably tall husband were dashed. I worked in a card shop in high school and remember several customers peering over the counter at the cash register to see if I was standing on something! By the age of twelve I was already 5'9", and I swore up and down that if I ever reached 6 feet in height I was just going to claim that I was 5'12" because that sounded shorter.

Well, this 5'12" person is in her 40s now, and there are still some things I dislike about being tall. Strangers think it is acceptable to greet me with the words, "Wow...you're really tall." I still stick out in pictures with my Sunday School class or other groups, so I've taken to sitting down so my height won't seem so obvious. I have to pay extra money for my tall-sized clothes because the regular size is too short. And many nights while cooking dinner, I hit my head on the vent-a-hood above the stove. "Why couldn't God have made me just a little shorter?" I wonder.

Isn't it the same for all of us at times? Don't we seem to find it difficult to accept ourselves exactly the way God made us? If we are tall, we want to be shorter. If we are short, we want to be taller. If we have straight hair, we wish it had more body. If we have curly hair, we pay to have it straightened. The list goes on and on! In Psalm 139:13-14 the psalmist says this about God: "For You created my inmost being; You knit me together in my mother's womb. I praise You because I am fearfully and wonderfully made; Your works are wonderful, I know that full well." If He created my inmost being and knit all my parts together in my mother's womb, then He certainly had a reason for determining my height. I need to start accepting myself as God determined me to be, thanking Him for the positive aspects and not dwelling on the things I see as negatives.

So over the years I've tried to not only accept my height, but also appreciate it. I can always reach the very top shelf in the closet, I'm easy to find in a crowd, and if I happen to gain five pounds it's not quite so noticeable! Now that I think about it, I guess I do like some things about being 6' tall. In fact, I have found that if I ever meet a woman who rivals me in height, I tend to stretch myself up a little higher, actually wanting to be the tallest!

Psalm 100:3 declares, "It is He who made us, and we are His." May we bask in the knowledge that we are His and strive to bring God glory exactly as He created us.

———✦———

Memory Verse:
"I praise You because I am fearfully and wonderfully made; Your works are wonderful, I know that full well" (Psalm 139:14).

———✦———

MONDAY: Read Psalm 139:1-6, 13-18. Meditate on God's Word and listen to what He has to say to you. Using the text as a guide, spend time in praise, confession and thanksgiving.

Pray for yourself, asking God to help you accept yourself exactly as He created you: I praise You today, Father God, as my Creator. You, who merely spoke and the world came into existence, also had a desire to create me. It is reassuring to know that nothing "was hidden from You when I was made in the secret place" (Psalm 139:15), and that "You are familiar with all my ways" (Psalm 139:3b). You did not neglect a single detail about the way I was created, nor are You unaware of a single day ahead of me... "All the days ordained for me were written in Your book before one of them came to be" (Psalm 139:16). Forgive me, Father, when I express dissatisfaction or disappointment in the way You created me. Your Word declares in Colossians 1:16 that all things were created by You and for You, so who am I to question my height, facial features, or body structure? Instead of trying to change myself, may I strive to use my body to bring You glory in everything I say and do (I Corinthians 10:31). Thank you for this earthly vessel, which was designed exactly as You planned it to be.

JOURNAL: _____

_____

_____

TUESDAY: Read Genesis 1:26-31 & 2:4-7. Meditate on God's Word and listen to what He has to say to you. Using the text as a guide, spend time in praise, confession and thanksgiving.

Pray for your husband, that he would accept both the way God created him and also his God-given role as "head" of his household: Creator God, Your Word tells us in Genesis 1:27, "So God created man in His own image, in the image of God He created him." May my husband grasp the reality of this verse, that he was created in the very image of God! May he rest in that knowledge, especially when a spirit of dissatisfaction rears its ugly head or the enemy tries to fill his mind with doubts. I praise You for, "You are worthy, our Lord and God, to receive glory and honor and power, for You created all things, and by Your will they were created and have their being" (Revelation 4:11). May my husband desire to "have his being" in You and You alone, accepting with humility his rightful place to rule "over all the earth," and more specifically, as head over his household (Ephesians

5:23). I pray that he would depend on You for every breath he takes, just as You "breathed into his nostrils the breath of life" (Genesis 2:7) at creation.
JOURNAL: _____

_____

_____

⸺◦◦◦⸺

WEDNESDAY: Read Gen 2:18-24. Meditate on God's Word and listen to what He has to say to you. Using the text as a guide, spend time in praise, confession and thanksgiving.

Pray for your marriage, that you and your husband would accept your unique roles, while finding delight in being "one flesh": Father, I praise You that in Your divine wisdom You knew from the very beginning that "it is not good for the man to be alone," so You made a "helper suitable for him" (Genesis 2:18). Thank You for choosing me to be that "helper" or companion for my husband. What an awesome thing that You formed woman from one of man's ribs, making her "bone of his bones and flesh of his flesh" (Genesis 2:23). The marriage relationship goes beyond surface level, beyond a mere partnership of two separate individuals...in marriage a man and woman are actually joined together, to be united as one. Thank You that on the day my husband and I were married, we too became one flesh. I pray that we would take that blessing, that privilege seriously, always striving to honor You first and then one another. May we not "compete" with each other, or quarrel with our Maker (Isaiah 45:9) about our God-given roles, but accept what You have for each of us. And may I be a "suitable helper" for him all of my days.
JOURNAL: _____

_____

_____

⸺◦◦◦⸺

THURSDAY: Read Isaiah 43:1-7. Meditate on God's Word and listen to what He has to say to you. Using the text as a guide, spend time in praise, confession and thanksgiving.

51

Pray for your children, asking God to give them eyes to see themselves for the wonderful creations they are: Father, You say in Jeremiah 1:5, "Before I formed you in the womb, I knew you, before you were born I set you apart." Thank You for this reminder that You are the One who formed my children in my womb, in Your perfect wisdom and according to Your perfect design. Thank You that even before they were born, You knew them and set them apart for Your glory. Help me to teach these truths to my children while they are young, reminding them often how very special and wonderful they are. May they know that they are precious and honored in Your sight and that You love them (Isaiah 43:4), exactly as they are. How reassuring to know that You have summoned them by name; they are <u>Yours</u> (Isaiah 43:1)! I pray that if they are tempted to look down on themselves for qualities they dislike, they would remember the truth that they are Your "workmanship, created in Christ Jesus to do good works" (Ephesians 2:10).

JOURNAL: _____

_____

_____

FRIDAY: Read Psalm 104:24-35. Meditate on God's Word and listen to what He has to say to you. Using the text as a guide, spend time in praise, confession and thanksgiving.

Pray for someone you know who struggles with poor self-image: Thank you, Lord Jesus, for putting _____ in my life. How I pray that this person could see himself for the wonderful creation You made him to be! Please use me to speak the words of reassurance and acceptance that he longs to hear, and to remind him of the unconditional love and perfect plan You have for him. May _____ look to You alone for fulfillment, because "when You open Your hand, [we] are satisfied with good things" (Psalm 104:28). The world offers dissatisfaction, rejection and feelings of worthlessness. But You offer satisfaction, acceptance and a reminder of who we really are in Christ... chosen, royal, holy, belonging to You (I Peter 2:9). When this dear person is unhappy with something about his outward appearance, may he remember that "man looks at the outward appearance, but the Lord looks at the heart" (I Samuel 16:7). Help _____ to be more concerned with the condition of his heart than with the way he looks. And through a fresh acceptance of who he is, may he be able to sing praise to You as long as he lives (Psalm 104:33)!

JOURNAL: _____

_____

_____

SATURDAY: A Day of Application

Read Psalm 95:1-7.

Name one thing about yourself that you do not like or with which you are dissatisfied. It can be a physical characteristic, a personality trait, or something you see as a limitation:

_____

_____

Thank God for this quality or feature, recognizing that He made you exactly as He wanted you to be:

_____

_____

Finally, "bow down in worship...kneel before the Lord [your] Maker" (Psalm 95:6):

_____

_____

SUNDAY: A Day of Praise

Read Psalm 148:1-14.

Praise God as Elohim - The Triune God, Creator - the One Who brought the universe and all matter and life in it into existence.

WRITE OUT YOUR PRAYER OF PRAISE HERE:

_____

_____

CHECK YOURSELF! WRITE YOUR MEMORY VERSE HERE:

_____

_____

Spiritual Growth

"In fact, though by this time you ought to be teachers, you need someone to teach you the elementary truths of God's Word all over again. You need milk, not solid food! But solid food is for the mature, who by constant use have trained themselves to distinguish good from evil" (Hebrews 5:12 & 14).

JUST GROW UP!

When you get right down to it, I am just not interested in electronics. I am very content to leave control of the remote and DVD player up to my husband and three sons and do not want to take the time to learn about new features and controls. My husband got a home stereo system for Christmas, which has just added to my confusion about which remote to use and which channel the television must be set on in order to use which feature. I long for the old days when I could just pick up one remote and change the channel. I feel the same way when it comes to computers, cell phones and cameras. The more advanced they get the more overloaded I feel!

Not too long ago I bought my first laptop computer. After many years of working on a desktop, it took me awhile to become accustomed to using the laptop's touch pad instead of the mouse I knew so well. I had noticed a little vertical line on the right side of the touch pad, and while I wondered what it was for, I never attempted to figure it out. A few weeks later, my 10-year-old son asked if he could use the new laptop. Within seconds, he discovered that the vertical line gave the user the ability to instantly scroll down the page. I could not believe that he, at 10 years of age, was able to figure it out that quickly when I had puzzled over it for weeks! It is so humbling that my boys' grasp of anything electrical is superior to mine. I know that if I would just take the time to read the instruction manual, or even go through the on-line tutorial, I could figure out how to operate these things on my own. But content to rely on those around me for help, I have basically refused to just grow up when it comes to electronics. I don't want to take the time to sit down and learn anything new!

In the classic children's story about Peter Pan there is a scene where all the boys are singing, "I'll never grow up, never grow up, never grow up!"[4] Just as those children didn't want to grow up and assume any responsibility, and I don't want to grow up and learn how to use all the electronics that are flooding my home, I believe that Christians sometimes adopt a similar mentality when it comes to spiritual growth. Whether the root of the problem lies with fear, confusion, apathy, lack of training, or just plain laziness, spiritual growth is minimal if not completely nonexistant. An honest profession of faith in Jesus Christ might have taken place years before, but without an effort to dig into God's Word consistently, nothing new has been learned in quite some time. "In fact, though by this time you ought to be teachers, you need someone to teach you the elementary truths of God's Word all over again. You need milk, not solid food! But solid food is for the mature, who by constant use have trained themselves to distinguish good from evil" (Hebrews 5:12 & 14).

Let's not be content to keep on drinking milk forever! God never intended for us to remain as children who must always rely on the teaching of others. It is high time we assumed some responsibility and started taking in the solid food of His Word for ourselves. Day by day, truth by truth, we can "grow up in [our] salvation" (I Peter 2:2) as God intended us to.

Memory Verse:

"But solid food is for the mature, who by constant use have trained themselves to distinguish good from evil" (Hebrews 5:14).

MONDAY: Read Hebrews 5:11-6:3. Meditate on God's Word and listen to what He has to say to you. Using the text as a guide, spend time in praise, confession and thanksgiving.

Pray for yourself, to be motivated to grow up in your salvation: Father God, please forgive me when my laziness and apathy make me slow to learn as a believer. Forgive me when I am content to sit back and feed off of the "milk" of others, rather than digging into Your Word for solid food of my own. I don't want to be a baby anymore! Therefore, I determine to "leave the elementary teachings about Christ and go on to maturity" (Hebrews 6:1). I determine to get into Your Word, hide it in my heart, and line my life up with Your teachings. Thank you that I do not have to rely on others to teach me... Your Word says, "But the Counselor, the Holy Spirit, whom the Father will send in my name, will teach you all things and will remind you of everything I have said to you" (John 14:26). How comforting to know that my spiritual maturity is not up to me alone! I can trust that "He who began a good work in [me] will carry it on to completion until the day of Christ Jesus" (Philippians 1:6). Please help me to be found faithful to grow spiritually this week, showing obedience and diligence to the very end.

JOURNAL: _____

_____

_____

———⊸∘⊶———

TUESDAY: Read Luke 8:4-15. Meditate on God's Word and listen to what He has to say to you. Using the text as a guide, spend time in praise, confession and thanksgiving.

Pray for your husband to mature spiritually: Lord Jesus, thank You that we have Your very words at our disposal. Thank you for the parables You shared with Your believers as You lived and walked upon this earth, that we can continue to learn from 2000 years later. Oh Father, how I pray that You would till up the soil of my husband's heart! When the seed of Your Word is scattered in his life, may it take root because his heart has been found to be full of "good soil," noble and true. May my husband "hear the Word, retain it, and by persevering produce a crop" (Luke 8:15)...a crop full of obedience, righteousness and purity. Help him, Father, in the face of life's worries, riches and pleasures. May such earthly concerns never choke him, preventing the spiritual growth and maturity (Luke 8:14) You desire. Rather, may my husband's roots in Your Word be so strong that his faith keeps him grounded, assuring a harvest of growth. I pray that he would always "stand firm in all the will of God, mature and fully assured" (Colossians 4:12).

JOURNAL: _____

_____

_____

WEDNESDAY: Read II Peter 1:3-11. Meditate on God's Word and listen to what He has to say to you. Using the text as a guide, spend time in praise, confession and thanksgiving.

Pray for your household, to be ever increasing in knowledge of the Lord Jesus: Father, I praise You that by Your divine power You have "given us everything we need for life and godliness" (II Peter 1:3). I am ever thankful for Your Holy Spirit at work in Your children, providing us with the capacity and ability to grow in spiritual understanding. We must not neglect or underestimate this Power that is within us! Please encourage those in our home to make every effort to add to our faith goodness, then knowledge, self-control, perseverance, godliness, brotherly kindness and love. "For if you possess these qualities in increasing measure, they will keep you from being ineffective and unproductive in your knowledge of our Lord Jesus Christ" (II Peter 1:8). God forbid that we know You personally, yet remain ineffective or unproductive as Your children! As one member of our family exhibits spiritual growth, may the rest of us be motivated to grow as well. And I pray that one day, each of us will "receive a rich welcome into the eternal kingdom of our Lord and Savior Jesus Christ" (II Peter 1:11).

JOURNAL: _____

_____

_____

THURSDAY: Read II Timothy 3:14-17 & I Peter 2:1-3. Meditate on God's Word and listen to what He has to say to you. Using the text as a guide, spend time in praise, confession and thanksgiving.

Pray for your children to grow spiritually as well as physically: Lord Jesus, it seems like my children are growing up so fast! Every year is a milestone, bringing mastery of new life skills and opening doors of increased independence. As I witness my children grow in body, I also see them growing experientially in their knowledge of You – Your faithfulness, Your provision, and Your love. They have tasted for themselves that You are good, and I pray that those little tastes will fuel a craving within each one of them to grow even more (I Peter 2:2-3). May my children "continue in what [they] have learned and have become convinced of" (II Timothy 3:14)...that the holy Scriptures which give wisdom for salvation will also give wisdom for all of life. "All Scripture is God-breathed and is useful for teaching, rebuking, correcting and training in righteousness, so that the man of God may be thoroughly equipped for every good work" (II Timothy 3:16). May my children be mature and equipped, because they have sought out Your Word and responded in obedience.

JOURNAL: _____

_____

_____

FRIDAY: Read Ephesians 4:11-16. Meditate on God's Word and listen to what He has to say to you. Using the text as a guide, spend time in praise, confession and thanksgiving.

Pray for your church to be spiritually mature, attaining to the whole measure of the fullness of Christ: Father God, thank You so much for my church home. How wonderful to have like-minded brothers and sisters, with whom I share a common bond in Christ! You have given each of us different skills and abilities, but all for the same purpose: "so that the body of Christ may be built up until we all reach unity in the faith in the knowledge of the Son of God and become mature" (Ephesians 4:12-13). Forgive me when I allow laziness or fear to get in the way of using my spiritual gifts for Your glory. For only as each part of Your church does its work, can Your body grow and build itself up in love. May my church stand firmly on the solid rock of Christ Jesus, not "blown here and there by every wind of teaching and by the cunning and craftiness of men in their deceitful scheming" (Ephesians 4:14). Rather, may we be spiritually mature and "in all things grow up into Him who is the Head, that is Christ" (Ephesians 4:15).

JOURNAL: _____

_____

_____

SATURDAY: A Day of Application

Read I Timothy 4:7-8.

Are you training yourself to be godly, determining to grow up spiritually?

If not, confess your lack of spiritual growth to the Lord, asking Him to give you the desire to "grow up in your salvation":

_____

_____

_____

Just as you must train in order to become physically fit, so you must train to become spiritually fit. In what ways will you determine to train yourself in the future?

- Daily quiet time? _____
- Daily reading God's Word? _____
- Daily time of prayer? _____
- Memorizing scripture? _____
- Corporate worship? _____
- Other? _____

Journal:

_____

_____

SUNDAY: A Day of Praise

Read Philippians 1:6 & 2:12-13.

Praise God that He is at work in you to help you grow up spiritually!

WRITE OUT YOUR PRAYER OF PRAISE HERE:

_____

_____

_____

CHECK YOURSELF! WRITE YOUR MEMORY VERSE HERE:

_____

_____

Making Prayer a Priority

"Therefore confess your sins to each other and pray for each other so that you may be healed. The prayer of a righteous man is powerful and effective" (James 5:16).

FAIL NOT TO PRAY

When my first child entered kindergarten, I began to participate in a group called *Moms in Prayer* (formerly known as *Moms in Touch*)[5]. Founded by Fern Nichols in 1984, this group began with just two or three moms who felt the burden to pray for their children and their children's school. Now 28 years later, *Moms in Prayer* has grown into an international organization encouraging moms in every state across the United States and in 140 other countries to unite in prayer with like-minded believers. During *Moms in Prayer* we spend time praising the Lord for who He is, rehearsing the qualities of His great character and reminding ourselves of His many incredible attributes. We bow before Him in silent confession, repenting of our sinfulness and grasping hold of His forgiveness. Knowing that every good and perfect gift is from above, we pour out our thanks to the One Who has given us all things. Finally, we bring our children before God, asking Him to bless them, protect them and conform them to the image of His Son. Lamentations 2:19 says, "…Lift up your hands to Him for the lives of your children…" It is a joy and privilege to be a part of this group, assured that each time we meet God hears our prayers and promises to answer us.

Participation in *Moms in Prayer* over the past nine years has dramatically transformed my prayer life! By making praise and thanksgiving the priority of prayer, before times of intercession, it has helped me get my focus off of self and on to Christ. As I am faced with my own shortcomings in light of His perfection, I realize afresh my great need for talking with Him moment by moment throughout each day. As I focus on praying Scripture, God changes my desires to look more like His, equipping me to pray for His will in my children's lives rather than my own. And as I have seen God answer requests on behalf of our children time and time again, it has opened my eyes to see that our prayers really do make a difference! The Bible says, "Therefore confess your sins to each other and pray for each other so that you may be healed. The prayer of a righteous man is powerful and effective" (James 5:16).

Prayer has been defined as communication with God. Really think about that for just a moment…God, Creator of heaven and earth, Sustainer and Giver of life, the Lord Most High, allows His children access to His throne of grace at any time of day or night, to speak to Him unhindered and unhurried. Not only does He allow us to come to Him, He delights when we do! "The prayer of the upright pleases Him" (Proverbs 15:8).

I've heard it said that prayer is the Christian's greatest privilege, greatest responsibility, greatest weapon of warfare, yet sadly, the most neglected area of Christian life. Dear sister, take delight in the privilege of being able to "cast all your anxiety on Him because He cares for you" (I Peter 5:7)! Live up to the responsibility of praying for others so that you will not "sin against the Lord by failing to pray…" (I Samuel 12:23)! Grasp hold of your greatest weapon of warfare by calling on the mighty power of God through prayer on bended knee! Prayer is our extreme privilege, responsibility and weapon of warfare as we walk in this lost and dying world…may we not neglect it.

Memory Verse:

"Therefore confess your sins to each other and pray for each other so that you may be healed. The prayer of a righteous man is powerful and effective" (James 5:16).

MONDAY: Read James 5:13-18. Meditate on God's Word and listen to what He has to say to you. Using the text as a guide, spend time in praise, confession and thanksgiving.

Pray for yourself, to truly value prayer and make it a daily priority: Oh Father, forgive me for the countless times I neglect the great privilege and responsibility of prayer! Forgive me when I declare that I am too busy to spend time with You, or when I lack the faith that my prayers will even make a difference. James 5:17 teaches that "Elijah was a man just like us," and his earnest prayers brought miraculous results! What an awesome God You are to listen to the simple prayers of ordinary people and promise that those prayers are both "powerful and effective" (James 5:16). It is my desire to be in constant, ongoing communication with You from the moment I wake up in the morning to the time I lie down to sleep at night. Help me develop the discipline of learning to "pray continually" (I Thessalonians 5:17), and remind me to keep my heart clean before You "so that nothing will hinder [my] prayers" (I Peter 3:7). Thank you that You allow Your children to come to You in times of trouble, sickness, and even sin, promising help when we come to You in confession and faith.

JOURNAL: _____

_____

_____

—————

TUESDAY: Read Daniel 9:1-3, 20-23. Meditate on God's Word and listen to what He has to say to you. Using the text as a guide, spend time in praise, confession and thanksgiving.

Pray for your husband, to turn to God in prayer and trust Him for an answer: Lord Jesus, thank you for this example from Your Word of Daniel, who "turned to the Lord God and pleaded with Him in prayer and petition" (Daniel 9:3). Daniel's prayer was serious business. He didn't just casually mention his need...he fasted and confessed the peoples' sin, begging for Your favor, forgiveness and help. Oh Father, may my husband be a man like Daniel, understanding that You alone are the answer in times of need. May he pray earnestly, dedicating himself to prayer and truly believing that You hear the prayers of the righteous (Proverbs 15:29). And when he does Lord, please answer his prayers as

You answered Daniel! "As soon as [he] began to pray, an answer was given" (Daniel 9:23). I pray that my husband would develop the habit of turning to you moment by moment throughout his day. Bind back the enemy with his lies that our prayers don't matter. For Your Word declares, "The eyes of the Lord are on the righteous and his ears are attentive to their prayer" (I Peter 3:12).

JOURNAL: _____

_____

_____

———◦◦◦◦———

WEDNESDAY: Read Matthew 6:5-13. Meditate on God's Word and listen to what He has to say to you. Using the text as a guide, spend time in praise, confession and thanksgiving.

Pray for those in your household, to have the proper attitude and understanding of prayer: Father, thank You that Your Word gives us instruction on how to pray! Jesus taught that prayer is meant to be private communication with You, not a public demonstration before others. "And when you pray, do not be like the hypocrites, for they love to pray...to be seen by men" (Matthew 6:5). You are to be our only audience! Thank You that we don't have to pray with grand words and lofty speech in order for You to hear us and know our need. In fact, You know what we need before we even ask You (Matthew 6:8). Convict my husband and me to teach our children about prayer by example. They need to hear us pray first thing in the morning, before meals, and at bedtime. I want them to know that we can and should pray about anything at anytime! May we be careful to follow Jesus' model on prayer, including praise, confession, and thanksgiving along with requests for help, provision, and forgiveness. Mature us to the point where we can pray, "Your will be done" (Matthew 6:10) even when it differs from our own.

JOURNAL: _____

_____

_____

———◦◦◦◦———

THURSDAY: Read Psalm 32:6-11. Meditate on God's Word and listen to what He has to say to you. Using the text as a guide, spend time in praise, confession and thanksgiving.

Pray for your children, to experience intimacy with God through prayer: Heavenly Father, the psalmist said, "You are my hiding place; You will protect me from trouble" (Psalm 32:7). Oh, how I want my children to know You as "Abba Father," the One they can run to in times of need! You promise in Your Word, "I will instruct you and teach you in the way you should go; I will counsel you and watch over you" (Psalm 32:8). I pray that my children would understand that they can turn to You for wisdom and direction. From personal experience King David declared: "Pour out your hearts to Him, for God is our refuge" (Psalm 62:8.) In like manner I pray that my children would learn to confide in You as one trusts a best friend. Please help them comprehend that prayer is the key to a closer walk with You! Only as they develop the discipline of spending time at Your feet, will they be able to experience the wonderful privilege of hearing from You personally. May they respond to Your invitation in Jeremiah 33:3: "Call to me and I will answer you and tell you great and unsearchable things you do not know."

JOURNAL: _____

_____

_____

FRIDAY: Read Ephesians 6:18-20. Meditate on God's Word and listen to what He has to say to you. Using the text as a guide, spend time in praise, confession and thanksgiving.

Pray for your church, to be faithful in prayer: Lord Jesus, I heard someone say once that "Prayer is the work!" We get so busy sometimes trying to do things for You, spending hours working in our own strength, when it would be much more effective to spend our time in prayer asking You to work through us. Forgive us when we depend more on our abilities than on Your mighty power. Remind us as a church to "pray in the Spirit on all occasions with all kinds of prayers and requests...be alert and always keep on praying for all the saints" (Ephesians 6:18). This verse shows the importance of three things: we must be rightly related to You if we are to be able to pray "in the Spirit"; we must stay informed and remain diligent in our prayers if we are to "be alert and keep on praying"; and we must have a global perspective if we are to "pray for all the saints". Help us think outside our church, outside our city and our country, praying for believers around the world. We must depend on prayer to unleash Your power, enabling us to "fearlessly make known the mystery of the Gospel" (Ephesians 6:19) wherever we go.

JOURNAL: _____

_____

_____

SATURDAY: A Day of Application

Read Matthew 14:23, Mark 1:35 and Mark 14:35-36.

If Jesus, the very Son of God, felt it necessary to spend time in prayer, shouldn't we? What do you learn from each of these verses about prayer?

1) _____

2) _____

3) _____

Are you making prayer a priority? If not, confess your neglect of spending time with the Lord. Thank Him for the privilege, responsibility and mighty power of prayer and commit to start making it a top priority:

_____

_____

SUNDAY: A Day of Praise

Read Romans 8:26-34.

Praise the Lord that He is our Intercessor! "The Spirit himself intercedes for us with groans that words cannot express" (v.26); "the Spirit intercedes for the saints in accordance with God's will" (v.27); and Jesus Christ "is at the right hand of God and is also interceding for us" (v.34).

WRITE OUT YOUR PRAYER OF PRAISE HERE:

_____

_____

_____

CHECK YOURSELF! WRITE YOUR MEMORY VERSE HERE:

_____

_____

Waiting on God and Expecting Him to Work

"Give ear to my words, O Lord, consider my sighing. Listen to my cry for help, my King and my God, for to You I pray. In the morning, O Lord, You hear my voice; in the morning I lay my requests before You and wait in expectation" (Psalm 5:1-3).

GHEE, I DIDN'T KNOW YOU COULD JUMP!

My children call my mother, their maternal grandmother, "Ghee." One day when my mother was keeping the boys for me, she decided to set up a badminton net in her backyard to play with the kids. As they were playing, one of the boys sent a birdie flying over my mother's head. When she jumped up to hit the birdie, my youngest son Alec exclaimed in surprise, "Ghee, I didn't know you could jump!" He did not expect her to jump so he was surprised to see that she was able!

And so often it is with us and the Lord.... we do not expect Him to work, do not expect Him to do something great, so when He does, we are surprised! Or, we never experience the wonderful thing He had planned to do in our lives because instead of waiting on Him we took matters into our own hands. How many times have we gotten down on our knees in prayer, poured out our hearts to Him, asking Him to take care of our need and work on our behalf - *move mountains even* - only to get up and go about our business as usual? We ask God to work, but then we set out trying to figure out a solution on our own. Oh ladies, it should not be! I have been dealing with just this issue for the past several weeks. My husband and I are praying about a big decision that will affect our entire family, and I have been literally begging God to tell us what to do. His still small voice spoke clearly to me during last week's church service... "Heather, you keep asking Me, but are you really expecting an answer?" Wow, conviction came immediately and pierced deep. I had been asking, over and over again, but I really wasn't putting myself in a position to hear an answer. I have purposely tried to face each day since anticipating a clear response from my Lord – perhaps today will be the day He reveals His will.

As we come to the Lord, asking Him to hear us, we would do well to remember to Whom we are talking...He is King of kings, Lord of lords, all powerful, all mighty, and completely able. And if that isn't enough, He cares deeply about us and what happens to us. He does hear His children when we call out to Him, and He does work on our behalf. So when we lay our requests at His feet, we ought to be waiting in expectation (Psalm 5:3) to see what He will do!

So what are your expectations from the Lord today? Are you just expecting the same old quiet time with Him, while voicing the same old prayers that really lack any conviction or trust? Or are you truly expecting God to do something today, perhaps something new and wonderful that you could never foresee on your own? I have found that the lower I set my expectations, the lower the result. Sometimes we set low expectations to protect ourselves from getting hurt or disappointed. But it takes a little risk, a little daring, dare I say a little faith, to set yourself up for expecting God to do something good or even great! So the next time you are tempted to get up off your knees and find a quick solution to whatever it was you were praying about, why don't you sit back down and do a little expectant waiting? After all, He is able to do immeasurably more for us than all we can ask or even imagine according to His power that is at work within us (Ephesians 3:20)!

Memory Verse:
"In the morning, O Lord, You hear my voice; in the morning I lay my requests before You and wait in expectation" (Psalm 5:3).

MONDAY: Read Isaiah 30:1-5, 15-21. Meditate on God's Word and listen to what He has to say to you. Using the text as a guide, spend time in praise, confession and thanksgiving.

Pray for yourself, that you would wait on God to work in your life, expecting great things: Oh Father, thank You for the privilege of coming before You at any time of day or night, and finding You there waiting to receive me! But how many times have I bowed before You, Lord, asking You to work, and then trying to figure out a solution on my own. Forgive me. Help me to wait on You. I have often behaved like an obstinate child, carrying out plans that are not Yours and doing things without consulting You (Isaiah 30:1-2). Even though it scares me not to take matters in my own hands, I determine today to start waiting on You, fully expecting You to work. I claim Your promise that says, "Whether you turn to the right or to the left, your ears will hear a voice behind you saying, 'This is the way; walk in it'" (Isaiah 30:21). Thank You for this reminder from Your Word: "Yet the Lord longs to be gracious to you; He rises to show you compassion. For the Lord is a God of justice. Blessed are all who wait for Him!" (Isaiah 30:18).

JOURNAL: _____

_____

_____

TUESDAY: Read Psalm 40:1-8. Meditate on God's Word and listen to what He has to say to you. Using the text as a guide, spend time in praise, confession and thanksgiving.

Pray for your husband, that he would look to the Lord, waiting on Him and His timing: Heavenly Father, I pray that my husband would be a blessed man, who makes You his trust...who does not turn aside to false gods (Psalm 40:4). May he not be misled or deceived into thinking that he can handle things alone, or even that he should not trouble You with every decision. How wonderful that nothing is too little or too big to bring before Your throne, and that You delight when Your children come to You for help, direction, or assurance. Psalm 40:5 says, "Many, O Lord my God, are the wonders You have done. The things You planned for us no one can recount to You; were I to speak and tell of them, they would be too many to declare." May he not miss out on a single one of the things You had planned for him because he chose his own path. Rather, may my husband come to You often, laying his requests at Your feet, and then waiting patiently for You to turn and hear his cry (Psalm 40:1).

JOURNAL: _____

_____

_____

WEDNESDAY: Read Habakkuk 1:1-4; 2:1-3. Meditate on God's Word and listen to what He has to say to you. Using the text as a guide, spend time in praise, confession and thanksgiving.

Pray for your marriage, that together you and your husband will station yourselves to hear from God: Father I praise You that like Habakkuk, my husband and I can pour out our complaints before You. We do not have to hide our feelings or pretend that everything is okay… we can bare our hearts and our hurts, trusting You to understand and come to our aide. In Habakkuk 2:1, the prophet declared, "I will stand at my watch and station myself on the ramparts; I will look to see what He will say to me, and what answer I am to give to this complaint." Father, I see that after Habakkuk voiced his prayer to You he stood as a "watchman," patiently waiting for Your answer. May my husband and I adopt the same attitude, keeping ourselves in the very best position to hear from You....daily on our knees waiting for Your response. And even "though it linger," may we wait for it; trusting that "it will certainly come and will not delay" (Habakkuk 2:3b). So this morning, O Lord, we recognize that You do hear our voices. We lay this request for our family before You, and wait in expectation: _____

_____.

JOURNAL: _____

_____

_____

—————⚬⚬⚬—————

THURSDAY: Read Lamentations 3:19-26.   Meditate on God's
Word and listen to what He has to say to you. Using the text as a
guide, spend time in praise, confession and thanksgiving.

Pray for your children, to wait on God in times of trouble: Lord Jesus,
You know how I hate it when difficult things come across my children's
path. How I want to shield them from any pain or hardship! I know that
"in this world [we] will have trouble"… so my heart is full of praise that
You reassure us to "take heart!" because You "have overcome the world"
(John 16:33). Help me to teach my children that they can be confident
of Your love for them and Your unfailing compassion toward them. Use
me to remind them of past instances where You proved Yourself mighty
to work in their lives. Then, when troubles come their way and their soul
is downcast within them (Lamentations 3:20), they can remember Your
faithfulness to them and have hope. Please open their eyes to see You at
work, so that they might give You all the credit for each and every blessing, each and every answer to their prayers. May my children learn to
look to You every morning and say to themselves, "The Lord is my por-
tion; therefore I will wait for Him" (Lamentations 3:24).

JOURNAL: _____

_____

_____

—————⚬⚬⚬—————

FRIDAY: Read Psalm 130:1-8. Meditate on God's Word and listen to
what He has to say to you. Using the text as a guide, spend time
in praise, confession and thanksgiving.

Pray for your nation, to turn back to the Lord and wait on Him: Oh
Father, how I praise You this morning for Your unfailing love! "With

You there is forgiveness" (Psalm 130:4), and with You there is full redemption! (Psalm 130:7). It grieves me to look at our world today and see how far we have drifted from You and Your commands for us. I pray that there would be a fresh awareness of sin in this nation, an overwhelming understanding of our separation from You apart from Christ. May people fall on their faces before You, broken by their own sinfulness and depravity, their pride and independence. For only then, through attitudes of confession and repentance, can You hear us out of the depths and redeem our nation from all our sin. May we wait for You, and in Your Word put our hope, "more than watchmen wait for the morning" (Psalm 130:6). We cling to Your promise that "Christ was sacrificed once to take away the sins of many people; and He will appear a second time, not to bear sin, but to bring salvation to those who are waiting for Him" (Hebrews 9:28). Oh Lord, our hope is in You alone.

JOURNAL: _____

_____

_____

SATURDAY: A Day of Application

Read Proverbs 16:1-9.

Are you guilty of asking the Lord for help and then never waiting on Him or expecting Him to work?

_____

_____

Take it a step further... are you guilty of never even consulting Him in the first place?

_____

_____

Ask God to show you a specific area of your life where you are making your own plans with the wrong motives (v.2) instead of waiting on Him:

_____

_____

Confess this as sin and repent.

Commit this concern to the Lord, waiting on Him to direct your path. Write out your prayer of commitment here:

_____

_____

SUNDAY: A Day of Praise

Read Deuteronomy 10:12-17.

Praise God that He is Adonai - The Lord and Master. And as such, He is worthy to be waited on and is very capable of working on your behalf.

WRITE OUT YOUR PRAYER OF PRAISE HERE:

_____

_____

CHECK YOURSELF! WRITE YOUR MEMORY VERSE HERE:

_____

_____

Memorizing and Meditating on God's Word

"Do not let this Book of the Law depart from your mouth; mediate on it day and night, so that you may be careful to do everything written in it. Then you will be prosperous and successful" (Joshua 1:8).

I CAN HARDLY REMEMBER MY NAME, LET ALONE A BIBLE VERSE!

A common complaint among pregnant women, older women, and just plain women in general is that their memory is completely shot. They are very forgetful and their ability to remember anything is completely gone. And it is no wonder...how many birthdays, phone numbers, social security numbers, locker combinations (for when our kids forget!), PIN numbers, insurance ID numbers, and computer passwords can we continue to cram into our heads? At some point, our brains will surely explode with all the data. I am quite good at "putting something somewhere for safekeeping," only to forget where the safe place was! Of course we can't remember where we put that important note/check/receipt/fill in the blank...we can barely remember our names at times!

But of all the important things we need to remember, God's Word definitely tops the list. There is no greater thing that we can spend our time doing than memorizing Scripture. When I accepted the Lord as my Savior at the age of 15, my mother gave me a little journal. It is dated July 13, 1984 and I still keep it with all of my devotional materials. The very first entry is Philippians 4:13: "I can do everything through Him

Who gives me strength." My piano teacher wrote that Scripture reference at the bottom of one of my work sheets, and I remember opening my Bible as soon as she left to find out what that verse said. It was one of the first verses I ever memorized. Now, more than 25 years later, I value Scripture memory more highly than ever. It is a discipline that requires diligence and persistence, but the rewards are great! When I meditate on and memorize God's Word, several wonderful things happen:

1.) The Lord speaks to me through His Word, giving me His perspective on an issue.
2.) The Lord brings His Word back to my mind at a later time when I most need it: to bring comfort, direction, encouragement or warning.
3.) I have God's Word at my disposal to use in prayer at any time of the day or night.
4.) God uses His Word in me to change me into the image of His Son by teaching me, rebuking me, correcting me and training me in righteousness (II Timothy 3:16).

Even more importantly, I am obeying His command to "fix these words of Mine in your hearts and minds" (Deuteronomy 11:18). Did you get that? God **commands** us to memorize His Word, so when we do not do it we are being disobedient. And nothing has transformed my prayer life like memorizing Scripture. Now when I pray, I can pray God's own Word back to Him!

In my Sunday School class we have named ourselves "Women of the Word". It is not a title to be taken lightly....if we are to be women of God's Word then we must know God's Word. We must determine to follow God's command to not let this Book of the Law depart from our mouths, but to meditate on it day and night, so that we will be careful to do everything written in it (Joshua 1:8). May we correctly handle His Word and honestly declare to our Lord, "Oh, how I love Your law! I meditate on it all day long" (Psalm 119:97).

Memory Verse:

"Do not let this Book of the Law depart from your mouth; meditate on it day and night, so that you may be careful to do everything written in it" (Joshua 1:8).

———

MONDAY: Read Joshua 1:1-9. Meditate on God's Word and listen to what He has to say to you. Using the text as a guide, spend time in praise, confession and thanksgiving.

Pray for yourself, that you would obey God's command to memorize Scripture: Lord Jesus, thank You for the precious gift of Your Word! How reassuring to know that You said, "Heaven and earth will pass away, but My Words will never pass away" (Mark 13:31). What a blessing it is to have my own copy of the Bible, Your very Words, that I can turn to at any moment. And on top of that, You have given Your children the ability to memorize Your Word, so that we are able to have it with us always! Forgive me Lord, when I neglect this privilege. Forgive me when I do not have the desire or take the time to study and memorize Your Word, disobeying Your command to do so. When I feel overwhelmed or unable to memorize a verse of Scripture, remind me that "I can do everything through Him Who gives me strength" (Philippians 4:13). As I memorize Your Word, I pray I would be careful to do everything written in it, never turning "from it to the right or to the left" (Joshua 1:7). And as I meditate on Your Word I know I can expect to gain the wisdom needed for daily decisions, because "the unfolding of Your Words gives light" (Psalm 119:130).

JOURNAL: _____

_____

———

TUESDAY: Read Psalm 1:1-6. Meditate on God's Word and listen to what He has to say to you. Using the text as a guide, spend time in praise, confession and thanksgiving.

Pray for your husband, that God's Word would be his delight: Father, what a wonderful picture of the man who finds his delight "in the law of the Lord, and on His law he meditates day and night" (Psalm 1:2). May my husband be such a man! A man who turns not to the wicked for advice or to the ungodly for companionship, but rather to You and Your Word. I pray that he would guard his daily quiet time and make Scripture reading one of his top priorities, allowing You time to speak directly to him. "For the Word of God is living and active. Sharper than any double-edged sword, it penetrates even to dividing soul and spirit, joints and marrow; it judges the thoughts and attitudes of the heart" (Hebrews 4:12). May my husband determine to "let the word of Christ dwell in [him] richly" (Colossians 3:16) so that Your Living Word can guide, teach, correct and encourage him. Then, he will be strong like a well-watered tree, fruitful and prosperous in whatever he does (Psalm 1:3). I praise You, Lord Jesus, that even though we live in a world where "the grass withers and the flowers fall...the Word of our God stands forever" (Isaiah 40:8)!

JOURNAL: _____

WEDNESDAY: Read Psalm 119:97-112. Meditate on His Word and listen to what He has to say to you. Using the text as a guide, spend time in praise, confession and thanksgiving.

Pray for your marriage, that you and your husband would highly esteem God's Word and uphold it before all who enter your home: Father, I join with the psalmist in declaring, "How sweet are Your words to my taste, sweeter than honey to my mouth!" (Psalm 119:103). How I long for the sweetness of Your Words to fill my home, making it a joyful and loving place to be! As You told the Israelites to write Your commands on the doorframes of their houses (Deuteronomy 6:9), so I want to place Scripture around my house where all who enter can read it and be blessed. Father, my husband and I know that we need Your wisdom in order to lead our family, and that wisdom is found in Your Word. It is "a lamp to my feet and a light for my path" (Psalm 119:105), providing clarity and direction for every decision that must be made. May we not be lazy with Your Word, only turning to it in times of crisis or need, but determine to "meditate on it all day long" (Psalm 119:97b). As we strive to understand and uphold Your Word, please accept, O Lord, the willing praise from our mouths, and teach us your laws (Psalm 119:108).

JOURNAL: _____

_____

———◦◦◦◦———

THURSDAY: Read Psalm 119:1-18. Meditate on His Word and listen to what He has to say to you. Using the text as a guide, spend time in praise, confession and thanksgiving.

Pray for your children to find great joy and delight in God's Word: Lord Jesus, I praise you for Your willingness to give us Your written Word! It is so comforting to know as a parent, that Your Word will always be there for my children, even after I am gone. And it is the very best "instruction manual" that I could ever leave for them! "How can a young man keep his way pure? By living according to Your Word" (Psalm 119:9). Oh Father, how I long for my children to live pure and blameless lives, pleasing You in all their ways. May my husband and I teach them from a very young age to hide Your Word in their hearts that they might not sin against You (Psalm 119:11). As they grow and learn the value of meditating on Your precepts (Psalm 119:15), I pray that You would open their eyes that they may see wonderful things in Your law (Psalm 119:18). May they never see Your Word as a burden, but rather as a blessing... something they long for, filling them with joy and delight. Then my children will be ready to receive Your blessings along with those who keep Your statutes and seek You with all their hearts (Psalm 119:2).

JOURNAL: _____

_____

———◦◦◦◦———

FRIDAY: Read II Peter 1:12-21. Meditate on His Word and listen to what He has to say to you. Using the text as a guide, spend time in praise, confession and thanksgiving.

Pray for your church to take a stand for God's Word: Lord Jesus, thank You for the eyewitness accounts recorded in Scripture of those who spent time with You as You walked on this earth! And thank You for this affirmation that everything written in the Bible came directly from You: "No prophecy of Scripture came about by the prophet's own interpretation. For prophecy never had its origin in the will of man, but men spoke from God as they were carried along by the Holy Spirit" (II Peter 1:20-21). It is so important that we know Your Word and have it hidden in our hearts, so that we can boldly stand up for the inerrancy and accuracy of Scripture. I pray that we would heed Moses' warning to the Israelites: "Do not add to what I command you and do not subtract from it" (Deuteronomy 4:2), but always keep Your commands fully. May we never be guilty of picking and choosing from Your Word, deeming some of it as "politically incorrect" or irrelevant in our world today. Rather, may we as a church body stand up for Your Word, knowing that we would "do well to pay attention to it, as to a light shining in a dark place, until the day dawns and the Morning Star," Jesus Christ, returns (II Peter 1:19).

JOURNAL: _____

_____

_____

SATURDAY: A Day of Application

Read II Timothy 2:15.

Can you stand as one approved, who does not need to be ashamed at the way you handle God's Word? Or have you neglected His Word and His command to hide His Words in your heart?

_____

_____

_____

If you have not been following God's command to memorize and meditate on His Word, why not start today? Write out this week's memory verse here:

_____

_____

Ask someone to be your accountability partner, holding you responsible every week for memorizing a new verse. Write his or her name here:

_____

_____

SUNDAY: A Day of Praise

Read Hebrews 4:12-13.

Praise God that His word is Living and Active - alive, effective, penetrating. Praise Him that His Word that "judges the thoughts and attitudes of the heart" (Hebrews 4:12) also works in us to change us more and more into the image of His Son.

WRITE OUT YOUR PRAYER OF PRAISE HERE:

_____

_____

CHECK YOURSELF! WRITE YOUR MEMORY VERSE HERE:

_____

_____

Patience

"Therefore, as God's chosen people, holy and dearly loved,
clothe yourselves with compassion, kindness, humility,
gentleness and patience" (Colossians 3:12).

WOULD YOU HURRY UP ALREADY?

It was taking forever, and my patience was wearing very thin. My neighborhood grocery store was in the middle of a huge remodeling project, and I could not find what I needed. Everything in the store had been rearranged, the noise of the jack hammers made it difficult to even think, and I had exactly 14 minutes left to grab what I needed, make it through the checkout line, and be in the carpool line to pick my boys up from school. Making a snap decision to forego the last thing on my list, I headed toward the front of the store to check-out. The express lane did not move at "express speed", and I did a very poor job of waiting patiently for my turn. The lady in front of me was taking her sweet time to write a check, and I inwardly stewed as the minutes ticked by. I don't know what I would have done if she had wanted a price check!

If patience is a virtue, I'm definitely not very virtuous. It is something I have struggled with all of my life and must make a constant matter of prayer. I really do want to be more patient, but everyone is just getting in my way! Opportunities for cultivating patience are all around me. When my 6-year-old son wants to pour the milk over his cereal, missing the bowl and creating a sour mess, I need patience. When the phone rings incessantly and emergencies arise, interrupting my carefully planned schedule, I yearn for patience. When I bring a matter repeatedly before the Lord and nothing seems to change, I pray for patience. But not only should I pray, asking the Lord to help me be more patient,

God's Word also reminds me that patience is something I purposely put on, much like the clothes I choose to wear each day. "Therefore, as God's chosen people, holy and dearly loved, clothe yourselves with compassion, kindness, humility, gentleness and *patience*" (Colossians 3:12). A patient attitude doesn't appear overnight (this is the voice of experience talking here)! But as I intentionally "put it on," bringing every trying situation before the Lord, He can then transform my lowly body to make it look more like His glorious body (Philippians 3:21).

I've spent a lot of my life praying for patience in dealing with other people, but it has recently dawned on me that I also need to pray for patience in dealing with myself. Instead of going through life in a hurry, I want to allow myself the time to do a task and do it well instead of rushing through it. Instead of beating myself up when I fail, I want to accept my mistakes and use them as learning experiences, patiently giving God time to mold me into the creation He wants me to be. The Lord has grown in me a more patient attitude over the years, but I still have a long way to go. And the more I get in the way, the more I choose to don the clothes of irritability and impatience, the slower the process!

So today, I determine to clothe myself with patience, relinquishing my "hurry up" attitude to the Lord, and asking Him to help me slow down in dealing with myself and with others. I am so thankful that "He who began a good work" in me promises to "carry it on to completion until the day of Christ Jesus" (Philippians 1:6).

***

Memory Verse:
"Therefore, as God's chosen people, holy and dearly loved, clothe yourselves with compassion, kindness, humility, gentleness and patience" (Colossians 3:12).

***

MONDAY: Read Colossians 3:5-14. Meditate on God's Word and listen to what He has to say to you. Using the text as a guide, spend time in praise, confession and thanksgiving.

Pray for yourself, asking God to work in you to be patient with others and with yourself: Father God, I praise You that as a believer I have been "raised with Christ" and my "life is now hidden with Christ" in You (Colossians 3:1&3)! Thank You that I am one of Your "chosen people, holy and dearly loved" (Colossians 3:12), and that You are ever patient with me. May I not take these wonderful blessings for granted! I know that I must make the choice every day to take off my "old self with its practices" of impatience, irritability, and hurriedness, and "put on the new self, which is being renewed in knowledge in the image of its Creator" (Colossians 3:9-10). I want to look more like You every day, so today I choose to wear the clothes of compassion, kindness, humility, gentleness and **patience.** May Your Holy Spirit convict me at the first hint of impatience or irritability, whether in dealing with others or with myself. I do not want to hurry through life and miss Your best for me. Lord Jesus, I ask You to equip me with everything good for doing Your will and work in me what is pleasing to You (Hebrews 13:21).

JOURNAL: _____

_____

TUESDAY: Read Colossians 1:9-13. Meditate on God's Word and listen to what He has to say to you. Using the text as a guide, spend time in praise, confession and thanksgiving.

Pray endurance and patience for your husband: Father, thank You that You qualify Your children "to share in the inheritance of the saints in the kingdom of light" (Colossians 1:12)! And as children of the light, we ought to be shining forth Your love, Your compassion, and Your patience as we walk this earth. I pray for my dear husband today, asking You to fill him "with the knowledge of [Your] will through all spiritual wisdom and understanding" (Colossians 1:9). Your Word says that "a man's wisdom gives him patience; it is to his glory to overlook an offense" (Proverbs 19:11). So I place my husband in Your very capable hands, asking You to strengthen him "with all power according to [Your] glorious might so that [he] may have great endurance and patience" (Colossians 1:11). During the work day, may he look to You continually for endurance in dealing with trying issues. In the evenings at home, help him to have patience when interacting with his family after a difficult day. And on self-examination, please reveal to him where he is not being patient enough with himself.

JOURNAL: _____

_____

———❧———

WEDNESDAY: Read Romans 12:9-18. Meditate on God's Word and listen to what He has to say to you. Using the text as a guide, spend time in praise, confession and thanksgiving.

Pray for those in your household, to deal patiently with one another: Father, You have blessed me so much with each member of my family! It truly is my desire that we "live in harmony with one another" (Romans 12:16). Your Word clearly teaches that such living requires several things: loving sincerely, honoring others above self, and practicing patience in light of short-comings. So I pray that each one of us would determine to "be joyful in hope, patient in affliction, faithful in prayer" (Romans 12:12). Please give my husband and me patience in dealing with our children and their unhurried manner. Remind us to patiently allow them the time to make decisions for themselves. I would never want my children to remember me for my impatience with them, but for the time and attention I lovingly offered. In patient wisdom may we allow You to work in them without stepping in to intervene. And may my husband and I set a godly example of dealing patiently with one another, so that our children would be motivated to follow suit.

JOURNAL: _____

_____

———❧———

THURSDAY: Read James 5:7-11. Meditate on God's Word and listen to what He has to say to you. Using the text as a guide, spend time in praise, confession and thanksgiving.

Pray for your children, to be patient with where God has them at the present time: Father, as I think about my children, I remember how difficult it was to be a child at times. When I was very young, I wanted to be "big" like my older sister. When I reached the teen years, I yearned for the freedom and responsibility that came with adulthood. Impatient for the next step, I was tempted to throw off childish things in a race for maturity. Oh, how I see the same impulses in my own children! At times I want to yell out, "Just slow down! You're growing up too fast!" So I ask You, Father, please help my children to be content where they are right now. I want them to enjoy the lack of responsibility and ease of life as a child, not hurry through it. I am so thankful that You are the Farmer, working in my children's lives behind the scenes. And one day, at the proper time, each one of them will yield their own valuable crop (James 5:7). May my children be patient to wait on Your perfect timing so that they don't miss out on Your best for them. Please, Father, help all of us to "be patient and stand firm, because the Lord's coming is near" (James 5:8).

JOURNAL: _____

_____

FRIDAY: Read II Corinthians 6:3-10. Meditate on God's Word and listen to what He has to say to you. Using the text as a guide, spend time in praise, confession and thanksgiving.

Pray for your pastor, to have patience in enduring the hardships of his calling: Father God, thank you so much for this man You have chosen to shepherd my church. His job is not an easy one... there are times that it demands all of his strength, all of his time, and certainly all of his patience as he deals with very imperfect people. So I lift him up to You today, praying that as Your servant, he would commend himself in every way: in great endurance; in troubles; in hard work and sleepless nights; in purity, understanding and patience; in the Holy Spirit and in sincere love (II Corinthians 6:4-6). When attacked by the evil one, remind him to fight back in "truthful speech and in the power of God; with weapons of righteousness" in his hands (II Corinthians 6:7). In times of both "glory and dishonor, bad report and good report" (II Corinthians 6:8), may he remain faithful to You. I pray that You would enable him to stand firm, never allowing his ministry to be discredited because of his own sin. And if he is tempted to give up in the face of difficulty, remind him that his "light and momentary troubles are achieving for [him] an eternal glory that far outweighs them all" (II Corinthians 4:17)!

JOURNAL: _____

SATURDAY: A Day of Application

Read Ephesians 4:1-3.

Name one area in which you need patience:

_____

Name one person with whom you need patience:

_____

Name one thing that you are trying to "hurry" in your life:

_____

Pray and ask the Lord to help you "clothe yourself with patience" (Colossians 3:12):

_____

Determine to "live a life worthy of the calling you have received" (Ephesians 4:1) by being willing to change anything about your life that does not please God. Write out your prayer of commitment here:

_____

_____

SUNDAY: A Day of Praise

Read II Peter 3:9-15.

Praise God that He is so patient with us! Praise God that He does not want anyone to die without repenting of their sin and receiving salvation through Jesus Christ.

WRITE OUT YOUR PRAYER OF PRAISE HERE:

_____

_____

_____

CHECK YOURSELF! WRITE YOUR MEMORY VERSE HERE:

_____

_____

Being a Godly Example

"Follow my example, as I follow the example of Christ"
(I Corinthians 11:1).

THE VALUE OF A PATTERN!

I sew a little bit from time to time and have greatly learned to appreciate the value of a pattern when making something I have never made before. The measurements have already been made, the amount of fabric and notions needed have already been calculated, and the step-by-step instructions written on the pattern package tell me exactly what to do. As long as I follow the pattern, I will end up with the item I wanted to make! But every once in a while, I venture out on my own and try to make something without a pattern. Without fail, I end up making a lot of mistakes and the results are less than perfect. Doing it my own way and learning by trial and error, the process is much longer and doesn't produce exactly what I had envisioned.

In much the same way of having a pattern to follow in sewing, so having an example to follow as Christians is an invaluable and much needed resource. Jesus Christ is our Perfect Example, and His Word is our "pattern" for living. With our eyes fixed firmly on Him, we have a model to pursue as we strive to live godly lives in accordance with His Word. The apostle Paul understood that as he followed Christ's example, he would become an example worth following as well: "Follow my example, as I follow the example of Christ" (I Corinthians 11:1).

Having other believers who are dedicated in their pursuit of Christ gives us flesh and blood examples that we so desperately need. When I was a 15 year-old teenager new to a relationship with Jesus, my youth pastor "Tic" opened my eyes to see Christ as the very real and personal God He is. By honestly sharing experiences from his own life, he demonstrated a humility before the Lord that I long to live up to. Then as a single young adult, I met a woman who was completely "on fire" for the Lord, with a love and zeal for our God that could not be contained! Cheri became my Sunday School teacher and began to teach me how to study God's Word and apply it to my life. Week after week as she poured her life into mine, I developed a growing intimacy with Christ and a desire to see others come to know Him too. When I was the busy mother of three young children, my Women's Minister, Amy, was the example I needed to begin teaching other women. She shared with me her own testimony of agreeing to teach, even though it took her out of her comfort zone. Amy was a model to me of obedience in the face of uncertainty. Her gentle admonition that I not delay in using the gifts God had given me was the motivation I needed to step out in faith and obey what God was asking of me. Later, when my first child entered kindergarten, another mom from my church asked me if I would like to start praying with her. The first time I heard Denise open her mouth in prayer, I was amazed at her knowledge of Scripture and jealous of her ability to recall so much of it from memory. In watching her, I was motivated to get serious about hiding God's Word in my heart so that I would have it ready to pray whenever a need arose.

You see, each of these precious believers taught me by example. ...it was as I saw them live in daily pursuit of the Lord, following Him to the best of their ability, that I had the desire to do so also. Don't you want to be an example worth following? I know I do! So "let us fix our eyes on Jesus" (Hebrews 12:2), the Perfect Example, and learn from those who have walked before us in faith and dependency on Him.

Memory Verse:
"Follow my example, as I follow the example of Christ"
(I Corinthians 11:1).

MONDAY: Read I Corinthians 10:31-11:1. Meditate on God's Word and listen to what He has to say to you. Using the text as a guide, spend time in praise, confession and thanksgiving.

Pray for yourself, to follow the example of Christ so that you will be a godly example before others: Lord Jesus, thank You for being our Perfect Example! "The Word became flesh and made His dwelling among us" (John 1:14), giving us a model to follow as we walk this earth. Thank You, too, for the examples of other Christians You have placed in my life who daily strive to live for You. It is my prayer that others will be able to "follow my example, as I follow the example of Christ" (I Corinthians 11:1). Remind me that others are watching! So whether I eat or drink or whatever I do, I should do it all for the glory of God (I Corinthians 10:31). Please forbid that I "cause anyone to stumble" (I Corinthians 10:32) because I have set the wrong example of worldly living! I yield myself afresh to You, asking You to equip me, motivate me, and use me in any way that You see fit. Please give me the discipline to stay in Your Word, the boldness to proclaim it, and the determination to live it! May I be an example worth following all the days of my life.

JOURNAL: _____

_____

_____

———————

TUESDAY: Read Philippians 3:12-17. Meditate on God's Word and listen to what He has to say to you. Using the text as a guide, spend time in praise, confession and thanksgiving.

Pray for your husband, to "live up to what [he] has already attained" (Philippians 3:16) and be an example before others: Father, it is so easy to get bogged down in the concerns of this life. I know that husbands often feel a great burden of responsibility to provide for their families. So I pray for my dear husband, that You would give him the stamina and strength that he needs to "press on toward the goal to win the prize for which God has called [him] heavenward in Christ Jesus" (Philippians 3:14).

Help him to forget what is behind – past failures that cause him regret, as well as past victories that deceive him into believing he has already done enough. Encourage him to strain toward what is ahead (Philippians 3:13) – the goal of knowing Christ more intimately, becoming more like Christ, and being all that Christ has in mind for him. May my husband "take note of those who live according to the pattern" (Philippians 3:17b) laid out in Scripture, and may he have the desire to follow their example as they follow Christ. And in everything may he set an example by doing what is good (Titus 2:7).

JOURNAL: _____

_____

⸺◦◦◦⸺

WEDNESDAY: Read I Corinthians 10:1-11. Meditate on God's Word and listen to what He has to say to you. Using the text as a guide, spend time in praise, confession and thanksgiving.

Pray for those in your household, to look to God's Word and learn from the examples of those who have walked before you: Father, in Your great wisdom and understanding of how we best learn, You included flesh and blood examples for us in Your Word. Thank You for the privilege of being able to read and study the accounts of men and women who determined to follow You wholeheartedly. May my husband and I teach our children to emulate these godly examples by putting into practice what we have learned or received or heard or seen in them (Philippians 4:9). But I think I am even more thankful for the many accounts recorded for us in Scripture where Your children have failed! For "these things occurred as examples to keep us from setting our hearts on evil things as they did" (I Corinthians 10:6). These things "were written down as warnings for us" (I Corinthians 10:11), so may we never dismiss them lightly! There is great wisdom in learning from the mistakes of others, so please help us to be both teachable and diligent in studying Your Word.

JOURNAL: _____

_____

⸺◦◦◦⸺

THURSDAY: Read Psalm 78:1-7. Meditate on God's Word and listen to what He has to say to you. Using the text as a guide, spend time in praise, confession and thanksgiving.

Pray for your children, to accept God's Word and pass it on to the next generation: Heavenly Father, You "commanded our forefathers to teach (Your laws to) their children, so the next generation would know them...and they in turn would tell their children" (Psalm 78:5-6). It is abundantly clear that the continuation of this cycle depends on us! May my husband and I not fall short in this responsibility, but teach our children Your Word with contagious enthusiasm. I pray that the things they hear from us they will "keep as the pattern of sound teaching, with faith and love in Christ Jesus" (II Timothy 1:13). As our children grow and their realm of influence broadens, please bring godly role models into their lives who will walk before them in purity, in discipline, and in dedication to You. I beg You, Father, protect them from anyone who would lead them away from the truth of Your Word! My children need to know that even from a young age they are setting an example for others to follow. I pray that they would take this responsibility seriously. May they never let anyone look down on them because they are young, but "set an example for the believers in speech, in life, in love, in faith and in purity" (I Timothy 4:12).

JOURNAL: _____

_____

_____

FRIDAY: Read I Thessalonians 1:1-10. Meditate on God's Word and listen to what He has to say to you. Using the text as a guide, spend time in praise, confession and thanksgiving.

Pray for your church, to be a model for other believers to follow: Father, what an amazing example the church of the Thessalonians was! They embodied faith, hope and love in the midst of severe suffering, and as a result, the power of the Holy Spirit fell upon them in a mighty way.

How I pray that my church would be like that…a church whose work is produced by faith, whose labor is prompted by love, and whose endurance is inspired by hope in our Lord Jesus Christ (I Thessalonians 1:3). Through the power of the Holy Spirit may we stand firm in our faith, be bold in sharing the Good News, and live as godly examples to this lost and dying world. May we imitate You as the Thessalonians did (I Thessalonians 1:6), so that we will become a model worth following. I pray that Your message would ring out from us not only in nearby cities, but that our faith in God would become known everywhere (I Thessalonians 1:8). May we wait in daily expectation of Your Son from heaven, the One Who was "raised from the dead – Jesus, Who rescues us from the coming wrath" (I Thessalonians 1:10).

JOURNAL: _____

_____

_____

SATURDAY: A Day of Application

Read Titus 2:1-8. Teach…train…be an example. "In everything set them an example by doing what is good" (verse 7). What kind of example are you being? Are you taking seriously your responsibility to teach and train others by example?

_____

If you know that you have been setting the wrong example before your children, friends, and others in your sphere of influence, confess it before the Lord and ask Him to forgive you. Write out your prayer here:

_____

_____

What kind of example are you following? A godly one or an ungodly one?

_____

Commit your life afresh to the Lord and determine to line up your life with His in every way. Then you will be able to say, "Follow my example, as I follow the example of Christ" (I Corinthians 11:1). Write out your prayer of commitment here:

_____

_____

SUNDAY: A Day of Praise

Read John 13:12-15.

Praise the Lord that He is our Perfect Example! Praise Him that He never asks us to do anything that He was not willing to do Himself.

WRITE OUT YOUR PRAYER OF PRAISE HERE:

_____

_____

_____

CHECK YOURSELF! WRITE YOUR MEMORY VERSE HERE:

_____

_____

Cultivating Relationships

"Two are better than one, because they have a good return for their work: If one falls down, his friend can help him up. But pity the man who falls and has no one to help him up!" (Ecclesiastes 4:9-10)

IT'S WORTH THE EFFORT!

Every year, my college girl friends and I designate a weekend, usually in the fall, to escape the normalcy of life and meet in a neutral location for a little "female bonding". A few times we have strayed from our typical routine when one of us has gotten married or had a baby, but usually the weekend is totally devoted to three simple things: shopping, eating and most importantly, talking! Away from the distractions and responsibilities of home, there are no time limits on our conversation. Deana, Angela, Laurie and I are free to talk without leaving out a single detail. Whether we are crying over disappointments or laughing until our sides hurt, the 25 years since college seem to disappear, making us feel like 18 year-olds again. We usually have to start planning our trip months ahead of time, but like a breath of fresh air, our time together never fails to leave me feeling refreshed, encouraged and loved.

The Lord has certainly blessed me over the years by giving me wonderful companions at different stages in my life. Through church, my children's school, my neighborhood, and especially within my own extended family, close relationships are a great blessing. Ecclesiastes 4:9-10 says, "Two are better than one, because they have a good return for their work: If one falls down, his friend can help him up. But pity the man who falls and has no one to help him up!" Simply put, ladies, we need other people. God Himself said, "It is not good for the man to be alone" (Genesis 2:18). But "superwomen" that we are, we try to convince ourselves that we can handle things on our own, that we are big girls who don't need any support, and that we just don't have the time to cultivate relationships in our busy lives. Lacking the time and energy to devote ourselves to one more thing, we stay home from neighborhood gatherings, neglect spending time with those we love, or allow past friendships to get swallowed up by present responsibilities.

I've heard it said that if a person has five close friends in her life, she should consider herself lucky. In my opinion, if she finds a few godly friends she is truly blessed! Devoted, loyal, like-minded, be there "through thick and thin" friends are not easy to come by. My own mother and sister are those dear friends who love me unconditionally, drop everything else for me in my time of need, and take my side no matter what. For a more unbiased point of view (which is sometimes difficult for family members!) I turn to my "oldest" friend Kelly, who has been my friend since the 8th grade. She listens attentively, accepts me exactly the way I am, and walks with me through the ups and downs of this life. Even though we no longer live in the same city, we make a point of maintaining our close friendship by calling each other weekly and visiting as often as we can.

Will it take some time and planning to maintain old friendships? Certainly! Will it take a little effort to begin a new one? Of course! But from personal experience I can testify that it will definitely be worth it. So pick up the phone today and plan some "girl time" of your own!

Memory Verse:
"Two are better than one, because they have a good return for their work: If one falls down, his friend can help him up. But pity the man who falls and has no one to help him up!"
(Ecclesiastes 4:9-10).

MONDAY: Read Ecclesiastes 4:8-12. Meditate on God's Word and listen to what He has to say to you. Using the text as a guide, spend time in praise, confession and thanksgiving.

Pray for yourself, to desire and develop godly relationships: Father, I praise You as the God Who knew from the very beginning that we would need companionship. To hold another's hand, feel a loving embrace, share a laugh or shed a tear, at times we yearn for "flesh and blood" as we walk through the ups and downs of this life. How very thankful I am for the friends You have placed in my path. Forgive me when I take those friends for granted, neglecting the time and effort to reach out and show that I care. Your Word says that "a friend loves at all times, and a brother is born for adversity" (Proverbs 17:17). Help me to be that kind of friend, and please bless me with that kind of friend! When I am tempted to go it alone, please remind me that I am weak and need the strength and support of others. "Though one may be overpowered, two can defend themselves. A cord of three strands is not quickly broken" (Ecclesiastes 4:12). And with You as that "third strand" in the relationship, we are strongest of all!

JOURNAL: _____

_____

_____

TUESDAY: Read Exodus 4:10-16. Meditate on God's Word and listen to what He has to say to you. Using the text as a guide, spend time in praise, confession and thanksgiving.

Pray for your husband, to reach out to others for companionship and support: Lord Jesus, our world today tells men to strive for independence, to claw their way to the top at the expense of others, and to rely on no one but themselves. How very contrary to Your Word! In fact, when calling Your own disciples, You "sent them out two by two" (Mark 6:7), giving them a partner to accomplish the work You had for them. I am thankful for this account from Exodus, which honestly portrays Moses' reluctance to do the job You called him to. Exasperated with Moses but knowing his fears and limitations, You assured him that he would not have to do the work alone: "(Aaron) is already on his way to meet you" (Exodus 4:14). Knowing that there would be obstacles and opposition, You prepared the way ahead of time so that support would be there when needed. In like manner, I pray that You would provide the companionship and support for my husband that he needs. May he resist the temptation to stand alone and build up walls of independence, instead reaching out in friendship and love to those You have placed in his life.

JOURNAL: _____

_____

_____

WEDNESDAY: Read Genesis 2:18-24. Meditate on God's Word and listen to what He has to say to you. Using the text as a guide, spend time in praise, confession and thanksgiving.

Pray for your marriage, that you and your husband would satisfy one another's need for companionship: Father God, as I read this passage, my mind envisions Adam surrounded by all the animals you created, looking for the perfect one to be his companion. "But for Adam no suitable helper was found" (Genesis 2:20b). So You made Adam fall into a deep sleep, removed one of his ribs, and fashioned a woman... bone of his bones and flesh of his flesh (Genesis 2:23). Adam now had a "suitable helper" and lifelong companion. Father, thank You for the man You have given me as my partner and friend. Thank You that You found in me a "suitable helper" for him, and You found in my husband the perfect man to be my soulmate. Your Word says, "He who finds a wife finds what is good and receives favor from the Lord" (Proverbs 18:22). You call me "good" Lord, and I want to be Your instrument of goodness and blessing in my husband's life! I pray that we would be able to joyfully declare, "This is my lover, this is my friend" (Song of Songs 5:16). Please reveal to each of us any way we fall short, so that we can fulfill one another's need for companionship in every way.

JOURNAL: _____

_____

_____

THURSDAY: Read I Samuel 18:1-4; 20:41-42. Meditate on God's Word and listen to what He has to say to you. Using the text as a guide, spend time in praise, confession and thanksgiving.

Pray for your children, to pursue godly friendships: Lord Jesus, what a precious friendship David and Jonathan shared! Your Word says, "Jonathan became one in spirit with David, and he loved him as himself" (I Samuel 18:1). These two men swore "friendship with each other in the name of the Lord" (I Samuel 20:42). Oh how I pray for such godly friendships for each of my children! May they be drawn to those who love You and disinterested in those who follow after worldliness. For "don't you know that friendship with the world is hatred toward God? Anyone who chooses to be a friend of the world becomes an enemy of God" (James 4:4). I pray that they would desire the right kind of friends and be protected from the wrong ones. Help them to connect with "like-minded" believers...at school, at work, wherever they go. May my children understand that it is not the number of friends one has that matters, but it is the loyalty of friends that is important. "A man of many companions may come to ruin, but there is a friend who sticks closer than a brother" (Proverbs 18:24).

JOURNAL: _____

_____

_____

FRIDAY: Read II Corinthians 6:14-18. Meditate on God's Word and listen to what He has to say to you. Using the text as a guide, spend time in praise, confession and thanksgiving.

Pray for your children, to seek out other believers in marriage: Father, Your Word is crystal clear: "Do not be yoked together with unbelievers" (II Corinthians 6:14). I can think of no more important relationship than marriage where I want my children to be "equally yoked". Please Lord, do whatever it takes to keep my children from the wrong mate and save them for the right one. May they choose to not even casually date unbelievers, but "come out from them and be separate" (II Corinthians 6:17). Help them to understand that this command is not meant to limit them but to protect them! It is hard enough to maintain unity in marriage with a like-minded spouse – how much more difficult with someone who neither knows You nor strives to live according to Your commands. I pray that the future spouses of each one of my children will experience an early salvation in a loving home and be devoted to sexual purity until marriage. May Christ be honored in their future homes so that You "will live with them and walk among them" (II Corinthians 6:16b).

JOURNAL: _____

_____

_____

SATURDAY: A Day of Application

Read Proverbs 27:6, 9, 10 & 17.

Do you have companions/godly friendships in your life? Those who will speak the truth in love, sharpen you "as iron sharpens iron", and be there for you in time of need?

_____

If so, spend some time thanking the Lord for blessing you with each one:

_____

_____

If not, pray and ask the Lord to give you a friend like Jonathan was to David – a friend in the Lord!

_____

_____

Are you a godly and dependable friend to others? _____ Do you invest time and effort in order to maintain the friendships that you have? _____ Make a plan right now to call a friend and set aside some time to spend together:

_____

_____

SUNDAY: A Day of Praise

Read John 15:12-15 & Exodus 33:11.

Praise the Lord that He is your Friend! He is always ready and willing to offer love, acceptance, comfort, encouragement and companionship. "The Lord would speak to Moses face to face, as a man speaks with his friend" (Exodus 33:11).

WRITE OUT YOUR PRAYER OF PRAISE HERE:

_____

_____

CHECK YOURSELF! WRITE YOUR MEMORY VERSE HERE:

_____

_____

WEEK FOURTEEN
Listening to God

"As Jesus and His disciples were on their way, He came to a village where a woman named Martha opened her home to Him. She had a sister called Mary who sat at the Lord's feet listening to what He said. But Martha was distracted by all the preparations that had to be made" (Luke 10:38-40).

TOO BUSY TO LISTEN

I received a phone call one day as I was doing chores around the house. When I answered the phone, an automated voice advised me to secure paper and pen because in 9 seconds I would be given some very important information. Now, as usual when I receive an automated phone call I was tempted to just hang up...I was busy and already in the middle of another task. But my curiosity got the best of me and I reluctantly found paper and pen in case the message really was important. After waiting impatiently for 9 seconds, I was informed that there was a recall on some food I had purchased at my local grocery store. The food was contaminated and needed to be thrown away. "Wow," I thought to myself, "I'm glad I listened. It would have been terrible if my family got sick because we ate that spoiled food!"

That phone call made me stop and consider how I interact with God. Daily I pray and spend time in His Word, but how well do I actually listen for Him to speak to me? I was tempted to hang up on that automated phone call because I thought I probably didn't even need to hear the instructions... that they wouldn't be relevant or worthwhile. In much the same way, I sometimes fail to approach the Lord for instructions or listen for His voice because I really don't believe I need any help. "I've got a lot to do today so I better get started!" Or "I'm capable enough to make this decision without anyone else telling me what to do."

The account of Martha and Mary in Luke chapter 10 is a great example of this. For Martha, there was so much to do! Martha had to prepare a meal for a group of hungry men, and I'm sure she wanted it to be perfect. She had bread to bake, chickens to pluck, salad to toss, a table to set, tea to brew and a house to clean, for goodness sake. After all, Jesus was visiting! Overwhelmed by all the preparations that had to be made, Martha came to Jesus complaining that Mary was just sitting around, leaving all the work for her to do alone. "Tell her to help me!" Martha demanded. "Martha, Martha," the Lord answered, "you are worried and upset about many things, but only one thing is needed. Mary has chosen what is better" (Luke 10:41-42). What was that one thing Mary had chosen to do? She chose to sit at the Lord's feet and listen.

Ouch! And so it is with us. We have work to do, groceries to buy, houses to clean, clothes to wash, committee meetings to attend, errands to run, lessons to prepare, workouts to fit in, etc. The question for all of us is this: How much time in our day do we actually spend before the Lord, listening to Him speak to us? He is our Lord and Master, after all, so shouldn't we be asking Him for direction or guidance on what we are to do? At the end of the day we might be able to check many things off our lists, but if none of them mattered to God, we've wasted our day. Now, this is not an excuse to let dirty dishes take over the kitchen and dirty clothes pile up in the laundry room! But before we get "distracted with all the preparations that have to be made," before we begin a task that God might not even be interested in, we do well to prepare ourselves for the day by worshiping our Lord and listening to what He has to say to us. We must determine to be more like Mary than Martha and choose what is better!

Memory Verse:
"She had a sister called Mary, who sat at the Lord's feet listening to what He said. But Martha was distracted by all the preparations that had to be made" (Luke 10:39-40).

MONDAY: Read Luke 10:38-42. Meditate on God's Word and listen to what He has to say to you. Using the text as a guide, spend time in praise, confession and thanksgiving.

Pray for yourself, to choose what is better and daily spend time listening to the Lord: Oh Lord Jesus, I am so guilty of not taking the time to sit at Your feet, listening to what You want to say to me. I know that I often rush into the day, hurrying to get everything done on my "to-do" list. I recognize that I have often complained to You as Martha did, that I have too much work to do and nobody will help me! Father, forgive me for neglecting this awesome privilege of listening to You speak. Thank You that You would even desire to speak to me, a sinner…if only I would listen to what You want to say to me! I am so thankful that You promise never to put more on me in one day than I can handle. If I feel overwhelmed, if I become "worried and upset about many things," it is because I have put too much on myself, not You. Please help me to be more like Mary who "has chosen what is better" (Luke 10:42). You, Lord Jesus, are the One who is worthy of my time and attention. I determine to sit quietly before You this morning, listening for Your voice.

JOURNAL: _____

_____

_____

TUESDAY: Read Ezekiel 2:1-8. Meditate on God's Word and listen to what He has to say to you. Using the text as a guide, spend time in praise, confession and thanksgiving.

Pray for your husband, to turn his ear toward God and listen for His voice: Heavenly Father, I pray for my dear husband today. Just as You spoke to Ezekiel saying, "But you, son of man, listen to what I say to you" (Ezekiel 2:8), so You want to speak to my husband. Oh, that he would have ears to hear! May he not be like those in Jeremiah 5:21 "who have eyes but do not see, who have ears but do not hear." Rather, may my husband wait to hear Your voice and listen intently to Your words of direction for his life. If you have something difficult for him to hear, I pray that he would not close his ears to Your truth, but open his heart for Your examination. If you have something difficult for him to do, may he not be afraid to obey Your voice. Use me to remind him that whatever You are commanding him today is not too difficult for him or beyond his reach (Deuteronomy 30:11). As the leader of our home, he needs to hear direction from You. May he be hungry for Your voice so that he will always lead our family as You direct.

JOURNAL: _____

_____

_____

———⚬⚬⚬———

WEDNESDAY: Read Isaiah 66:1-4. Meditate on God's Word and listen to what He has to say to you. Using the text as a guide, spend time in praise, confession and thanksgiving.

Pray for those in your household, to properly respond when God speaks: Lord, as I read these verses I am reminded of Your greatness. Heaven is indeed Your throne and the earth is merely Your footstool (Isaiah 66:1). Who are we to choose our own way and refuse to listen to Your Word? You say in Scripture, "For when I called, no one answered, when I spoke, no one listened" (Isaiah 66:4). Oh Lord, please forgive us when we are found guilty of such a response. In our home may Your Words be our very sustenance, fulfilling what was said in Deuteronomy 8:3 that "man does not live on bread alone but on every word that comes from the mouth of the Lord." I pray that my husband and I would depend on Your Word for guidance and value what You say more than any other opinion we might hear. I want our children to witness what it means to live in daily anticipation of hearing Your voice. And when You do speak, that the only proper response should be to tremble…tremble in humility that the God of the universe would speak to us! Please remind us daily to "be quick to listen, slow to speak" (James 1:19).

JOURNAL: _____

_____

_____

———⚬⚬⚬———

THURSDAY: Read I Samuel 3:1-10. Meditate on God's Word and listen to what He has to say to you. Using the text as a guide, spend time in praise, confession and thanksgiving.

Pray for your children to be like Samuel, listening for the Lord's voice: Father, in Samuel 3:1 it says, "In those days the word of the Lord was rare." Oh what a privilege we have "in these days" of being able to read Your written Word anytime we wish! And not only that, You say, "Call to Me and I will answer you and tell you great and unsearchable things you do not know" (Jeremiah 33:3). But also "in these days" there are so many distractions, so much noise and activity going on all the time, that we must focus more than ever before to wait on You and hear Your voice. It is such a temptation to have a one-sided conversation with You, doing all of the talking and none of the listening. Help me to teach my children that prayer was never meant to be this way! Just as they ask me questions and wait for my response, so they should ask of You and wait for Your answer. May they be ready to hear Your voice as Samuel was, saying "Speak Lord, for your servant is listening" (I Samuel 3:9).

JOURNAL: _____

_____

_____

FRIDAY: Read Deuteronomy 4:32-40. Meditate on God's Word and listen to what He has to say to you. Using the text as a guide, spend time in praise, confession and thanksgiving.

Pray for your church, that God's faithfulness to speak to His children in the past will reassure your church members of His desire to speak to them today: Father, thank You for this reminder of how You have spoken to Your children since the beginning of time. "Has any other people heard the voice of God speaking" (Deuteronomy 4:33) as the Israelites did when You led them out of Egypt and into the Promised Land? No! Others serve gods "made by the hands of men. They have mouths, but cannot speak...nor can they utter a sound with their throats"

(Psalm 115:4b-7). Quite the contrary, we serve the Living God who "does speak – now one way, now another – though man may not perceive it" (Job 33:14). How I pray that the members of my church would not miss it when You speak. When our pastor shares the messages You have laid on his heart, and we hear Your voice to discipline us (Deuteronomy 4:36) may we respond in humble obedience. When the choir sings praises to Your name, and we hear Your voice of faithfulness, may we never fail to give You thanks. And as Your sheep, may we be careful to listen to Your voice; You know us, and we follow You (John 10:27).

JOURNAL: _____

_____

_____

SATURDAY: A Day of Application

Read Luke 9:28-36.

In Luke 9:35 God says, "This is my Son, whom I have chosen; listen to Him!"

Do you often fail to take the time to listen to the Lord Jesus? If so, confess it here:

_____

_____

Commit some extra time to the Lord today, just to sit at His feet and listen to what He has to say to You. Do your best to clear your mind and focus on Him. Have paper and pen ready to write down anything that He says to you or brings to your mind. "Speak Lord Jesus, for your servant is listening":

_____

_____

SUNDAY: A Day of Praise

Read Job 33:13-18.

"Before they call I will answer; while they are still speaking I will hear" (Isaiah 65:24).

Praise God as the great Communicator...He speaks, He hears, and He answers.

WRITE OUT YOUR PRAYER OF PRAISE HERE:

_____

_____

_____

CHECK YOURSELF! WRITE YOUR MEMORY VERSE HERE:

_____

_____

Protection

"For He will command His angels concerning you to guard you in all your ways; they will lift you up in their hands, so that you will not strike your foot against a stone" (Psalm 91:11-12).

STITCHES AND BROKEN ARMS

One summer, the night before my family was to go on vacation, my two oldest boys were having a race to see who could run around my in-laws' house the fastest. They were running in opposite directions around the house, with the start and finish line at the golf cart parked in front. It was a close race, so my oldest son Ian was still going full steam when he reached the golf cart finish line. His leg hit the golf cart first, at the exact place where a small piece of metal protruded for the trailer hitch. He didn't even have time to rejoice over the big win, as the pain of his injury was immediate. That innocent looking trailer hitch had torn Ian's flesh open down to the bone, and we spent the rest of the night in the emergency room getting his leg stitched up!

It wasn't our first trip to the ER, but I sure hoped and prayed it would be our last. After a broken arm and two other minor surgeries among the three boys, a friend said I should count myself lucky that there hadn't been more hospital visits. But I know better than to attribute good luck as the reason we had not been subjected to more time on the examination table. Psalm 91:11-12 says, "For He will command His angels concerning you to guard you in all your ways; they will lift you up in their hands, so that you will not strike your foot against a stone." Praise God that He is the Commander in Chief of a host of angels too numerous for me to count! It is wonderfully reassuring to know that I can ask the Lord to command His army of angels to guard my children wherever they are. Who knows how many times they have been lifted up and protected from a possible injury that I was never even aware of?

My husband and I have spent a lot of time praying for our boys over the past thirteen years, and I imagine that prayers for protection have definitely topped the list. When my children were infants, I prayed that God would protect them from injury or disease, from falling out of their cribs, and from SIDS (Sudden Infant Death Syndrome). When they were toddlers, I prayed that they would be safe from going out in the street, from having bad dreams, and from catching viruses from other runny-nosed kids at Mother's Day Out. When they started school, I changed my prayers to protection on the playground, protection from bullies, and protection from being abducted by a child molester. As they enter the teen years, I have now added protection from peer pressure, protection from drugs and alcohol, and protection from pre-marital sex. And how I pray that our God would protect my children from the evil one in every area of their lives! (We will actually deal with this topic in Week 43.) I can work myself up into quite a state imagining all kinds of terrible things that could happen to them, but I know that the very best thing I can do when these ideas pop into my mind is to bring them to God in prayer. He is Lord, and they are His.

I would do anything in my power to protect my children, but I also know that my power is very limited. "Great is our Lord and mighty in power; His understanding has no limit" (Psalm 147:5). Thank God that both His understanding of our concerns and His power to care for our children are limitless. Not only is He able to protect our children when we are not, He is also willing!

Memory Verse:
"For He will command His angels concerning you to guard you in all your ways; they will lift you up in their hands, so that you will not strike your foot against a stone"
(Psalm 91:11-12).

MONDAY: Read Psalm 40:11-17. Meditate on God's Word and listen to what He has to say to you. Using the text as a guide, spend time in praise, confession and thanksgiving.

Pray for yourself, asking God to help you trust Him as your Protector: Father, it is such a comfort to know that You, the God of power and might, are my Protector, my Deliverer, and my Shield. Nothing crosses my path that has not first been filtered through Your loving hands. Please forgive me when I forget these truths and allow myself to be consumed with fear and anxiety. Forgive me when I foolishly try to set up my own means of protection instead of asking for Your intervention. When "troubles without number surround me" (Psalm 40:12), help me to remember that I am not alone! "You are my help and my deliverer; O my God, do not delay" (Psalm 40:17). Please Father, protect me from bodily harm so that I can be here for my family. Protect me from the emotional turmoil that sometimes comes from being a woman. Protect me from being lured into worldliness. And please protect me from myself, when I am my own worst enemy! I cling to Your Promise that says, "I will lie down and sleep in peace, for You alone, O Lord, make me dwell in safety" (Psalm 4:8).

JOURNAL: _____

_____

_____

TUESDAY: Read Psalm 140:1-8. Meditate on God's Word and listen to what He has to say to you. Using the text as a guide, spend time in praise, confession and thanksgiving.

Pray for God's protection over your husband: Lord Jesus, I realize that I often look to my husband as my protector. Thank you for his bodily presence that makes me feel safe. But he needs protection too! So I lift him up to You, my Lord and my God, asking You to keep him from the hands of the wicked; protect him from men of violence who plan to trip his feet (Psalm 140:4). If anyone intends to harm him, I pray that You, our Strong Deliverer, would shield his head and not let their plans succeed

(Psalm 140:7-8). Please protect him from physical harm as he works and goes about his day. Whenever he gets behind the wheel of his car, I pray that You would protect him on his entire journey and in every city through which he travels (Joshua 24:17). I ask You to protect his mind and his heart from anything that would damage his relationship with You or with me. I pray that You would protect him from injury or disease, keeping him healthy and strong for many years to come. And in the day of difficulty, will You be his hiding place and protect him from trouble (Psalm 32:7).

JOURNAL: _____

_____

_____

WEDNESDAY: Read Psalm 35:1-10. Meditate on God's Word and listen to what He has to say to you. Using the text as a guide, spend time in praise, confession and thanksgiving.

Pray for your home and those in your household, to be protected at all times: Lord, I cling to Your Words in Psalm 35:10 that say, "You rescue the poor from those too strong for them, the poor and needy from those who rob them." Our world is so full of evil today, and the news is full of reports of burglaries, attacks, and crimes too heinous to even think about. Oh how I pray that You will "take up shield and buckler; arise and come to [our] aid" (Psalm 35:2), preventing such terrible things from happening to us. If anyone means to enter our home and do my family harm, I beg You Lord, to send Your angel to drive them away (Psalm 35:5). As You gave Your children "a wall of protection in Judah and Jerusalem" (Ezra 9:9), so give us a wall of protection around our home. And I pray that You also protect the physical structure of our home from being damaged in any type of natural disaster. May our testimony be like that of Job who had "a hedge around him and his household" and all that he had on every side (Job 1:10).

JOURNAL: _____

_____

_____

THURSDAY: Read Psalm 91:1-16. Meditate on God's Word and listen to what He has to say to you. Using the text as a guide, spend time in praise, confession and thanksgiving.

Pray for your children, to be covered with God's protection: Oh Father, I remember so well when my first child was born, and the overwhelming love I had for him right from the start! I knew I would do anything possible to protect this child from harm. But I quickly became aware that I was powerless to protect him from everything and needed Someone greater than me to stand at his defense. So I ask You, Lord Jesus, to protect my children. I am so thankful that You are "my refuge and my fortress, my God in whom I trust" (Psalm 91:2). I pray that You would cover my children with Your feathers so that under Your wings they will find refuge (Psalm 91:4). Please protect them physically, from injury or harm. Protect them emotionally, from unkind words and feelings of despair. Protect them spiritually, from anyone who would say or do anything to lead them astray. I ask You, Almighty God, to spread your protection over my children… "surround them with Your favor as with a shield" (Psalm 5:11-12). Protect them from making poor decisions, from forming ungodly relationships, and from becoming addicted to worldly passions. If my children ever find themselves in a scary place, remind them that they can call upon You and You will answer them; You will be with them in trouble and deliver them (Psalm 91:15).

JOURNAL: _____

_____

_____

FRIDAY: Read Psalm 27:1-8. Meditate on God's Word and listen to what He has to say to you. Using the text as a guide, spend time in praise, confession and thanksgiving.

Pray for the protection of your country: Lord Jesus, thank You for this land in which we live. As a nation that was founded on You and Christian principles, I pray that we would look to You and You alone for protection of this country. Show us where we have become overly confident and self-reliant, trusting in our own strength rather than depending on You. It is not by our might nor by our power, but by Your Spirit (Zechariah 4:6) that we might be protected from opposition or harm. So I pray that in the day of trouble, You would keep us safe in Your dwelling (Psalm 27:5) because we acknowledge Your name. Oh Lord, protect us from the spread of false religions. Protect us from the temptation to go astray, seeking to fulfill the lust of the flesh. Protect our country from the threat of attack, war, and terrorism. If and when enemies and foes attack us, may they stumble and fall (Psalm 27:2). II Samuel 22:31 says that You are "a shield for all who take refuge in You" – so please shield us from natural disasters like flood, earthquake, or tornadoes. Please hear our voices when we call, O Lord; be merciful to us and answer us (Psalm 27:7).

JOURNAL: _____

_____

_____

SATURDAY: A Day of Application

Read Psalm 3:1-8. Do you feel overwhelmed by foes/potential foes this morning? Do you feel like there are "tens of thousands drawn up against [you] on every side?" (v.6) Do these feelings cause you to lie awake at night, unable to sleep?

_____

If so, commit the matter to the Lord right now, asking Him to shield and protect you:

_____

Have you been exhausting yourself with worry and effort in trying to protect your children? If so, it is time to recommit them into His hands. Read Hosea 2:6. Pray and ask the Lord to block your child's path with thornbushes, protecting him/her from every possible danger - physically, emotionally and spiritually, seen and unseen. Pray that God would put a wall of protection around your child, so that the wrong people could not find their way to your child, and that your child cannot find his/her way to them.

Write out your own prayer of protection here:

_____

_____

SUNDAY: A Day of Praise

Read Psalm 71:1-8.

Praise God as Your Protector & Shield.

WRITE OUT YOUR PRAYER OF PRAISE HERE:

_____

_____

_____

CHECK YOURSELF! WRITE YOUR MEMORY VERSE HERE:

_____

_____

WEEK SIXTEEN
Forgiveness

"Bear with each other and forgive whatever grievances you may have against one another. Forgive as the Lord forgave you. And over all these virtues put on love, which binds them together in perfect unity" (Colossians 3:13-14).

PLAYING THE "GRACE" CARD

The man was bitter and angry, merely tolerating life and the people around him. For the past seventeen years he had been consumed with regret and unforgiveness when his son was run over and killed by a drug dealer fleeing the police in a car chase. Now years later, the man lived as if the accident had just happened, daily reviewing the events in his mind. The criminal had gone to jail to serve time for the crime, and essentially, so had the man. Erecting his own prison walls of unforgiveness and hostility, he was held captive by his grief and despair. Growing more and more bitter at the world around him, he seemed unable even to love the son and wife he had left. Projecting his anger through prejudice and hatred, he was an empty shell of a man with no hope and nothing to live for.

As I watched the events of the movie, "The Grace Card," unfold before my eyes, my heart hurt for the man. Trying to put myself in his shoes, I wondered how I would react… would I be able to forgive and move on? Or would I too, drown in bitterness and despair? Convinced that only God could turn these tragic events around and bring healing to the broken man, I sat glued to my seat, anxiously awaiting the outcome.

Our God does not disappoint! After experiencing the unconditional love and undeserving kindness of a coworker, the bereft father began to understand his own need for the very grace of God. In his anguish the man finally called out to the Lord, Who answered by setting the man free (Psalm 118:5). Free from his self-imposed prison of anger and bitterness. Free from the heavy weight of unforgiveness on his weary shoulders. And free to experience the abundant life that Christ intended for him. The movie closed by challenging viewers to extend "the grace card" – offering to pray for, forgive, and be a friend to those around them - especially to those who are undeserving and unloving in return.

I must admit, forgiveness is not foremost in my mind when I have been hurt, betrayed or mocked by another. And those feelings of unforgiveness just intensify when someone I love has been hurt! My flesh rises up against me, whispering words of revenge and anger, while shutting others out who try to help. But God's Word says, "Bear with each other and forgive whatever grievances you may have against one another. Forgive as the Lord forgave you. And over all these virtues put on love, which binds them together in perfect unity" (Colossians 3:13-14). The Lord never asks anything of us that He is not willing to do Himself. So out of humble gratitude that He is always willing to forgive us, shouldn't we be willing to forgive others?

The act of forgiveness is as much for the forgiver as for the one in need of forgiveness. When we refuse to grant it, we are disobeying our Lord and hurting ourselves by living in bondage to our emotions. But when we choose to forgive, *even when it is not asked of us*, we have the victory!

Memory Verse:
"Bear with each other and forgive whatever grievances you may have against one another. Forgive as the Lord forgave you"
(Colossians 3:13).

MONDAY: Read Luke 23:13-26, 32-43. Meditate on God's Word and listen to what He has to say to you. Using the text as a guide, spend time in praise, confession and thanksgiving.

Pray for yourself, to offer forgiveness to others as Christ Jesus offers it to you: I praise You, Lord Jesus, for setting the ultimate example of forgiveness! Pronounced innocent by both Herod and Pilate, committing no crime worthy of the death penalty, still the people demanded Your life. They shouted, "Crucify Him! Crucify Him!" Like a Lamb led away to the slaughter, You were "despised and rejected by men" (Isaiah 53:3), You were mocked, You were insulted, You were beaten, You were "pierced for our transgressions...crushed for our iniquities" (Isaiah 53:5) and finally, You were crucified. And what was Your response to it all? You said, "Father, forgive them, for they do not know what they are doing" (Luke 23:34). Oh Lord Jesus, that You would have such mercy, such forgiveness, such love! That even in the very midst of Your agony and suffering, You were pleading with the Father on our behalf. Thank You, Lord Jesus! Your great act of forgiveness makes me realize just how unforgiving I can be toward those who hurt me. Please work in me to develop a forgiving spirit, no matter how great the offense.

JOURNAL: _____

_____

_____

————————

TUESDAY: Read Acts 6:8-15, 7:54-60. Meditate on God's Word and listen to what He has to say to you. Using the text as a guide, spend time in praise, confession and thanksgiving.

Pray for your husband, to develop a forgiving spirit like that of Stephen: Lord Jesus, Stephen had every earthly reason to be angry and bitter with those who opposed him. They argued with him, persuaded others to give false testimony about him, dragged him out of the city, and then stoned him to death. But Scripture says that while they were stoning him, Stephen cried out, "Lord, do not hold this sin against them" (Acts 7:60). *In the very moment* that they were hurting him, Stephen was asking You to forgive them! How contrary to human nature! Only You could enable someone to react that way. So I pray for my dear husband, asking You to develop such a forgiving spirit in him. May he be known as "a man full of God's grace and power" (Acts 6:8). Open his eyes to see others as You do: as sinners, in desperate need of salvation. Open his mind to understand that "it is to his glory to overlook an offense" (Proverbs 19:11) and offer forgiveness when wronged. May he be so full of Your Holy Spirit that "his face is like the face of an angel" (Acts 6:15), shining with Your love, Your grace, and Your mercy.

JOURNAL: _____

_____

_____

WEDNESDAY: Read Romans 12:14-21. Meditate on God's Word and listen to what He has to say to you. Using the text as a guide, spend time in praise, confession and thanksgiving.

Pray for your household to be characterized by forgiveness and not revenge: Father God, Your Words in this passage fly in the face of my flesh and the teachings of this world in which we live. To "bless those who persecute you; bless and do not curse" (Romans 12:14) is the last thing on my mind when someone in my family has been wronged. But Your Word is clear: "do not repay anyone evil for evil...do not take revenge" (Romans 12:17&19). On the contrary: "If your enemy is hungry, feed him; if he is thirsty, give him something to drink" (Romans 12:20). So I humbly approach Your throne for help, fully aware that no one in my house can do this without the work of the Holy Spirit. Please help me and my husband to model humility and love in our dealings with others, setting an example of forgiveness before our children. May we "spur one another on toward love and good deeds" (Hebrews 10:24), thinking of ways to return curses with blessings. And may we be as willing to offer forgiveness to those within our home as we are to offer it to others.

JOURNAL: _____

_____

_____

THURSDAY: Read Matthew 18:21-35. Meditate on God's Word and listen to what He has to say to you. Using the text as a guide, spend time in praise, confession and thanksgiving.

Pray for your children, to be forgiving of others and forgiven by our Lord: Father, I am sure that Peter thought he was being generous when he asked You if he should forgive a brother up to seven times. Your answer to forgive "not seven times, but seventy-seven times" (Matthew 18:22) was surely as hard to accept then as it is now! How I pray that my children would always be willing to forgive – no matter how many times it is asked of them. When they have a tendency to start keeping track of offenses, remind them that "If you, O Lord, kept a record of sins, O Lord, who could stand? But with you there is forgiveness" (Psalm 130:3-4). Your Word warns: "For if you forgive men when they sin against you, your heavenly Father will also forgive you. But if you do not forgive men their sins, your Father will not forgive your sins" (Matthew 6:14-15). May my children not be like the servant who refused mercy on the one who owed him money, even after his own debt had been forgiven. Rather, may they find joy in offering forgiveness out of a heart of gratitude for all You have done for them.

JOURNAL: _____

_____

_____

FRIDAY: Read II Corinthians 2:5-11. Meditate on God's Word and listen to what He has to say to you. Using the text as a guide, spend time in praise, confession and thanksgiving.

Pray for your church, to be forgiving of brothers and sisters who have repented of past sin: Lord Jesus, Your Word teaches that when a person in our church family falls into sin, it is the responsibility of the church to discipline the offender to keep the church pure and bring the person back to repentance. But once repentance has taken place, it is now time for the church to accept and welcome him back into the church family. "You ought to forgive and comfort him, so that he will not be overwhelmed by excessive sorrow...reaffirm your love for him" (II Corinthians 2:7-8). Please Lord, convict us when we respond in judgment rather than in love. I pray that in my church, we would "stand the test and be obedient" (II Corinthians 2:9) to Your teachings in this matter. Help us to welcome such a one back into the fold with open arms and forgive "in order that Satan might not outwit us. For we are not unaware of his schemes" (II Corinthians 2:11) to tear us apart through unforgiveness and division. May we never give our enemy an opportunity to harm Your church – rather, may we stand firm in forgiveness and unity.

JOURNAL: _____

_____

_____

SATURDAY: A Day of Application

Read Luke 17:3-5.

Is there someone you are refusing or struggling to forgive?

_____

_____

Admit your struggle to the Lord as the apostles did saying, "Increase my faith!" (Luke 17:5). Confess it as sin:

_____

_____

Mark 11:25 says, "And when you stand praying, if you hold anything against anyone, forgive him, so that your Father in heaven may forgive you your sins." Write out your prayer here, asking God to help you forgive so that He will also forgive you your sins:

_____

_____

SUNDAY: A Day of Praise

Read Micah 7:18-19.

Praise God that He is our Forgiver!

WRITE OUT YOUR PRAYER OF PRAISE HERE:

_____

_____

_____

CHECK YOURSELF! WRITE YOUR MEMORY VERSE HERE:

_____

_____

Developing a Craving for God

"O God, You are my God, earnestly I seek You; my soul thirsts for You, my body longs for You, in a dry and weary land where there is no water" (Psalm 63:1).

CANDY COFFEE

When I lie down to go to sleep at night, I am already anticipating my first cup of coffee in the morning. I love coffee! I love the smell of it, I love the taste of it on my tongue, I love the warmth of it flowing down my throat, and I love the satisfaction it brings. I have two rattan chairs with over-sized cushions in my sitting room, and that is where I sit to drink my coffee and have my quiet time with the Lord every morning. I have come to call those chairs my "coffee chairs," and it is my favorite place to sit, pray, discuss the day with my husband, or talk on the phone with a friend. But no matter what I do there, it is always best to have coffee while doing it. In college, I trained myself to drink my coffee black, thinking that was the mature thing to do. I continued to drink it that way until I got pregnant with my first child, but during those nine months I completely lost my taste for coffee. It wasn't until I became pregnant with my second child that I began to crave coffee again, and this time, I wanted it loaded up with cream and sugar. I've never gotten away from coffee with all the extras and continue to drink it loaded up to this day.

Just as I have come to crave a cup of coffee as soon as I awake each morning, so should we wake up craving time with our Lord. It should be a time we anticipate before going to bed the night before. It should be a time we love to experience, that fills us with the warmth of His Presence. It should be a time we hate to miss, knowing that our day just isn't complete without Him. We should hunger for time alone with Him, thirst for time with the King of kings. It should be in a special place, away from the busyness of the household, with our Bible and all of our devotional materials nearby. And it shouldn't just be the bare minimum, like black coffee alone. Our time with our Lord is meant to be "loaded up" with extras so that our fellowship with the Lord is satisfying and sweet...extra words of praise and thanksgiving, unhurried time to read our Bibles and hear Him speak, and plenty of time to lay our requests at His feet and "wait in expectation" (Psalm 5:3). And when we rise from spending time with Him, we should be fully satisfied. For in Him alone can the "soul be satisfied as with the richest of foods" (Psalm 63:5).

I spent two years working as a Peace Corps Volunteer (PCV) in Africa after college. My favorite thing to do for breakfast while living there was to go to the corner omelet stand for a greasy egg, onion, and tomato omelet served on a French baguette. While the omelet was good, the best part of breakfast was the coffee that came with it. My fellow PCVs and I started calling it "candy coffee". This coffee was made with locally grown coffee beans and was very strong. In order to take away the bitterness, several cubes of sugar were added. The final touch was sweetened condensed milk, poured into a spoon till it was full and running over. All this was stirred together, and the result was so good it tasted like candy! And it definitely satisfied my thirst for something sweet.

So today, may your soul thirst for God, may your body long for Him, as "in a dry and weary land where there is no water" (Psalm 63:1). I pray that you would be anxious to rise early and meet with the Lord, determined not to leave until you are fully satisfied.

Memory Verse:
"O God, You are my God, earnestly I seek You; my soul thirsts for You, my body longs for You, in a dry and weary land where there is no water" (Psalm 63:1).

MONDAY: Read Psalm 63:1-11. Meditate on God's Word and listen to what He has to say to you. Using the text as a guide, spend time in praise, confession and thanksgiving.

Pray for yourself, asking God to make you thirsty for Him: Lord Jesus, You alone deserve my praise, because "Your love is better than life" itself (Psalm 63:3). How I pray that my desire for You would be like that of the psalmist, earnestly longing for You as a man without water would long for a drink. I confess that I often go elsewhere seeking to be filled, but I've learned that material things only give temporary satisfaction. Forgive my tendency to take my eyes off of You and onto the things of this world. Thank you, Father God, that You have filled my life with all manner of good things...family, friends, help for today, and best of all, the promise of an eternity with You! Truly, "my cup overflows" (Psalm 23:5). May I "think of You through the watches of the night" (Psalm 63:6) and may "my soul cling to You" (Psalm 63:8) throughout the day. I want to be so thirsty for You that I rise early each morning to spend time alone in Your Presence. And when I do, may my soul "be satisfied as with the richest of food" so that for the rest of the day "with singing lips my mouth will praise You" (Psalm 63:5).

JOURNAL: _____

_____

_____

TUESDAY: Read Psalm 42:1-8. Meditate on God's Word and listen to what He has to say to you. Using the text as a guide, spend time in praise, confession and thanksgiving.

Pray for your husband, to grow in his desire for the Lord and look to Him for help: Oh Father, may my dear husband pant for You as the deer pants for streams of water (Psalm 42:1). May he not be satisfied with just a little of You, but have an insatiable craving to know You more. May he have such a thirst for You that he can hardly wait to go and meet with You (Psalm 42:2) each morning! When things are going well, I pray that my husband would look to You first, honoring You with his praise and thanksgiving. When he faces troubles or difficulties, may he not rely on himself but put his hope in You (Psalm 42:5), Who can be trusted to work on his behalf. When he is downcast in his soul, may his first thought be to pour out his soul to You (Psalm 42:4), the One Who cares most deeply for him and Who understands the way he feels. Please keep him in my thoughts today so that I might continually lift him up in prayer, looking for ways to be a blessing to him.

JOURNAL: _____

_____

_____

———

WEDNESDAY: Read John 7:32-41a. Meditate on God's Word and listen to what He has to say to you. Using the text as a guide, spend time in praise, confession and thanksgiving.

Pray for your marriage, that you and your husband would motivate each other to spend time with God: Lord Jesus, I praise You as the Christ, the One Who came to offer eternal life to a lost and dying world. Your Word explains why we can never be completely satisfied with earthly things or pleasures: For You have "set eternity in the hearts of men" (Ecclesiastes 3:11), giving us a spiritual thirst that only You can satisfy. I pray that when my husband and I feel the void in our hearts and are thirsty, when we long to be filled with something, that we would come to You and drink (John 7:37). May we never go elsewhere seeking to quench that insatiable thirst, but encourage one another to fill our emptiness with You. Scripture says "as iron sharpens iron, so one man sharpens another" (Proverbs 27:17). I pray that when one of us spends time in Your Presence, it would motivate the other to get down on his knees as well. For only then can Your precious streams of living water flow from within us (John 7:38)! May our home be so full of Your Holy Spirit that You would flow out of us and into others.

JOURNAL: _____

_____

_____

———∘∘∘———

THURSDAY: Read Psalm 107:1-13. Meditate on God's Word and listen to what He has to say to you. Using the text as a guide, spend time in praise, confession and thanksgiving.

Pray for your children to long for a personal relationship with God and experience the satisfaction He alone can bring: Oh Lord, we give thanks to You, for You are good; Your love endures forever (Psalm 107:1)! Thank You for Your overwhelming goodness and unconditional love for each one of my children. As they grow up and get a taste of this world and its troubles, I pray that it would leave them hungry for something more... hungry for You. You alone can "satisfy the thirsty and fill the hungry with good things" (Psalm 107:9). So if they feel like they are wandering in the desert, unable to find a place to settle (Psalm 107:4), I pray that they would seek the solace of Your Word which brings clarity and direction. Or if they are sitting in darkness and in deepest gloom because they have rebelled against Your Words and despised Your counsel (Psalm 107:10-11), may they humble themselves and turn to Your Word which holds the keys to repentance and forgiveness. As they begin to taste and see that You are good (Psalm 34:8), please fill them with a longing for more of what You offer.

JOURNAL: _____

_____

_____

———∘∘∘———

FRIDAY: Read Revelation 21:1-8. Meditate on God's Word and listen to what He has to say to you. Using the text as a guide, spend time in praise, confession and thanksgiving.

Pray for your country, to have a hunger and thirst for the Living God: Oh Father, I praise You this morning as "the Alpha and the Omega, the Beginning and the End" (Revelation 21:6). What wonderful things You have planned for those who love You! How I yearn for the day that the dwelling of God will be with men, "and He will live with them" (Revelation 21:3)...no more tears, no more death, no more crying or pain. For behold, You will make everything new! (Revelation 21:5). Come quickly Lord Jesus, come! But as we await Your return, I pray that we would be a people who overcome the lure of this world with all its wickedness, standing firm in our faith until the very end (Mark 13:13). May the people of this country come to You thirsty, so that You can give us "to drink <u>without cost</u> from the spring of the water of life" (Revelation 21:6). You are that water, the Living Water, Who alone can satisfy our thirst so that we will never be thirsty again (John 4:10, 13). May all men long to have You as their God and desire to be Your children, so that no one will miss out on this glorious inheritance of eternal life!

JOURNAL: _____

_____

_____

SATURDAY: A Day of Application

Read Psalm 73:23-28.

Set aside some extra time to spend with the Lord today. Suggestions:

- Make yourself a cup of coffee or tea and settle down with God's Word.
- Take a walk by yourself and spend the time praising God.
- Drive to the park, find a secluded spot, and pour your heart out to the Lord.

The more time we spend with the Lord, the more time we want to spend with Him!

Make this verse your own words to the Lord: "Whom have I in heaven but You? And earth has nothing I desire besides You" (Psalm 73:25). Ask the Lord to give you more of a desire for Him:

_____

_____

SUNDAY: A Day of Praise

Read John 6:35, 47-51.

Praise Jesus that He is the Bread of Life. "Then Jesus declared, 'He who comes to Me will never go hungry, and he who believes in Me will never be thirsty'" (John 6:35).

WRITE OUT YOUR PRAYER OF PRAISE HERE:

_____

_____

_____

CHECK YOURSELF! WRITE YOUR MEMORY VERSE HERE:

_____

_____

Thought Life

"We demolish arguments and every pretension that sets itself up against the knowledge of God, and we take captive every thought to make it obedient to Christ" (II Corinthians 10:5).

TAKEN CAPTIVE!

The newspaper headline announced, "Five people taken captive by madman." I shuddered to think about the fate that awaited those prisoners. How terrible…to be taken against your will and forced into submission, all the while hoping against hope for someone to rescue you. Their enemy had stolen more than just their freedom. He had also taken their sense of confidence and peace, replacing them with feelings of desperation and fear. The normalcy of these prisoners' lives had come to an abrupt halt and life might never be the same again.

In much the same way, I realize that there have been many times in my life when I was being "held captive"…not bodily, but in my mind. Much like these prisoners captured by their enemy, the believer often falls captive in her thought life. The lure of this world, the sinfulness of our own flesh, and the temptations of our chief adversary, the devil, can pull us downward in a matter of moments. Take your focus off of Christ, even temporarily, and you become vulnerable to becoming a prisoner of sinful thinking, which then leads to sinful behavior. Confusion, doubt and anxiety replace the peace, certainty and order of your mind. Greed, selfishness and self-gratification replace giving, service, and living to please Christ. The world shouts out, "Live for self!" and "If it feels good, do it!" Years ago these would have been unacceptable standards, but over time we have come to accept these lies as truth. Television, magazines, and the internet relentlessly bombard us with temptations to overspend, overindulge, and gratify the flesh. Telling ourselves that "no one will know" or "no one will be hurt" we ignore our conscience and indulge in the very things we know we shouldn't. And all the while, our "enemy the devil prowls around like a roaring lion looking for someone to devour" (I Peter 5:8). With his lies and threats of unacceptance, he accuses us of taking "this Jesus thing" too seriously and lures us into believing that we must tolerate worldly thinking. Rendered helpless, we stand back and allow ourselves to be assaulted by doubt and become numb to the ungodly thinking around us.

The Apostle Paul wisely advised his reader on how to break free from such captivity: "We demolish arguments and every pretension that sets itself up against the knowledge of God, and we take captive every thought to make it obedient to Christ" (II Corinthians 10:5). Ladies, our Rescuer awaits! He is able to "demolish the arguments" that this world uses against us! He is able to refute the false claims of the evil one, casting light on his deception and lies. Under the examination of His Word, disobedient thoughts quickly flee! In bondage no longer, the Lord enables us to "take captive" every single thought, holding it up for inspection before His all-seeing eyes. Any thought that "sets itself up against the knowledge of Christ," any thought that does not hold up to the scrutiny of the truth of God's Word, can be quickly seized and dismissed before it does any damage!

The Lord promises "to proclaim freedom for the captives and release from darkness for the prisoners" (Isaiah 61:1). Refuse to give control of your mind to any other, instead taking captive every thought to make it obedient to Christ.

Memory Verse:
"We demolish arguments and every pretension that sets itself up against the knowledge of God, and we take captive every thought to make it obedient to Christ"
(II Corinthians 10:5).

MONDAY: Read Psalm 139:1-6. Meditate on God's Word and listen to what He has to say to you. Using the text as a guide, spend time in praise, confession and thanksgiving.

Pray for yourself, asking God to search your mind for any incorrect thinking: Father, what a reminder this passage is of Your omniscience. There is nothing You don't know about me! Not a single thought enters my mind without Your awareness, not a movement that I make escapes Your notice, and "before a word is on my tongue You know it completely" (Psalm 139:4). How foolish I am at times to think that I can hide my thoughts from You, my very Creator. Father, forgive me when I allow my mind to go down the wrong paths of incorrect thinking, listening to the lies of Satan and this world. I must daily submit my mind to Your Word which has the power to "judge the thoughts and attitudes of the heart" (Hebrews 4:12). May I not squirm under Your discerning eye, but allow Your Word to penetrate deeply to expose any ungodly thinking. Thank you that when I "take captive every thought to make it obedient to Christ" (II Corinthians 10:5) by purposely fixing my eyes on You, I gain Your perspective to see the truth clearly.

JOURNAL: _____

_____

_____

TUESDAY: Read Philippians 4:8-9. Meditate on God's Word and listen to what He has to say to you. Using the text as a guide, spend time in praise, confession and thanksgiving.

Pray for your husband, to give the Lord control of his mind and thoughts: Lord Jesus, just as I battle for control of my mind at times, so does my husband. Our enemy would like nothing better than to hold him captive with thoughts of material gain, sensual pleasure, and selfish ambition. May my husband recognize these thoughts for what they are: Satan's attempt to render him useless and ineffective in Your Kingdom. When he battles thoughts of boredom in his work or restlessness with where life has him, remind him that he can experience abundant life in Your presence! If he ever feels unworthy as I do, remind him that his worth is found in You alone. Your Word tells us how to combat such thoughts: "Whatever is true, whatever is noble, whatever is right, whatever is pure, whatever is lovely, whatever is admirable – if anything is excellent or praiseworthy – think about such things" (Philippians 4:8). Help my husband make the conscious choice to focus his thoughts on truth and goodness so that he will be able to sense Your Presence in a very real way.

JOURNAL: _____

_____

_____

———⊰◦⊱———

WEDNESDAY: Read Romans 8:5-11. Meditate on God's Word and listen to what He has to say to you. Using the text as a guide, spend time in praise, confession and thanksgiving.

Pray for those in your household, to have your minds set on what the Spirit desires: Oh Father, as believers in the Lord Jesus Christ we have Your very Spirit living within us! Thank you for this awesome privilege and precious gift. May we make every effort to humbly submit to Your Spirit, allowing You and You alone to guide our thinking. Your Word says that "the mind controlled by the Spirit is life and peace" (Romans 8:6)…how I desire for my home to be filled with life and peace, rather than death and hostility! I know that it is the responsibility of me and my husband to be examples of godly thinking before our children. What we teach them at home and model before them day by day will influence their thinking for the rest of their lives. So we ask You to test us, O Lord, and try us, examine our hearts and minds (Psalm 26:2). Please reveal anything in our lives that needs to change! As You uncover incorrect thinking and ungodly behavior, may we be obedient to change as Your Spirit directs.

JOURNAL: _____

_____

_____

———◁◦▷———

THURSDAY: Read Colossians 2:6-10. Meditate on God's Word and listen to what He has to say to you. Using the text as a guide, spend time in praise, confession and thanksgiving.

Pray for your children, to live for Christ and never fall prey to false thinking: Oh Father, I know that this world holds a battle for the minds of my children! False teachers are everywhere, just looking for the opportunity to plant their lies and mislead the masses. I pray Your Word, begging that no one take my children "captive through hollow and deceptive philosophy, which depends on human tradition and the basic principles of this world rather than on Christ" (Colossians 2:8). Please make me and my husband aware if our children are tempted to follow any kind of false teaching. Burden us to pray for them and warn them to "come to their senses and escape from the trap of the devil, who has taken them captive to do his will" (II Timothy 2:26). We must take a stand against any incorrect beliefs our children bring home! I pray we would never back down from our responsibility of correcting any ungodly thinking that we see in our children. It is up to us to uphold the truth of Your Word....may we be determined to do it boldly and consistently.

JOURNAL: _____

_____

_____

———◁◦▷———

FRIDAY: Read Philippians 3:17-4:1. Meditate on God's Word and listen to what He has to say to you. Using the text as a guide, spend time in praise, confession and thanksgiving.

Pray for your church, to keep your mind fixed on the heaven that awaits you! Father God, we are all too aware that "many live as enemies of the cross of Christ. Their destiny is destruction, their god is their stomach, and their glory is in their shame. Their mind is on earthly things" (Philippians 3:18-19). This world would love for Your church to join them...to be given over "to a depraved mind, to do what ought not to be done" (Romans 1:28), and to blur the distinctions between right and wrong. Oh, may we not fall victim in the church to the temptations of this world to downplay our beliefs with earthly thinking! We must constantly be on our guard to keep You at the forefront of our minds. Rebuke us with Your heavy hand of conviction if we fall into "thinking differently" than we should...make it clear to us (Philippians 3:15) so that we can correct our beliefs to line up with Your Word. May the members of my church presently live as citizens of heaven, eagerly awaiting our Savior, the Lord Jesus Christ (Philippians 3:20). Please Father, help us stand firm until the end!

JOURNAL: _____

_____

_____

SATURDAY: A Day of Application

Read Isaiah 55:8-9.

The Lord declares, "For my thoughts are not your thoughts." Ask God to reveal any incorrect thinking in your life. Record it below and defeat the ungodly thought with Scripture.

Example: Ungodly thought: God doesn't care about me.

Truth from scripture: Psalm 139:1-6.

1) _____

2) _____

3) _____

Commit to "take captive every thought to make it obedient to Christ" (II Corinthians 10:5). Write out your prayer of commitment here:

_____

_____

SUNDAY: A Day of Praise

Read Colossians 1:13-14.

Praise God as our Rescuer! He rescues us from the dominion of darkness, from the power of sin, and from the captivity of our own ungodly thinking.

WRITE OUT YOUR PRAYER OF PRAISE HERE:

_____

_____

_____

CHECK YOURSELF! WRITE YOUR MEMORY VERSE HERE:

_____

_____

Trusting God

"This is what the Lord says – He who made a way through the sea, a path through the mighty waters, who drew out the chariots and horses, the army and reinforcements together, and they lay there, never to rise again, extinguished, snuffed out like a wick: Forget the former things; do not dwell on the past. See, I am doing a new thing! Now it springs up; do you not perceive it? I am making a way in the desert and streams in the wasteland" (Isaiah 43:16-19).

A NEW THING

After my husband and I had our third child, our house began to feel a little cramped. We started discussing the possibility of moving to a bigger house in a neighborhood closer to our children's school. For about a month we went back and forth on the issue, some days feeling like we should just stay put, and other days feeling like we should go ahead and put our house on the market. My husband and I had different concerns. Being in sales and paid by commission, the amount of money my husband makes in a given month can change dramatically. So the major concern he had was whether or not we could afford it. My concerns centered more on our family....how will the kids adjust? Who will our new neighbors be? Will we be able to find something we like?

One morning in my quiet time I brought the matter before the Lord once again. We had been praying that God would show us His will on the matter, trusting that if we proceeded as He directed, we would be fine. As I prayed through my list of pros and cons, I got hung up on one thought: we have been so happy here for 11 years, would change be the best thing? Immediately, God spoke His Word to my soul that I had memorized some time before: "Forget the former things; do not dwell on the past. See, I am doing a new thing!" (Isaiah 43:18). It was the green light from God that I needed to move forward, reassured that God did indeed have something new for our family. We contacted a realtor and put our house on the market, ready for it to sell quickly.

But the days turned into weeks, and the weeks turned into months, without a single offer. In 2007 the housing market was in a recession, and the outlook for selling was bleak. After four months of waiting for the "new thing" God had for us, I began to pray more earnestly. "Did we hear you correctly Lord? Why isn't our house selling?" God led me back to study this same passage from Isaiah 43:18, and this time I saw something new. The very next verse says this, "I will make a way in the desert and streams in the wasteland" (Isaiah 43:19). The housing market might look like a deserted wasteland to me, but God could make a way if it was His will for our house to sell. Armed with that Scripture, I prayed God's Word back to Him every time it came to mind, trusting God to make a "way in the desert and streams in the wasteland" of the housing market. On the very last day of our six month contract with our realtor, we received a very reasonable offer and accepted. Six weeks later we moved into our new roomier house, just three minutes from the school, amazed at how God can and will work on our behalf.

I am so glad that I did not cling to the former things and only focus on the past. I just love the "new things" God has for us when we choose to trust Him!

Memory Verse:
"Forget the former things; do not dwell on the past. See, I am doing a new thing! Now it springs up; do you not perceive it? I am making a way in the desert and streams in the wasteland"
(Isaiah 43:18-19).

MONDAY: Read Isaiah 43:14-25. Meditate on God's Word and listen to what He has to say to you. Using the text as a guide, spend time in praise, confession and thanksgiving.

Pray for yourself, asking God to help you trust Him more fully: Oh Father God, how I praise You this morning as the One Who can be trusted in every area of my life. After all, You are my Redeemer, my Holy One, my Creator, and my King! Forgive me when I do not call upon You, when I burden You with my sin and weary You with my offenses (Isaiah 43:24) instead of blessing You with offerings of thanksgiving and trust. I do not want to be like the one spoken of in Zephaniah 3:2: "She does not trust in the Lord, she does not draw near to her God." You alone can be depended on to be trustworthy 100% of the time. Thank You for the great things You have accomplished in my life that were seemingly impossible. Please bring those to my mind any time I lack confidence in Your ability to work. Prick my heart if I have been resisting "a new thing" that You have been leading me to do. May I step out in faith, trusting You with all of the details that seem impossible to overcome. "With man this is impossible, but with God all things are possible" (Matthew 19:26). I don't want to miss a single thing You have for me!

JOURNAL: _____

_____

TUESDAY: Read Daniel 6:1-23. Meditate on God's Word and listen to what He has to say to you. Using the text as a guide, spend time in praise, confession and thanksgiving.

Pray for your husband, that he would trust in God as Daniel did: I praise You, Father God, as the Rescuer, the Deliverer, the One Who can "shut the mouths of lions!" I pray that when my husband is up against difficult and overwhelming circumstances, that his first response would be to turn to You. I'm sure there are times when he feels like Daniel, "cast into a lion's den" with absolutely no way to escape. When he finds himself in that kind of situation, standing inches away from something that threatens to tear him apart, I pray that he would emerge unharmed. Then we can boldly declare, "no wound was found on him because he had trusted in his God" (Daniel 6:23)! May he bring before You all of his concerns for his family, his health, and his job, including his hopes and fears, trusting You to be beside him every step of the way. I pray that daily, in good times and in bad, he would get down on his knees and pray, giving thanks to You (Daniel 6:10). And when his head hits the pillow at night, may he sleep soundly because he has "no fear of bad news; his heart is steadfast, trusting in the Lord" (Ps 112:7).

JOURNAL: _____

_____

_____

WEDNESDAY: Read II Samuel 7:18-29. (If time permits, also read verses 1-17). Meditate on God's Word and listen to what He has to say to you. Using the text as a guide, spend time in praise, confession and thanksgiving.

Pray to the Lord, trusting Him with your marriage and your household: I praise You Lord, for "there is no one like You, and there is no God but You" (II Samuel 7:22). I echo King David's prayer and offer it as my own this morning: "Who am I, O Sovereign Lord, and what is my family, that you have brought me thus far?" (II Samuel 7:18). When I look back and think about the mistakes You saved me from, the wrong choices You kept me from making, I am so very thankful that You have established this house for me. Thank you for blessing me with my husband, our children, and our home. I give them all back to You, trusting You to continue to care for us and our needs. As my husband and I trust You with our marriage, I pray that our commitment to one another would grow stronger every day. As we strive to build our home according to Your commandments, I pray that You will "be pleased to bless the house of your servants" (II Samuel 7:29). And when our days on this earth come to an end, we trust that the future home You are preparing for us in heaven awaits our arrival! (John 14:1-2).

JOURNAL: _____

_____

THURSDAY: Read Psalm 22:1-11, 22-24. Meditate on God's Word and listen to what He has to say to you. Using the text as a guide, spend time in praise, confession and thanksgiving.

Pray for your children, to trust in God so that He will direct their paths: Lord Jesus, I praise You as the One Who is trustworthy and true! You have not hidden Your face from us, but have listened to our cry for help (Psalm 22:24). May I be diligent to share examples of Your faithfulness and trustworthiness with my children so that they will understand that You are worthy of their trust as well. Whatever is going on in their lives at this very moment...whether it is difficulty at school, problems with friends, or uncertainty about the future....may they look to You in trust and experience Your deliverance. I pray that their testimony would be that "in You they trusted and were not disappointed" (Psalm 22:5). As my children experience Your faithfulness, may they be compelled to declare Your name to their brothers and proclaim Your righteousness to a people yet unborn (Psalm 22:22, 31). I pray that my children will trust in You with all their hearts and lean not on their own understanding, but in all their ways acknowledge You, so that You will direct their paths (Proverbs 3:5-6).

JOURNAL: _____

_____

_____

FRIDAY: Read Exodus 14:1-14, 30-31. Meditate on God's Word and listen to what He has to say to you. Using the text as a guide, spend time in praise, confession and thanksgiving.

Pray for your pastor, trusting him as God's man to lead your church: Father, I thank You for my pastor. Just as You chose Moses to lead the Israelites out of Egypt, so You have chosen my pastor to lead our church congregation. I pray that You would enable him to stand firm in the faith as Moses did, trusting You to work even if his people begin to falter. Please use my pastor to speak truth into our lives, reminding us that when difficulties arise we need not fear. For You will fight for us; we need only to be still (Exodus 14:14). The Bible says, "And when the Israelites saw the great power the Lord displayed against the Egyptians, the people feared the Lord and put their trust in him and in Moses his servant" (Exodus 14:31). May my pastor trust in You, so that we may trust in him. Help him guard his time alone with You each day, in order to gain the strength he needs when so many people are depending on him. Remind the members of our congregation to be faithful in praying for him and his family. And may our church be able to say, "Some trust in chariots and some in horses, but we trust in the name of the Lord our God" (Psalm 20:7).

JOURNAL: _____

_____

_____

SATURDAY: A Day of Application

Read Psalm 37:1-11.

Name one thing that you are struggling to trust God with:

_____

_____

Commit this issue to the Lord and place your trust in Him (Psalm 37:5). Write out your prayer here:

_____

_____

_____

Now, "be still before the Lord and wait patiently for Him" (Psalm 37:7). Every time this concern comes to mind, repeat your statement of trust.

SUNDAY: A Day of Praise

Read Psalm 84:1-12.

Praise God as Lord Almighty, worthy of our trust. Definition of "trust" - assured reliance on the character, ability, strength, or truth of someone or something; one in which confidence is placed. "O Lord Almighty, blessed is the man who trusts in You" (Psalm 84:12).

WRITE OUT YOUR PRAYER OF PRAISE HERE:

_____

_____

_____

CHECK YOURSELF! WRITE YOUR MEMORY VERSE HERE:

_____

_____

Rejoicing in the Lord

"Though the fig tree does not bud and there are no grapes on the vines, though the olive crop fails and the fields produce no food, though there are no sheep in the pen and no cattle in the stalls, yet I will rejoice in the Lord, I will be joyful in God my Savior"
(Habakkuk 3:17-18).

HOT AND WEARY

It was the end of the summer, and my husband and I were hot and weary. It seemed like everything in our house was going wrong. First it was the air conditioner…it had been the hottest summer on record in Memphis for the past 10 years, with temperatures over 100 degrees for days on end, and our downstairs unit had been broken for an entire month. Daily we awaited a decision from the home warranty company, hoping and praying that our unit was covered under their plan and we would not have to dish out thousands of dollars to replace it on our own. Then it was the lawnmower…the pull cord snapped in two, causing my husband extra toil out in the hot sun (and then, two weeks later it happened again!) Next came the dishwasher, seeming to run for hours on end, but leaving a white residue all over my plates and silverware. Follow that up with an inexplicable infestation of flies (that left my husband and me bewildered but our boys delighted as they challenged each other to see who could kill the most), and I was close to my breaking point. So when a flying squirrel found his way into the air conditioning vent in our bedroom and kept us awake two nights running, it was the last straw. "Will all of these problems ever end?" we asked each other in dismay. "Lord, what's going to go wrong next?"

On the verge of going to sit in my "pouting corner," I read these verses from Habakkuk 3:17-18 in my daily quiet time: "Though the fig tree does not bud and there are no grapes on the vines, though the olive crop fails and the fields produce no food, though there are no sheep in the pen and no cattle in the stalls, yet I will rejoice in the Lord, I will be joyful in God my Savior." I might not have had any fruitless fig trees or empty stalls in my barn, but I certainly had some issues of my own. And God's Word was reminding me to be joyful in the midst of them!

We so often see joy as something that accompanies blessing and prosperity, not inconveniences and adversity! But the psalmist in these verses from Habakkuk declared that he would rejoice in the Lord *in spite of* difficult circumstances. Why? Why would he rejoice in the Lord when his crops had failed and he had no food to eat? Because, dear sister, our joy comes not from our present situation, but from our position in Christ! Our joy comes from knowing the Lord personally as our Savior! Our joy comes from knowing Who God is... He is the King of Kings and Lord of Lords....He is my Creator and my Redeemer...He is preparing a place for me in heaven at this very moment... He has given me His righteousness in exchange for my sin... and He has made me to be His heir and co-heir with Christ. My circumstances can change like the wind, but the stability of my Lord will last forever! And that is something to rejoice about!

"You turned my wailing into dancing; You removed my sackcloth and clothed me with joy" (Psalm 30:11). I am so thankful for a God Who is able to give me joy no matter what is going on at this very moment. So here is my statement of joy at the end of the summer of 2010: "Though the air conditioner is broken and it is hot in my house, though the dishes are dirty and the grass is tall, though the flies bother me all day and the squirrels keep me up at night, yet I will rejoice in the Lord, I will be joyful in God my Savior." Amen!

Memory Verse:
"Be joyful always; pray continually; give thanks in all circumstances, for this is God's will for you in Christ Jesus"
(I Thessalonians 5:16-18).

MONDAY: Read Psalm 96:1-13. Meditate on God's Word and listen to what He has to say to you. Using the text as a guide, spend time in praise, confession and thanksgiving.

Pray for yourself to have a joyful attitude, rejoicing always in the Lord: Father, Your Word says, "Let the heavens rejoice, let the earth be glad; let the sea resound, and all that is in it; let the fields be jubilant, and everything in them. Then all the trees of the forest will sing for joy" (Psalm 96:11-12). Truly, Oh Lord, if I remain silent, the rocks will cry out to proclaim Your majesty! "For great is the Lord and most worthy of praise" (Psalm 96:4). Forgive me, Father, when I lapse into an attitude of complaining, rather than having a joy-filled heart that rejoices in You alone. Forgive me, Lord Jesus, when I only think to praise You when things are going well. As the trees of the forest sing for You, so I determine to sing for joy to You today. No matter what happens - no matter what breaks, no matter what problems arise - I will rejoice because You are worthy of my praise. I will "sing to the Lord, praise His name; proclaim His salvation day after day." I will "declare His glory among the nations, His marvelous deeds among all peoples" (Psalm 96:2-3).

JOURNAL: _____

_____

_____

TUESDAY: Read Romans 5:1-5. Meditate on God's Word and listen to what He has to say to you. Using the text as a guide, spend time in praise, confession and thanksgiving.

Pray for your husband, to have joy regardless of what is going on in his life: Father God, I am so thankful for my husband and for the joy You have brought into my life because of him. Oh how I want him to be happy! You know how I hate to see him loaded down with the cares of this world, problems at work, or times of unrest. Thank you that my husband can cast his cares on You, because You care for him (I Peter 5:7). When trouble strikes, I pray that You would "restore to [him] the joy of Your salvation" (Ps 51:12). Use me to remind him that this world is not the end...a future home awaits him in heaven! And while it is easy to rejoice in the hope we have in You, You also tell us to "rejoice in our sufferings" (Romans 5:3) because they produce perseverance, then character, then hope. "For our light and momentary troubles are achieving for us an eternal glory that far outweighs them all" (II Corinthians 4:17). Please help my husband to fix his eyes "not on what is seen, but on what is unseen. For what is seen is temporary, but what is unseen is eternal" (II Corinthians 4:18).

JOURNAL: _____

_____

_____

———————

WEDNESDAY: Read Psalm 149:1-5. Meditate on God's Word and listen to what He has to say to you. Using the text as a guide, spend time in praise, confession and thanksgiving.

Pray for the attitude in your home to be one of joy: Father, we rejoice in the honor that You bestow on us..."For the Lord takes delight in His people; He crowns the humble with salvation" (Psalm 149:4). We know that we are not deserving of Your favor or Your grace, and we humbly bow before You as our King. It is our desire that You receive praise in our home, and that we never miss a chance to rejoice in You or Your provision. How I pray that my husband and I would find joy in our marriage, always careful to focus on what we have and not on what we don't have. May we be good examples of joy-filled lives before our children and find joy in being together as a family. If joy is lacking in our home, remind us that it doesn't have to be that way. Your Word says "a cheerful look brings joy to the heart" (Proverbs 15:30), so may we determine to look cheerfully at one another! I pray that we will not be too timid to praise Your name with dancing, or make music to You (Psalm 149:3) before men. Rather, may we wake up with praise on our lips, and fall asleep at night "singing for joy on [our] beds" (Psalm 149:5).

JOURNAL: _____

_____

_____

―――∘⧫∘―――

THURSDAY: Read Psalm 30:1-12. Meditate on God's Word and listen to what He has to say to you. Using the text as a guide, spend time in praise, confession and thanksgiving.

Pray for your children, to understand that God is able to turn sadness into joy: Oh Father God, how I love my children! You know how I desire only good things for them, and how I would like to spare them from every possible sadness or pain. But I know that is not possible... for "in this world [we] will have trouble" (John 16:33). So please Lord, when they come face to face with trials, help me to point them back to You. May they not harden their hearts in times of difficulty but cry out to You for help and mercy. Humble me enough to be willing to share my own difficult experiences so that they can see that "weeping may remain for a night, but rejoicing comes in the morning" (Psalm 30:5). I want my children to trust in Your ability to turn their "wailing into dancing"; You can remove their sackcloth and clothe them with joy (Psalm 30:11). Nothing is too difficult for You! You even promise that "in all things God works for the good of those who love Him" (Romans 8:28). So I thank You in advance for Your work on their behalf and for the joy You will bestow on them in the midst of trouble.

JOURNAL: _____

_____

_____

―――∘⧫∘―――

FRIDAY: Read Isaiah 35:1-10. Meditate on God's Word and listen to what He has to say to you. Using the text as a guide, spend time in praise, confession and thanksgiving.

Pray for your church, to live in the reality of the joy we will experience in the coming kingdom: Oh Father, thank You for this glimpse of what is in store for Your children! This chapter is a beautiful picture of Your coming Kingdom – soon and very soon we are going to see our King! How can we help but rejoice when we focus our minds on things to come.... "Then will the eyes of the blind be opened, and the ears of the deaf unstopped. Then will the lame leap like a deer, and the mute tongue shout for joy" (Isaiah 35:5-6)! There will be nothing unclean or wicked there... we will have fear of nothing and want for nothing. Thank You, Lord Jesus, that You will make ALL things new. Thank You that Your redeemed "will enter Zion with singing; everlasting joy will crown [our] heads. Gladness and joy will overtake [us], and sorrow and sighing will flee away" (Isaiah 35:10). May our church on earth live joyful lives in front of a lost world, announcing to all who will hear that the best is yet to come!

JOURNAL: _____

_____

_____

SATURDAY: Day of Application

Read Habakkuk 3:17-18.

Do you have a tendency to be joyful and rejoice in the Lord only when things are going well? _____ If so, confess it here:

_____

_____

Write out your own commitment to praise God no matter what is going wrong. Using the outline from Habakkuk 3:17-18 as a guide, fill in these blanks with your own present difficulties.

Though _____

And _____

Though _____

And _____

Though _____

And _____

Yet I will rejoice in the Lord, I will be joyful in God my Savior!

Journal: _____

SUNDAY: A Day of Praise

Read Isaiah 62:5 and Zephaniah 3:17.

Praise God that He rejoices over you!

WRITE OUT YOUR PRAYER OF PRAISE HERE:

_____

_____

_____

CHECK YOURSELF! WRITE YOUR MEMORY VERSE HERE:

_____

_____

Salvation

*"That if you confess with your mouth, "Jesus is Lord," and believe
in your heart that God raised Him from the dead, you will be saved.
For it is with your heart that you believe and are justified, and it is
with your mouth that you confess and are saved" (Romans 10:9-10).*

DID YOU HEAR?

I remember walking into a children's clothing store one afternoon and stumbling onto the biggest clearance sale I had ever seen. I frequently shopped at this store, and they always had good prices, but that day they had their best sale yet! Their already low prices were cut in half, and customers were to receive an additional 30% off the lowest price at the register. I dug my mobile phone out of my purse to call a friend... she would definitely want to hear about this! I shopped and shopped, finding one great bargain after another, excited to have found such great deals. I walked out of that store very pleased with myself for purchasing clothes that my children needed at rock bottom prices. And when I got home I couldn't wait to spread the news to other friends and relatives. "Did you hear? Our favorite clothing store is having a great sale, and I want to make sure you don't miss it!"

We often jump at the chance to share such good news with anyone who will listen. If I heard that $100 bills were being given out at the local grocery store, wouldn't I call up everyone I knew to tell them about it? Or if I had discovered the cure for cancer, wouldn't I shout it from the rooftop? Of course I would! Well, I have heard the very best news of all time....better than free money or even a cure for cancer. Jesus Christ died for our sins and has made a way for us to get to heaven! I want nothing more than for those I know and love to receive the free gift of salvation in Christ Jesus. More than good health, financial prosperity, or earthly blessing, I desire that everyone I know would have a personal relationship with the Lord.

Too many of us have grown up believing that if we would just go to church, just try to do our best, just give to the poor or help out in the community, God will look favorably on us and maybe, just maybe, allow us into heaven. This "works-based" belief system is not only wrong, it will forever separate us from God. All of the good works in the world are meaningless apart from surrendering your life to Jesus Christ. "For all have sinned and fall short of the glory of God" (Romans 3:23). You, dear friend, are a sinner. "For the wages of sin is death, but the gift of God is eternal life in Christ Jesus our Lord" (Romans 6:23). Your sinfulness will only earn you death and an eternal separation from God, no matter how many "good works" you do. Salvation is not something you earn… it is a gift to be received by faith in Christ Jesus! "But God demonstrates His own love for us in this: While we were still sinners, Christ died for us" (Romans 5:8). God made a way for sinful man to approach His holiness…He sent His only Son into this sinful world to die on the cross for my sin and for yours. "That if you confess with your mouth, "Jesus is Lord," and believe in your heart that God raised Him from the dead, you will be saved" (Romans 10:9). Will you finally confess Jesus as Lord of your life, turning your back on sin and placing your faith in Him alone for salvation?

Have YOU heard the Good News? "Everyone who calls on the name of the Lord will be saved" (Romans 10:13). This is the best news ever…please don't miss out on an eternity in heaven!

Memory Verse:
"That if you confess with your mouth, "Jesus is Lord," and believe in your heart that God raised Him from the dead, you will be saved" (Romans 10:9).

MONDAY: Read Revelation 3:20-22. Meditate on God's Word and listen to what He has to say to you. Using the text as a guide, spend time in praise, confession and thanksgiving.

Pray for yourself, asking the Lord to reveal the true condition of your heart: Do you know Jesus as your Savior, or are you lost? Lord Jesus, Your Word says: "He saved us, not because of righteous things we had done, but because of His mercy" (Titus 3:5). Thank you Lord, that salvation is not contingent upon my righteousness, but it is a free gift offered to anyone! I understand that in order to receive that gift, I must make a decision to trust You alone with my life. My salvation and eternity in heaven depend on my own personal repentance.... acknowledging that I am a sinner and that only You can save me. Lord Jesus, if You "stand at the door and knock" (Revelation 3:20) at this very moment, asking me to open my heart to You, may I not turn You away! Help me relinquish anything that is holding me back from inviting You to come into my life. I confess my need of You, and I turn away from my sinful ways. Please come into my life and save me. I cling to Your promise that, "If anyone acknowledges that Jesus is the Son of God, God lives in him and he in God" (I John 4:15).

JOURNAL: _____

_____

_____

———•◦•———

TUESDAY: Read John 3:1-8. Meditate on God's Word and listen to what He has to say to you. Using the text as a guide, spend time in praise, confession and thanksgiving.

Pray for your husband, to have a desire to know Christ: Oh Heavenly Father, just as Nicodemus came to Jesus seeking answers, so I pray that my husband would come to You. May he have a burden to know for certain where he will spend eternity. May he not put off living for You one more day. Give him an urgency to know the truth...the truth that will set him free! Jesus said, "I tell you the truth, no one can see the kingdom of God unless he is born again" (John 3:3). Like Nicodemus, may my husband shun anything that is holding him back from making You Lord of his life…whether it be misunderstanding about salvation, fear of what others may think, trusting in his own knowledge, or refusal to humble himself before Your mighty hand. "Salvation is found in no one else, for there is no other name under heaven given to men by which we must be saved" (Acts 4:12). If my husband already has a personal relationship with You, I thank You for the daily gift of eternal life that is afforded to him even now as he walks upon this earth.

JOURNAL: _____

_____

_____

—————◦∘◦—————

WEDNESDAY: Read Matthew 1:18-25. Meditate on God's Word and listen to what He has to say to you. Using the text as a guide, spend time in praise, confession and thanksgiving.

Pray for your household to be alive with God's presence: Oh Father, how I praise You for the miraculous birth of our Lord and Savior Jesus Christ! You chose two of the least likely candidates - a young virgin girl and a humble carpenter – to accomplish the most glorious event of all time. That You could use two such ordinary people to be the earthly parents of Your Son shows Your mighty power at work in those who love You! As I reflect on that I realize that it was their desire to yield to Your will that equipped them for the task at hand. In much the same way, my husband and I must yield completely to You and Your will as the only possible way to raise our children up for Your Kingdom. We must daily turn to You alone as our Savior and LORD – the One we should look to for direction at every turn. Just as Joseph and Mary experienced the reality of "God with us" (Matthew 1:23) as they raised Christ Himself in their home, I thank You that we can experience the reality of "God with us" if indeed the Holy Spirit lives in our hearts. It is my prayer that each person in our home would count themselves "dead to sin but alive to God in Christ Jesus" (Romans 6:11) because You live in each one of us!

JOURNAL: _____

_____

———❈———

THURSDAY: Read John 14:1-6. Meditate on God's Word and listen to what He has to say to you. Using the text as a guide, spend time in praise, confession and thanksgiving.

Pray for your children, to accept Christ as their personal Lord and Savior: Lord Jesus, I praise You today as "the Way and the Truth and the Life" (John 14:6). Thank You for humbling Yourself and becoming "obedient to death – even death on a cross!" (Philippians 2:8). Because of Your willingness to die for the sins of the world, anyone who accepts You as Lord will be saved from an eternity of torment in hell. Oh, what a Savior You are! Lord, it is my heart's desire that my children come to know You personally as soon as possible. You said in Your Word that "no one can come to Me unless the Father Who sent Me draws him" (John 6:44), so I ask that my children be drawn to You. Please God, I pray that You would open my children's "eyes and turn them from darkness to light, and from the power of Satan to [You], so that they may receive forgiveness of sins and a place among those who are sanctified by faith" in Christ Jesus (Acts 26:18). Nothing else matters if they miss salvation, so do whatever it takes to show them their need of You. And thank You Lord, that You are in heaven right now preparing a place for your children, and You promise to come back for us one day soon (John 14:3)!

JOURNAL: _____

_____

———❈———

FRIDAY: Read John 3:16-21. Meditate on God's Word and listen to what He has to say to you. Using the text as a guide, spend time in praise, confession and thanksgiving.

Pray for people around the world to hear the Good News of salvation: "For God so loved the world that He gave His one and only

Son, that whoever believes in Him shall not perish but have eternal life" (John 3:16). I stand amazed, Father God, that You could love this wicked world so much that You would voluntarily give up Your only Son as a Living Sacrifice to atone for our sins. "Look, the Lamb of God, who takes away the sins of the world! (John 1:29). Oh what a Savior! But Your Word is clear…"Whoever believes in the Son has eternal life, but whoever rejects the Son will not see life, for God's wrath remains on him" (John 3:36). Oh Father, forgive those who have chosen in their hearts to reject You, refusing to accept You or "putting it off" for another time. Make them so miserable in the darkness of their evil deeds that they would hunger for the Light of Jesus Christ. Thank You for Your patience with us, "not wanting anyone to perish, but everyone to come to repentance" (II Peter 3:9). May all men see that "the Son of Man came to seek and to save what was lost" (Luke 19:10).

JOURNAL: _____

_____

_____

SATURDAY: A Day of Application.

Read Ephesians 2:1-9.

"For it is by grace you have been saved, through faith – and this not from yourselves, it is the gift of God – not by works, so that no one can boast" (Ephesians 2:8-9).

In what are you trusting for salvation? Are you relying on your works and your own goodness, or have you placed your faith in Christ alone? Pray and ask the Lord to reveal to you if you are trusting in anyone or anything other than Him for salvation. Journal your thoughts/prayer here:

_____

_____

If the Lord is revealing to you that You do not know Him personally, go back and reread the prayer on Monday's lesson. Ask Jesus to come into your heart and be your Lord and Savior! Record the date here:

_____

Now go and tell somebody your Good News!

SUNDAY: A Day of Praise

Read John 10:7-15.

Praise Jesus as Savior: He is the "Gate" – the Way to salvation. He is the "Good Shepherd" – Who lay down His life for you!

WRITE OUT YOUR PRAYER OF PRAISE HERE:

_____

_____

_____

CHECK YOURSELF! WRITE YOUR MEMORY VERSE HERE:

_____

_____

Love for Others

"Be imitators of God, therefore, as dearly loved children and live a life of love, just as Christ loved us and gave Himself up for us as a fragrant offering and sacrifice to God"
(Ephesians 5:1-2).

LOVE IS POSITIVE ACTION

When I was engaged to be married, a sweet older woman in the faith gave me a wedding present that was quite different than the others I had received. It had been such fun to open all those traditional gifts of china, crystal, and silver, envisioning my future home complete with a new china cabinet to proudly display them all! But when her gift arrived, the package was so small and light that I knew immediately that this was not another piece of china or crystal to complete my requested 12-piece place setting. When I opened her gift I saw that it was a spice can, very similar to the kind that holds pepper or cinnamon, but this one was labeled, *LOVE –* Spice for Living ®. The ingredients were listed as faithfulness, gentleness, goodness, joy, kindness, patience, peace, perseverance, protection, trust, truthfulness and unselfishness. And although the can was empty of anything tangible, the net weight was listed as "immeasurable". On the back of the can was written: THE STORY BEHIND "LOVE" © ...*For many years a man watched his wife take a locked box down from the cupboard. She would unlock the box, take a pinch, sprinkle it over whatever she was cooking, relock the box and return it to its place. One day, while his wife was away, his curiosity got the best of him. He went to the cupboard, took the box down and opened it. To his surprise it was empty! He turned it over and on the bottom was written the word "LOVE". Don't keep your*

"LOVE" locked up in a cupboard. Keep it within easy reach and use generously."[6]

That little can of love has proven more valuable than all of the china and crystal I so desired (and every once in a while my husband reminds me that I need to actually use those dishes, not just display them!) What a wonderful reminder that love is something to be added to everything we say and do. As I take that can out of my cupboard and sprinkle a little on whatever dish I am making for dinner, it turns my thoughts toward those whom God has given to me to love. It prompts me to pray for them, to thank the Lord for blessing me with each one, and to serve them in a spirit of love.

When my husband and I were first married we attended a newlywed Sunday School class at our church. Almost weekly the teacher would remind us that "love is positive action." It is not just a lovey-dovey feeling of emotion; rather, it is something we do for others to prove that we care for them unconditionally, selflessly, sacrificially, and without thinking of receiving anything in return. Much like our dear Lord Jesus did for us when He died on the cross for our sins. "Be imitators of God, therefore, as dearly loved children and live a life of love, just as Christ loved us and gave Himself up for us as a fragrant offering and sacrifice to God" (Ephesians 5:1-2). The One Who dearly loves us wants us to imitate Him and live a life of love towards others. It will not always be easy, and it will not always be fair, but then neither was His sacrifice for us.

There are countless ways to show love to those around us every day, from making a batch of those favorite cookies, to doing someone else's chores for them, to forgiving when it is undeserved. So don't keep your love under lock and key...sprinkle a little (or a lot!) on everything you do, and your offerings of love will smell as good as those freshly baked cookies!

Memory Verse:
"Live a life of love, just as Christ loved us and gave Himself up for us as a fragrant offering and sacrifice to God" (Ephesians 5:2).

MONDAY: Read I Corinthians 13:1-8, 13. Meditate on God's Word and listen to what He has to say to you. Using the text as a guide, spend time in praise, confession and thanksgiving.

Pray for yourself, to make it your goal to imitate God and live a life of love: Father God, in reading this passage it is abundantly clear that love is supreme! It does not matter how much I give, how much I do, how much wisdom or faith I have, unless I have love, "I am nothing" and "I gain nothing" (I Corinthians 13:2 & 3). Oh Father, forgive me when my attitude or acts of service sound more like a clanging gong than a sweet melody because I have left out love, the most important thing. I want to be like You, Lord, and live a life of love, seeing others through Your eyes. Develop in me love that is patient and kind; love that does not envy or boast; love that is not proud, rude or self-seeking; love that is not easily angered and keeps no record of wrongs (I Corinthians 13:4-5). I know that I can never have this type of love on my own, apart from Your Holy Spirit! So please work in me, giving me a love for others that "always protects, always trusts, always hopes, always perseveres" (I Corinthians 13:7). I will praise You, Oh God, for You have "not rejected my prayer or withheld [Your] love from me!" (Psalm 66:20).

JOURNAL: _____

_____

_____

—————

TUESDAY: Read Matthew 22:34-40. Meditate on God's Word and listen to what He has to say to you. Using the text as a guide, spend time in praise, confession and thanksgiving.

Pray for your husband, to obey God's command to love Him and love others: Lord Jesus, it should come as no surprise that the two greatest commandments in all the Bible are the two You exemplified in Your own life. Thank You for being the Perfect Example of how to love! I pray fervently for my husband today, that he would love You, the Lord his God, with all his heart and with all his soul and with all his mind (Matthew 22:37). May he not hold back from intimacy with You and miss out on any of those things that "God has prepared for those who love Him" (I Corinthians 2:9). Then, as he walks more closely with You, the second command to "love your neighbor as yourself" (Matthew 22:39) will naturally follow. May he love his wife, "just as Christ loved the church" (Ephesians 5:25), love his children, and love others as himself. Your Word tells us that we have a "continuing debt to love one another" (Romans 13:8), so I pray that his indebtedness to You for salvation would be his motivation for loving those around him.

JOURNAL: _____

_____

_____

⸺⸺

WEDNESDAY: Read Matthew 5:43-48. Meditate on God's Word and listen to what He has to say to you. Using the text as a guide, spend time in praise, confession and thanksgiving.

Pray for those in your household, that you would be willing to love others even when it is not given in return: Oh Lord Jesus, this is one of Your most difficult commandments! Loving our enemies and praying for those who persecute us (Matthew 5:44) definitely do not come naturally. Please forgive us, Lord, when we put conditions on our love, just loving those who love us and only greeting our brothers (Matthews 5:46). To our shame, we look no different than the world You ask us to witness to! Please give me and my husband the power to love our enemies in the face of disagreement and even persecution, so that we can set the example for all those in our household. May we teach our children that "hatred stirs up dissension, but love covers over all wrongs" (Proverbs 10:12). Remind us to pray with our children when they are treated unfairly or hurt by others, trusting You to care for them instead of lashing out in retaliation. Thank You that Your love for us is never based on our performance or our love for You in return. Rather, Your love is perfect, as our heavenly Father is perfect (Matthew 5:48).

JOURNAL: _____

_____

_____

———◦◦◦◦———

THURSDAY: Read I John 4:7-21. Meditate on God's Word and listen to what He has to say to you. Using the text as a guide, spend time in praise, confession and thanksgiving.

Pray for your children, to have a deep love for one another: The Word of God says, "This is love: not that we loved God, but that He loved us and sent His Son as an atoning sacrifice for our sins" (I John 4:10). In light of this sacrifice, our response should be clear: "Since God so loved us, we also ought to love one another" (I John 4:11). Oh Father, I see my children growing up into very different individuals, with opposing likes and interests, and often getting on each other's nerves. It grieves me when I see them argue or belittle one another, showing little care or concern for the other's feelings. I pray that Your Holy Spirit would open their eyes to see the truth…"If anyone says, "I love God," yet hates his brother, he is a liar" and "Whoever loves God must also love his brother" (I John 4:20-21). May they not just say they love one another with their lips, but prove their love toward one another by their actions. As the years go by, may they grow to have sincere love for their siblings, loving one another deeply, from the heart (I Peter 1:22).

JOURNAL: _____

_____

_____

———◦◦◦◦———

FRIDAY: Read John 15:9-17. Meditate on God's Word and listen to what He has to say to you. Using the text as a guide, spend time in praise, confession and thanksgiving.

Pray for your church, to remain in God's love through obedience to His Word: "Your love, O Lord, reaches to the heavens, Your faithfulness to the skies....how priceless is Your unfailing love!" (Psalm 36:5 & 7). Oh Lord, Your love is perfect, unfailing, and without equal! And yet, knowing the sinners we are, You command us to love each other as You have loved us (John 15:12). Only through the mighty power of Your Holy Spirit within us could we ever attain to a love like Yours – a love that causes one to lay down his life for his friends (John 15:13). As Your church, we must take this command very seriously so that we can "bear fruit – fruit that will last" (John 15:16). So I pray that the members of my church would model lives of sincere love. May we "hate what is evil; cling to what is good. Be devoted to one another in brotherly love. Honor one another above [ourselves]" (Romans 12:9-10). May our love for one another and for unbelievers be contagious, so that "we may spur one another on toward love and good deeds" (Hebrews 10:24).

JOURNAL: _____

_____

_____

SATURDAY: A Day of Application

Read John 13:34-35.

Are you following God's command to love others? Does the way you treat those around you – from close family members to strangers on the street – prove that you are a disciple of the Lord Jesus Christ?

_____

If not, confess it to the Lord as sin and ask Him to give you His love for others. Write out your prayer here:

_____

_____

"Dear children, let us not love with words or tongue but with actions and in truth" (I John 3:18). Think of one thing you can do to show "positive action" toward someone in your life today. Write it here:

_____

Now do it, without expecting anything in return.

SUNDAY: A Day of Praise

Read I John 3:1-3, 16.

Praise God for His great love for you! Praise God that He calls you His child. Praise God that He was willing to lay down His life for you.

WRITE OUT YOUR PRAYER OF PRAISE HERE:

_____

_____

_____

CHECK YOURSELF! WRITE YOUR MEMORY VERSE HERE:

_____

_____

166

Wisdom and Discernment

"If any of you lacks wisdom, he should ask God, who gives generously to all without finding fault, and it will be given to him"
(James 1:5).

AN ORDINARY WOMAN BUT AN EXTRAORDINARY GOD

When the Lord originally laid it on my heart to write this book, all I could think was, "Who am I, Lord, to write a devotional book? I am just an ordinary woman, a wife and a mother, doing the best I can to take care of this family You have entrusted me with. What would I have to say that would matter one bit to anyone else?" So for quite some time as the Lord continually brought the idea back to my mind, I did my best to brush the thought away. Afraid to even consider putting myself out there and attempt such a daunting task, I had no shortage of excuses to offer up to my Lord. And the one that topped the list was a lack of wisdom. "I don't know what format to use, Lord. I don't know which passages to choose. I don't know what to say." And on and on and on. But as I brought each excuse before the Lord, He slowly but clearly organized my thoughts and directed me in the way I should go. Finally I relented, clinging to the fact that while I was just an ordinary woman, He was an extraordinary God who could be trusted to reveal the way one small step at a time.

James 1:5 says, "If any of you lacks wisdom, he should ask God, who gives generously to all without finding fault, and it will be given to him." When I finally quit fighting with the Lord and submitted to what He was asking of me, I clung to this verse for dear life! God not only promises to give His wisdom to anyone who asks for it, without finding fault, He also promises to give it generously, lavishly, abundantly! He will not just give us a little wisdom, just enough to keep us from making a horrible mistake; rather, He will give us great wisdom, in order to make the best possible decisions for our lives. What hope that gives ordinary people like you and me whom God often calls on to do things that take us out of our comfort zones and force us to make difficult decisions in uncharted territory.

In the book of Joshua, chapter 3, the Israelites are finally ready to enter the Promised Land after wandering in the desert for 40 years. The people are given this order: "When you see the ark of the covenant of the Lord your God…you are to move out from your positions and follow it. Then you will know which way to go, <u>since you have never been this way before</u>." (Joshua 3:3-4a). How many times are we called upon, as parents, as employees, as church members, as citizens to do something we have never done before? Almost every day! The decisions we face are endless… how should I handle this discipline situation with my rebellious child? How can I best prepare for this presentation at work? Where should we live? Should my husband accept this job offer? What great comfort is found in turning each and every decision over to the Lord. If we ask for wisdom, He promises to give it to us. Where He leads, we simply follow. We can step out in confidence, knowing that He will show us the right way to go.

"Whether you turn to the right or to the left, your ears will hear a voice behind you, saying, "This is the way; walk in it"" (Isaiah 30:21). May I clearly hear God's voice directing every one of my decisions because I have sought His face and asked Him what to do.

Memory Verse:
"If any of you lacks wisdom, he should ask God, who gives generously to all without finding fault, and it will be given to him"
(James 1:5).

MONDAY: Read Proverbs 2:1-10. Meditate on God's Word and listen to what He has to say to you. Using the text as a guide, spend time in praise, confession and thanksgiving.

Pray for yourself, to seek God's wisdom for every decision you face: Father I praise You as the Lord who "gives wisdom, and from His mouth come knowledge and understanding" (Proverbs 2:6). You, the Maker of heaven and earth, allow me to come seeking Your face, Your direction, whenever I need it! Oh Father forgive me when I "go my own way," failing to ask You for guidance. I willingly respond to Your rebuke and ask that You pour out Your heart to me, making Your thoughts known to me (Proverbs 1:23). When I am overwhelmed by the decisions I must make, remind me to lift them up to You, one by one. I am so thankful that even when I do not know the way to go, You do! "Nothing is too hard for You" (Jeremiah 32:17b). May I continually "look for (wisdom) as for silver and search for it as for hidden treasure" (Proverbs 2:4). I truly desire to "understand what is right and just and fair – every good path" (Proverbs 2:9). Help me to keep my eyes fixed on You, so that I can be a woman who "speaks with wisdom, and faithful instruction is on her tongue" (Proverbs 31:26).

JOURNAL: _____

_____

_____

TUESDAY: Read I Kings 3:5-14. Meditate on God's Word and listen to what He has to say to you. Using the text as a guide, spend time in praise, confession and thanksgiving.

Pray for your husband to have wisdom and insight like Solomon: Lord Jesus, Solomon could have asked for anything he wanted, and You would have given it to him. You truly are a God who can do anything! How very convicting that of all the things Solomon could have asked for – long life or wealth or victory over his enemies – he asked for wisdom and discernment. Oh Father, may my husband be a man like Solomon. May he seek

Your face each day, knowing that "The fear of the Lord is the beginning of wisdom; all who follow His precepts have good understanding" (Psalm 111:10). When my husband feels inadequate at work and does "not know how to carry out [his] duties" (I Kings 3:7b) please give him "wisdom and very great insight, and a breadth of understanding as measureless as the sand on the seashore" (I Kings 4:29). When faced with multiple decisions at home, please give him "a discerning heart to govern [his family] and to distinguish between right and wrong" (I Kings 3:9). And as he walks in Your ways and obeys Your statutes and commands (I Kings 3:14), please bless his life abundantly!

JOURNAL: _____

_____

_____

WEDNESDAY: Read Psalm 143:7-10. Meditate on God's Word and listen to what He has to say to you. Using the text as a guide, spend time in praise, confession and thanksgiving.

Pray for those in your household, to look to the Lord continually for instruction: In Proverbs 14:1 it says, "The wise woman builds her house, but with her own hands the foolish one tears hers down." Father God, please forgive me and my husband when we foolishly act in a way that brings destruction on our home. When we make decisions before consulting You, forgive us. When we strike out on our own, refusing the counsel of Your Word, rebuke us. It is up to us to show our children the great importance of seeking Your face and responding in humility and obedience. As we make every decision, please show us the way we should go, for to You we lift up our souls (Psalm 143:8b). Teach us to do Your will, for You are our God; may Your good Spirit lead us on level ground (Psalm 143:10). When the way ahead of us looks dark and treacherous, please remind us of this promise from Your Word: "I will lead the blind by ways they have not known, along unfamiliar paths I will guide them; I will turn the darkness into light before them and make the rough places smooth" (Isaiah 42:16).

JOURNAL: _____

_____

_____

———◦◦◦◦———

THURSDAY: Read Proverbs 23:19-25. Meditate on God's Word and listen to what He has to say to you. Using the text as a guide, spend time in praise, confession and thanksgiving.

Pray for your children, that they will listen to sound counsel and make wise decisions: Father, Your Word gives this strong warning: "The fear of the Lord is the beginning of knowledge, but fools despise wisdom and discipline" (Proverbs 1:7). How I pray that my children would fear You, Lord, and embrace the counsel in Your Word. May they listen "and be wise, and "keep [their] hearts on the right paths" (Proverbs 23:19). Give them the strength to reject the foolish lies of this world. Warn them when they are tempted to make bad decisions leading to such things as drunkenness, gluttony and laziness. Grant them understanding beyond their years, giving them the ability to discern truth from falsehood. The Bible says, "Listen to your father, who gave you life, and do not despise your mother when she is old" (Proverbs 23:22). May my husband and I prove ourselves to be a dependable source of wisdom because we have trusted in You! Years from now I pray that we will be able to look back with joy and delight because our children made wise choices that glorified You.

JOURNAL: _____

_____

_____

———◦◦◦◦———

FRIDAY: Read Proverbs 4:5-19. Meditate on God's Word and listen to what He has to say to you. Using the text as a guide, spend time in praise, confession and thanksgiving.

171

Pray for your president, to have great wisdom and discernment as he leads your country: Father, Your Word tells us that in Christ "are hidden all the treasures of wisdom and knowledge" (Colossians 2:3). Through You and You alone can we be certain of making wise decisions. So I pray for the president of this country, that He would know You personally and trust in You daily for direction in every situation placed before him. As he searches out the right way to go, please surround him with godly men and women who will speak the truth to him without reservation. In Proverbs 4:6 You say, "Do not forsake wisdom, and she will protect you" – oh how I pray that the decisions he makes will bring protection to our land! Please prevent him from any course of action that would "set foot on the path of the wicked or walk in the way of evil men" (Proverbs 4:14). Guide him in the way of wisdom and lead him along straight paths so that when he walks, his steps will not be hampered (Proverbs 4:11-12). When there is confusion, bring clarity; when there is doubt, bring assurance; and when there is indecision, may the right path "be like the first gleam of dawn, shining ever brighter" (Proverbs 4:18) before him.

JOURNAL: _____

_____

_____

SATURDAY: A Day of Application

Read Ephesians 1:15-19.

Pray for yourself, asking the Lord to "give you the Spirit of wisdom and revelation, so that you may know Him better" (v.17). Pray for spiritual illumination so that you can more fully grasp "the hope to which He has called you, the riches of His glorious inheritance in the saints, and His incomparably great power for us who believe" (v.18-19). Write out your prayer here:

_____

_____

Are you currently struggling with making a big decision and need the Lord's wisdom? Use these verses to pray and ask for His direction:

1) "Show me the way I should go, for to you I lift up my soul" (Psalm 143:8).

2) "Whether you turn to the right or to the left, your ears will hear a voice behind you, saying, "This is the way; walk in it" (Isaiah 30:21).

_____

_____

SUNDAY: A Day of Praise

Read Jeremiah 10:6-12.

"Oh, the depth of the riches of the wisdom and knowledge of God!" (Romans 11:33).

Praise God for His great wisdom. "Among all the wise men of the nations…there is no one like you" (Jeremiah 10:7b). None compares to Him!

WRITE OUT YOUR PRAYER OF PRAISE HERE:

_____

_____

CHECK YOURSELF! WRITE YOUR MEMORY VERSE HERE:

_____

_____

Self-Control

"I know that nothing good lives in me, that is, in my sinful nature.
For I have the desire to do what is good, but I cannot carry it out.
For what I do is not the good I want to do; no, the evil I do not want
to do – this I keep on doing. Now if I do what I do not want to
do, it is no longer I who do it, but it is sin living in me that does it"
(Romans 7:18-20).

WHY DID I EAT THAT?

Christmas break was over, the kids were back in school, and I had no more excuses. It was time to lose the extra pounds that I had gained while eating too many Christmas goodies and going out to eat too often. I woke up with fierce determination and renewed commitment to control my eating, choose healthier options and lose weight. The day started out pretty well, with my sensible bowl of raisin nut bran for breakfast. But just a few hours later I was in a rush to get out the door and run my errands. I thought I better grab something to take along for lunch when I got hungry. Leftover pizza from the refrigerator was the easiest and quickest option. Even though I wasn't hungry yet, I went ahead and ate it as soon as I got in the car. "It will be better freshly warmed from the microwave," I rationalized. I ate it too fast, ate more than I should have, and immediately regretted what I had done. "Why did I eat that?" I asked myself. Today was the day I was going to practice a little self-control and start eating better. "What is wrong with me?"

The Apostle Paul has just the words to convey my regret: "I do not understand what I do. For what I want to do I do not do, but what I hate I do" (Romans 7:15). When I woke up that morning I had no intention of eating leftover pizza for lunch. In fact, I hated myself for doing it! Yet, that is exactly what I had done. I had fallen back into old habits, allowing my lack of self-control to keep me feeling defeated. And so it is in other areas of my life....I determine to be more organized, memorize two Bible verses a week, arise extra early for my quiet time, compose a beautiful prayer to my Lord in my journal, and what really happens? I oversleep, barely have time to read the Bible verses, and only have time to write "Help!" in my prayer journal. The reality of it all is this: I am a sinner and without yielding to the controlling Presence of God's Holy Spirit within me I will never have the self-control I desire.

"So I find this law at work: When I want to do good, evil is right there with me. For in my inner being I delight in God's law; but I see another law at work in the members of my body, waging war against the law of my mind and making me a prisoner of the law of sin at work within my members. What a wretched [woman] I am! Who will rescue me from this body of death? Thanks be to God – through Jesus Christ our Lord!" (Romans 7:21-25). Amen! God's Word tells us that our Rescuer awaits to free us from the sin nature so that we can escape from whatever holds us back....even a shortage of self-control, determination, or restraint.

A lack of self-control has consequences on our relationships, our productivity, our health, our witness before others, and our ability to live victorious lives. But don't be defeated. Give the matter to the Lord and rely on His Spirit to help you overcome your fleshly tendencies! He is ready and willing to equip you with the self-control needed in all areas of life.

Memory Verse:
"I know that nothing good lives in me, that is, in my sinful nature. For I have the desire to do what is good, but I cannot carry it out"
(Romans 7:18).

MONDAY: Read Romans 8:1-11. Meditate on God's Word and listen to what He has to say to you. Using the text as a guide, spend time in praise, confession and thanksgiving.

Pray for yourself, to exercise self-control in all areas of your life by living according to the Spirit: Father God, this passage gives me such hope when I am faced with my own sinful tendencies. I praise You that "through Christ Jesus the law of the Spirit of life set me free from the law of sin and death" (Romans 8:2). As Your child, I do not have to be controlled by my flesh with its insatiable desires. Instead, I can exercise self-control by Your Spirit that lives within me, denying my flesh and submitting to You and Your control. Please point out any areas of my life that reveal a lack of self-control and restraint: Where there is overindulgence, rebuke me; where there is an unbridled tongue or uncontrolled anger, correct me; where there is laziness or apathy, convict me. May Your Holy Spirit help me in my weaknesses….interceding for me (Romans 8:26) to have the self-control I so desire. "The mind of the sinful man is death, but the mind controlled by the Spirit is life and peace" (Romans 8:6). Thank You for the peace and abundant life that come through yielding to You!

JOURNAL: _____

_____

_____

TUESDAY: Read Galatians 5:16-23. Meditate on God's Word and listen to what He has to say to you. Using the text as a guide, spend time in praise, confession and thanksgiving.

Pray for your husband, to live by the Spirit and so bear the Spirit's fruit of self-control: Father Your Word says, "Like a city whose walls are broken down is a man who lacks self-control" (Proverbs 25:28). This verse shows just how important it is for my husband to have self-control, for without it, he opens the way to destruction and leaves himself defenseless against the enemy. I pray then, that he would "live by the Spirit," so that he "will not gratify the desires of the sinful nature" (Galatians 5:16). May my husband make You his daily priority, allowing Your Word to shine light on all of his actions and attitudes. Convict him of any areas where he needs to practice more self-control in his life. In John 15:5 You say, "I am the vine; you are the branches. If a man remains in me and I in him, he will bear much fruit; apart from Me you can do nothing." So I pray that my husband would remain in You so that he can bear all of the fruit of Your Holy Spirit, especially self-control. May even he be surprised at Your ability to keep him calm in stress, to hold his tongue when angry, and to show restraint when his flesh tells him to do otherwise.

JOURNAL: _____

_____

_____

WEDNESDAY: Read I Timothy 3:1-11. Meditate on God's Word and listen to what He has to say to you. Using the text as a guide, spend time in praise, confession and thanksgiving.

Pray for your household, to be a training-ground for self-control: Lord Jesus, Your Word has much to say to those who desire to be "overseers" or leaders. Among many other things, men and women alike are told to be temperate and self-controlled. And as the "overseers" of our home, my husband and I are responsible both for modeling self-control and for requiring it from our children. Please help us to manage our family well and see that our children obey us with proper respect (I Timothy 3:4). May we not be extreme or excessive in our rules or punishments, but be fair and consistent in setting guidelines for our children. I pray that my husband and I would keep a tight rein on our feelings and emotions, exercising self-control and steadiness as we face the trials and complications each day brings. When there are outbursts, may Your Spirit lead us to correct in love and compassion. When we feel ourselves losing control, may we have the wisdom to step back and allow Your Spirit to calm us down before reacting sinfully. May we saturate ourselves in Your Word and prepare our minds for action and self-control (I Peter 1:13), very aware that our children are always watching and learning.

JOURNAL: _____

_____

_____

THURSDAY: Read II Timothy 3:1-9. Meditate on God's Word and listen to what He has to say to you. Using the text as a guide, spend time in praise, confession and thanksgiving.

Pray for your children, to exhibit self-control in an uncontrolled environment: Oh Father, when I read this description of the "last days" and look at the world around me, I am convinced that the last days are upon us! Our world today seems characterized by a lack of self-control: living to the extreme, overindulgence, little respect for authority and self-gratification at the cost of others. "Their folly will be clear to everyone" (II Timothy 3:9b) except themselves! How I pray that it will never be so for my children. Convict my husband and me to teach them to "be self-controlled and alert," knowing that their "enemy the devils prowls around like a roaring lion looking for someone to devour" (I Peter 5:8). Please remind my children to always think things through – not to act impulsively, but to consider the possible consequences ahead of time. May they "learn to control [their own bodies] in a way that is holy and honorable" (I Thessalonians 4:4) and refuse to be controlled by their emotions or by the opinions of others.

JOURNAL: _____

_____

_____

—————

FRIDAY: Read Titus 2:1-8. Meditate on God's Word and listen to what He has to say to you. Using the text as a guide, spend time in praise, confession and thanksgiving.

Pray for your church, to take seriously the responsibility of modeling and teaching self-control to the younger generation: Father, thank You for placing me in a body of believers that is my spiritual family… to love and encourage me, as well as train and correct me when needed. In these eight short verses from Titus the need for self-control is emphasized for everyone within the church, beginning with our elders: "Teach the older men to be temperate…self-controlled" (Titus 2:2). May older men take this responsibility seriously, knowing that right living must begin at the top if they are to "encourage the young men to be self-controlled" (Titus 2:6) as well! Likewise, it is the older women who must train the younger women in all areas, including self-control. Regardless of age, I pray that the members of my church would be aware of the influence we have on the next generation and take this responsibility seriously. We must go to You daily for a fresh filling of Your Holy Spirit. You alone have the power to enable us to exercise self-control "so that no one will malign the Word of God" (Titus 2:5).

JOURNAL: _____

_____

_____

SATURDAY: A Day of Application

Read Romans 7:15-20.

Name one area where you continually struggle with self-control: .

_____

Claim Psalm 46:1 as God's promise to help you in this area: "God is our refuge and strength, an ever present help in."

_____

Commit this area to the Lord, asking Him to help you exercise self-control in this area of struggle. Write out your prayer of commitment here:

_____

_____

SUNDAY: A Day of Praise

Read Deuteronomy 33:26-29.

Praise God that He is a very present help – ever present to guide believers by the indwelling Holy Spirit; always ready to correct and help when you are tempted to lose control.

WRITE OUT YOUR PRAYER OF PRAISE HERE:

_____

_____

_____

CHECK YOURSELF! WRITE YOUR MEMORY VERSE HERE:

_____

_____

WEEK TWENTY-FIVE
Confession and
Cleansing from Sin

"If we confess our sins, He is faithful and just and will forgive us our sins and purify us from all unrighteousness" (I John 1:9).

WHAT'S IN YOUR CLOSET?

It was the week after Christmas break, and I was doing some deep cleaning. We had rearranged the boys' rooms upstairs, and now I was faced with the daunting task of cleaning out all the closets to make them ready for use. There was one closet in particular that I dreaded: the "hand-me-down" closet where I stored all the clothes my older boys had outgrown until my youngest son could wear them. The problem was, in the past year or so I had taken to just opening the door and throwing things in, without taking the time to sort through them properly. Another closet was full of old toys, baseball cleats passed down from cousins, and years of past school papers. I needed to sort through everything, get it all organized, and decide what to keep and what to get rid of. My best friend Kelly called while I was knee-deep in old clothes. "Why did I ever start this," I moaned! The magnitude of the task was making me feel suffocated, and I regretted the mess I had allowed to build up over time.

But what a great feeling it was at the end of the day when everything was neat and orderly, cleared of all the clutter and all the mess! Clothes were stacked neatly in tubs and labeled with the correct sizes. I had a bag full of hand-me-downs for friends' kids at church and another bag for Goodwill. My boys would actually be able to use their closets now, and I could breathe easily without the chore weighing me down.

In much the same way, I think we have "closets" in our hearts where we store those things we do not want to deal with right now... things like unconfessed sin, feelings of guilt or accusation, regret or shame. Just as we throw things in the closets of our homes to deal with later, we often hold on to the clutter of sin and all of its baggage until it weighs us down just as heavily as old clothes. The Lord never intended for us to be bogged down with the weight of such things... forgiveness and cleansing are just a breath away! The Bible says, "If we confess our sins, He is faithful and just and will forgive us our sins and purify us from all unrighteousness" (I John 1:9). We can trust the Lord to forgive us when we come to Him in true confession and repentance. And once we have confessed our sin, God says, "I, even I am He who blots out your transgressions, for my own sake, and remembers your sins no more" (Isaiah 43:25). If God doesn't remember my past sin, then why should I? Satan loves to bring yesterday's mistakes into our minds to keep us trapped by guilt and shame; but if this sin has already been confessed, then by all means refuse to listen to him! Instead, "Let us draw near to God with a sincere heart in full assurance of faith, having our hearts sprinkled to cleanse us from a guilty conscience and having our bodies washed with pure water" (Hebrews 10:22). Our Lord and Savior is willing and able to clean away the mess left by our sin, including every stain of guilt, shame and remorse!

What a freeing experience to bow the knee before God the Father, receiving His complete forgiveness and feeling Him purify your heart. So what are you waiting for? Throw open the doors to your closets and start cleaning!

Memory Verse:
"If we confess our sins, He is faithful and just and will forgive us our sins and purify us from all unrighteousness" (I John 1:9).

MONDAY: Read Hebrews 10:19-23. Meditate on God's Word and listen to what He has to say to you. Using the text as a guide, spend time in praise, confession and thanksgiving.

Pray for yourself, asking the Lord to reveal any areas of your heart that need His cleansing: Oh Father, thank You for the precious blood of Jesus that enables me to approach You with confidence! (Hebrews 10:19). I praise You that Your Son is the Great High Priest who is able to take away once and for all the sins of the world! I do not need to cower in Your Presence – rather I can come boldly before Your throne of grace, asking forgiveness and receiving Your cleansing. I open my heart to Your examination this morning, knowing that You will deal with me gently but firmly. Where there is sin, may I come to You in confession, allowing You to "wash away all my iniquity and cleanse me from my sin" (Psalm 51:2). Where Satan reminds me of guilt or shame over sin that has already been dealt with, may I firmly rebuke him in the authority of Your Powerful Name. Where there is regret or remorse, may I remember that in all things (good and bad) You work "for the good of those who love you" (Romans 8:28). And may I "hold unswervingly to the hope [I] profess, for He who promised is faithful" (Hebrews 10:23)!

JOURNAL: _____

_____

_____

———◦◦◦———

TUESDAY: Read Psalm 51:1-9. Meditate on God's Word and listen to what He has to say to you. Using the text as a guide, spend time in praise, confession and thanksgiving.

Pray for your husband, to be rightly related to God through confession and repentance: Lord Jesus, as Creator, You know our propensity toward sin; yet as Redeemer, You prove Your ultimate love for us by taking the penalty of our sin on Yourself. What a mighty God You are! May we never minimize the tremendous gap between Your perfection and our unworthiness. Your Word says that "he who conceals his sins does not prosper, but whoever confesses and renounces them finds mercy" (Proverbs 28:13). So just as King David approached You in humility and honesty in regards to his sin, so may my husband come before Your throne seeking forgiveness and reconciliation when he has strayed away from You. Have mercy on my husband, O God, "according to Your unfailing love; according to Your great compassion blot out [his] transgressions" (Psalm 51:1). And after he has come to You in true repentance and confession, please lift the burden of sin from his back and remind him that he has been washed, "whiter than snow" (Psalm 51:7).

JOURNAL: _____

_____

_____

———◦◦◦◦———

WEDNESDAY: Read I John 1:5-10. Meditate on God's Word and listen to what He has to say to you. Using the text as a guide, spend time in praise, confession and thanksgiving.

Pray for your household, to be filled with the light of God's presence because you have confessed and been cleansed from sin: Father, we praise You as the God of light; in You "there is no darkness at all" (I John 1:5)! How I long for my home to be filled with the light of Your glory at all times. The Bible says, "If we walk in the light, as He is in the light, we have fellowship with one another, and the blood of Jesus, His Son, purifies us from all sin" (I John 1:7). I long for fellowship with You and with those in my home, so please show us any way that we are not walking in the truth. "If we claim to be without sin, we deceive ourselves and the truth is not in us" (I John 1:8). I pray that You would help my husband and me to humbly teach our children that we are sinners in need of Your forgiveness and cleansing. Then, by following our example, they too will confess and repent of sin. Thank You that, "If we confess our sins, You are faithful and just to forgive us our sins and purify us from all unrighteousness" (I John 1:9). May our home always be full of the light of Your presence and empty of guilt and shame over unconfessed sin.

JOURNAL: _____

_____

_____

———≡◦◦◦≡———

THURSDAY: Read Psalm 32:1-5. Meditate on God's Word and listen to what He has to say to you. Using the text as a guide, spend time in praise, confession and thanksgiving.

Pray for your children, to experience the relief and cleansing of confessed sin: Oh Father, I remember well my own times of grief and despair over unconfessed sin. The burden of it can be so heavy that day to day activities become almost too much to bear! But Your Word says, "Blessed is he whose transgressions are forgiven, whose sins are covered" (Psalm 32:1). Oh, how I want my children to be blessed! So I lift them up to You, asking You to convict them quickly when they go astray. May they have no "secret sins", but be caught when guilty so that they cannot continue in them. As the psalmist said, "It was good for me to be afflicted so that I might learn Your decrees" (Psalm 119:71). Better a minor lesson now than an extremely difficult and more serious one later. When my children sin, I pray that it would make them feel dirty and ashamed so that they will confess and repent. May my children acknowledge their sin to You and not try to cover up their iniquity (Psalm 32:5). And once You have forgiven them, remind them how thorough Your cleansing is! "As far as the east is from the west, so far has He removed our transgressions from us" (Psalm 103:12).

JOURNAL: _____

_____

_____

———≡◦◦◦≡———

FRIDAY: Read Colossians 1:18-23. Meditate on God's Word and listen to what He has to say to you. Using the text as a guide, spend time in praise, confession and thanksgiving.

Pray for your church, to look to Christ alone for reconciliation with the Father and a life free from guilt or accusation: Oh Father, may my church never lose sight of the fact that Your Son Jesus "is the head of the body, the church…so that in everything He might have the supremacy" (Colossians 1:18). May we keep Him as our top priority, our first love, our ruler and Lord. Thank You so much for reconciling Your church by Christ's physical body through death to present us holy in Your sight, "without blemish and free from accusation" (Colossians 1:22). It is a gift we do not deserve – that You would exchange His righteousness for our sin! "God made Him who had no sin to be sin for us, so that in Him we might become the righteousness of God" (II Corinthians 5:21). May we represent You well in this lost and fallen world, showing unbelievers the glorious hope and freedom that come from confessed and covered sin. I pray that we will continue in our faith, "established and firm, not moved from the hope held out in the Gospel" (Colossians 1:23) until our Lord Jesus returns to take us home.

JOURNAL: _____

_____

_____

SATURDAY: A Day of Application

Read Jeremiah 2:22: "Although you wash yourself with soda and use an abundance of soap, the stain of your guilt is still before me," declares the sovereign Lord."

Are you trying to clean yourself up on your own?

_____

You can only receive forgiveness and cleansing from the Lord.

Ask him to forgive you for your sins and allow Him to clean you!

"Though your sins are like scarlet, they shall be as white as snow; though they are red as crimson, they shall be like wool" (Isaiah 1:18).

Write out your prayer of confession here:

_____

_____

Are you still harboring guilt or shame for already confessed sin? Claim Hebrews 10:19-23 as God's promise that you are cleansed from a guilty conscience:

_____

_____

SUNDAY: A Day of Praise

Read Isaiah 44:21-23.

Praise God that He is able to make the vilest sinner clean! "I have swept away your offenses like a cloud, your sins like the morning mist" (v.22).

WRITE OUT YOUR PRAYER OF PRAISE HERE:

_____

_____

_____

CHECK YOURSELF! WRITE YOUR MEMORY VERSE HERE:

_____

_____

WEEK TWENTY-SIX
Relying on God's Power for Strength

"I am the vine; you are the branches. If any man remains in Me and I in him, he will bear much fruit; apart from Me you can do nothing" (John 15:5).

GET PLUGGED IN!

A few years ago I bought a fancy new blender that has a variety of uses. It can grate, beat, stir, puree, crumb, chop and mix. It has different buttons you can push if you're making a smoothie, a milkshake or an icy drink. So one night after dinner I decided to put that fancy blender to good use by making milkshakes for my family for dessert. I had already added the ice cream, milk and chocolate syrup, and my youngest son Alec was waiting patiently to start the blender. But when he pushed the "milkshake" button on the blender, nothing happened. It only took a few seconds for me to realize my mistake...I had not plugged the blender into the electrical outlet. The new blender was equipped to perform a variety of tasks, but without a source of power, it was completely incapable of doing anything.

Jesus said, "I am the vine; you are the branches. If any man remains in Me and I in him, he will bear much fruit; apart from Me, you can do nothing" (John 15:5). Just as my blender needed to be plugged in to a power source in order to work, so I must be plugged into my Power Source, the Lord Jesus Christ, in order to work. My blender cannot stir without power. My blender cannot puree without power. And I know from personal experience that my blender cannot beat a milkshake without power!

This earthly vessel that I am in cannot perform any of my roles without my Power Source either. Sure, I can try to function in and of my own strength, but failure or "burnout" always results. I cannot be a godly mother unless I am plugged in to the Lord Jesus to gain the patience and wisdom that I need. I cannot be a loving wife unless I am plugged in to God, relying on His love and His grace to filter through me. I cannot be a faithful Sunday School teacher unless I am plugged in to Him, asking His Holy Spirit to empower me to teach His Word. I cannot be a caring sister, a doting daughter, a kind neighbor...the list goes on and on. For apart from Him, I can do nothing.

Every morning we must get "plugged in" to our Power Source. We must rise early enough to bow the knee to our Lord and Savior Jesus Christ, not just asking Him to bless our day but to direct and control our day...to acknowledge that we cannot do anything of value by our strength alone! We need His power at work within us. We need Him to equip us for each and every one of our tasks. He promises us in His Word: "Remain in me, and I will remain in you. No branch can bear fruit by itself; it must remain in the vine. Neither can you bear fruit unless you remain in Me" (John 15:4). I so desire to bear good fruit for my Lord, the fruit of the Spirit that is "love, joy, peace, patience, kindness, goodness, faithfulness, gentleness and self-control" (Galatians 5:22). When I bear the fruit of impatience, irritability, unrest, selfishness and lack of joy, it is a sure indication that I am not plugged in!

What kind of fruit is growing on your vine? Determine to "remain in Him" today. Plug yourself in first thing in the morning, and He promises that He will not only remain with you, but you will bear fruit! After all, our fruit is what proves that we are His disciples (John 15:8).

Memory Verse:

"I am the vine; you are the branches. If any man remains in Me and I in him, he will bear much fruit; apart from Me you can do nothing" (John 15:5).

MONDAY: Read John 15:1-8. Meditate on God's Word and listen to what He has to say to you. Using the text as a guide, spend time in praise, confession and thanksgiving.

Pray for yourself, that you would turn to the Lord daily and yield to the pruning process that releases His power in your life: Lord Jesus, sometimes it is a lack of discipline that keeps me from turning to You...I oversleep or am too lazy to get out of bed in the morning. Sometimes it is misguided priorities....I allow other people or things to infringe on my time alone with You. But I must confess that most of all, it is sheer disobedience that keeps me from plugging into You and Your Word. For when I turn to You for strength and direction, You often reveal sin in my life that needs to be confessed and corrected. "I am the true vine, and my Father is the gardener. He cuts off every branch in me that bears no fruit, while every branch that does bear fruit He prunes so that it will be even more fruitful" (John 15:1-2). That pruning process hurts! Forgive me Lord, when I am unwilling to open my life to the scrutiny of Your Word. Conviction is always uncomfortable, but I know it is the only way for me to bear the abundance of fruit You desire to see in me. Please help me to yield to You, so that I can experience the power-filled life!

JOURNAL: _____

_____

_____

TUESDAY: Read Ephesians 3:14-21. Meditate on God's Word and listen to what He has to say to you. Using the text as a guide, spend time in praise, confession and thanksgiving.

Pray for your husband to look to God for strength rather than rely on himself: Father, there have been numerous times that I have looked to my husband for strength when my own was lacking. And while I'm thankful that he is there to support me in my time of need, it is my prayer that he understands that he can look to You for strength when his is lacking! Just because he is the head of the household, it does not mean that he must be "superman". He, too, needs Your power for each one of the tasks for which he is responsible. So I pray that out of Your glorious riches You would strengthen my husband with power through Your Spirit in his inner being (Ephesians 3:16). When he becomes overwhelmed by the weight of his responsibilities, may he remember that "with Your help [he] can advance against a troop"; with his God he can scale a wall (Psalm 18:29). I pray that my husband would have power to grasp the vastness of Your love for him, and comprehend that You are "able to do immeasurably more than all we ask or imagine" according to Your power that is at work within us (Ephesians 3:20).

JOURNAL: _____

_____

_____

——❦——

WEDNESDAY: Read Exodus 15:1-6, 19-21. Meditate on God's Word and listen to what He has to say to you. Using the text as a guide, spend time in praise, confession and thanksgiving.

Pray for those in your household, to be aware of and acknowledge the power of God on your lives: What a wonderful account of the power and strength of the awesome God we serve! Moses and his sister Miriam sang boldly of God's might, testifying before the Israelites that it was God and God alone who brought them safely through the Red Sea. "The Lord is my strength and my song; He has become my salvation. He is my God, and I will praise Him, my father's God, and I will exalt Him" (Exodus 15:2). They gave all of the glory and all of the honor to Whom it was due! Oh Father, how I pray that my husband and I would be like Moses and Miriam, declaring before those in our home that You are a God of great power. I want our children to see us constantly looking to You for help – and then join us in praising Your name boldly and unashamedly when You work! Give us the desire and strength to daily approach Your throne of grace, so that when You appear we may be confident and unashamed before You at Your coming (I John 2:28).

JOURNAL: _____

_____

_____

THURSDAY: Read Isaiah 40:25-31. Meditate on God's Word and listen to what He has to say to you. Using the text as a guide, spend time in praise, confession and thanksgiving.

Pray for your children to grasp the mighty power of God and turn to Him for strength: Father God, a mere glance toward the heavens is all that is needed to observe Your mighty power and strength. You, who call each star by name and never lose a single one of them, can most definitely exert Your power in the lives of my children! I am so thankful that You will never grow tired or weary of my prayers on their behalf; quite the contrary, You both understand and delight in my prayers for them. May it be a great comfort to my children to know that You give "strength to the weary and increase the power of the weak" (Isaiah 40:29). When they are overwhelmed at school or work and feel as if they bear the weight of the world on their shoulders, remind them that You are a very present help and source of power. "Even youths grow tired and weary, and young men stumble and fall; but those who hope in the Lord will renew their strength" (Isaiah 40:30-31). O Sovereign Lord, begin to show my children your greatness and Your strong hand (Deuteronomy 3:24).

JOURNAL: _____

_____

_____

FRIDAY: Read II Chronicles 20:1-12. Meditate on God's Word and listen to what He has to say to you. Using the text as a guide, spend time in praise, confession and thanksgiving.

Pray for your pastor, to seek God's help and strength in times of trouble: Father God, thank You for this man You called to be the pastor of my church. I'm sure his role is both a tremendous blessing and a tremendous burden at times! He needs Your strength, Lord Jesus. He needs Your power to face the vast armies that threaten Your church…whether the armies are made up of enemies from within, like worldliness, unbelief, or hypocrisy; or enemies from without, like opposition from unbelievers and our chief adversary, the devil. May he be like Jehoshaphat, who "resolved to inquire of the Lord" (II Chronicles 20:3) at every turn. When he feels weak, remind him to "be strong in the Lord and in His mighty power" (Ephesians 6:10). Use my church body to share the many ways You have exerted Your strength in the past, in order to reaffirm his faith in You in the present. In difficult times I pray that he would lead our church to collectively confess that "we have no power to face this vast army that is attacking us. We do not know what to do, but our eyes are upon You" (II Chronicles 20:12).

JOURNAL: _____

_____

_____

SATURDAY: A Day of Application

Read Jeremiah 32:17-27.

God says, "I am the Lord, the God of all mankind. Is anything too hard for me?" (Jeremiah 32:27).

Name something that seems too hard for you right now:

_____

_____

Give it to the Lord, claiming His promise from Philippians 4:13 - "I can do everything through Him who gives me strength":

_____

_____

SUNDAY: A Day of Praise

Read I Chronicles 29:10-13.

Praise God that He is El – The God of Power and Might. "In your hands are strength and power to exalt and give strength to all" (I Chronicles 29:12).

WRITE OUT YOUR PRAYER OF PRAISE HERE:

_____

_____

_____

CHECK YOURSELF! WRITE YOUR MEMORY VERSE HERE:

_____

_____

WEEK TWENTY-SEVEN
Purity and Holiness

---

*"Since we have these promises, dear friends, let us purify ourselves
from everything that contaminates body and spirit, perfecting holiness out of reverence for God"*
(II Corinthians 7:1).

STICKING OUT LIKE A SORE THUMB!

Fast food restaurants, strip malls, and gas stations crowded the streets as I drove home from my appointment. This area of town was newly developed, but construction had been going at break neck speed and new buildings and shops were everywhere. It was hard to believe that just a year or two ago, hardly anything was there but farm land and the occasional home. As my eyes scanned the street for somewhere to stop for lunch, I saw a sight that stuck out like a sore thumb. There, surrounded by newly poured asphalt and neon signs, stood two old silos on a plot of green grass. The silos looked like they had been there for a long, long time, covered in moss and ivy, weathered by years in the sun and the abuse of wind and rain. Tall and strong amidst the newly developed structures, they seemed to stand proudly for a past way of life. But next to all the "newness," they seemed odd, out-of-place. They just did not fit in with the current environment.

In much the same way, the biblical virtues of purity and holiness stand in stark contrast to the impurity and godlessness of our modern day culture. Innocence and a lack of worldly experience are ridiculed and deemed things of the past. Clinging to values our grandparents held dear earns us the labels of "old fashioned" and "prude". Previously not mentioned topics like sex before marriage and homosexuality are now so prevalent that they are totally accepted, even expected. If young people choose to follow God's command to abstain from sex until marriage, they are considered to be weird and behind the times. The saying "boys will be boys" is tossed lamely about behind snickers and winks, excusing if not encouraging teenage boys and young men to experiment with sex and pornography. Teenage girls and women of all ages are taught to dress provocatively, wielding sexuality as a tool to be lorded over men. In such an environment, the idea of keeping oneself pure seems behind the times, but that is exactly what Christians are called to do.

Definitions for the word "pure" include: free from contamination; and free from what weakens or pollutes. As Christians, we have been made holy by the blood of Jesus Christ and have been set apart by God for His use. We must deliberately and purposely keep ourselves from being polluted by the worldly influences all around us. If we do not, we become weakened at best, and totally ineffective for Christ at worst.

The Bible says: "Since we have these promises, dear friends, let us purify ourselves from everything that contaminates body and spirit, perfecting holiness out of reverence for God" (II Corinthians 7:1). What are the promises spoken of in this verse? That we, as believers, are the very temple of the living God! "I will live with them and walk among them, and I will be their God, and they will be my people" (II Corinthians 6:16). The Living God promises to live within me, walk through this difficult life by my side, and be there at every turn and twist in the road. His very Presence makes me holy, and I should represent Him well by striving to keep His temple pure...even if it means I might stick out like a sore thumb!

Memory Verse:
"Let us purify ourselves from everything that contaminates body and spirit, perfecting holiness out of reverence for God"
(II Corinthians 7:1).

MONDAY: Read I Peter 3:1-6. Meditate on God's Word and listen to what He has to say to you. Using the text as a guide, spend time in praise, confession and thanksgiving.

Pray for yourself, committing to keep your mind and body pure out of reverence for God: Heavenly Father, what a reminder this passage is of the influence I have on those around me. The Bible is clear: the purity and reverence of my life, demonstrated by a willingness to submit to my husband, affects both him and any others I come in contact with during the day. May my behavior always lead others toward You and never away from You. I desire to obey Your command to set a godly example "in speech, in life, in love, in faith and in *purity*" (I Timothy 4:12). Please point out any area of sin in my life - ranging from impure thoughts to acceptance of worldly behavior that is contrary to Your Word - so that I can purify myself from anything that contaminates body and spirit (II Corinthians 7:1). Thank You for reminding women that the condition of the inner self is much more important than our outward adornment. "The unfading beauty of a gentle and quiet spirit... is of great worth in God's sight. For this is the way the holy women of the past who put their hope in God used to make themselves beautiful" (I Peter 3:5). May my beauty come from You!

JOURNAL: _____

_____

_____

—————————

TUESDAY: Read I Thessalonians 4:1-8. Meditate on God's Word and listen to what He has to say to you. Using the text as a guide, spend time in praise, confession and thanksgiving.

Pray for your husband, to fully yield to the sanctifying work of the Holy Spirit: Father, Your Word says, "It is God's will that you should be sanctified...avoid sexual immorality... control [your] own body in a way that is holy and honorable" (I Thessalonians 4:3-4). So it is my prayer today that my husband fully yield to Your Holy Spirit as You work in him, conforming him to the image of Christ in every way. May

197

my husband hold up each area of his life for Your careful examination and quickly repent if You convict him of any impurity or unholiness. When he sees immorality in the lives of his friends or coworkers, please help him stand strong in the face of temptation. May he never share in the sins of others, but keep himself pure (I Timothy 5:22). I pray that You would put godly men in his life who would help him keep his eyes fixed on You, not on this world. "For God did not call us to be impure, but to live a holy life" (I Thessalonians 4:7). Please guard his eyes, his ears, his lips, and his heart from the impurities of this world, so that he may "live in order to please God" (I Thessalonians 4:1).

JOURNAL: _____

_____

_____

WEDNESDAY: Read I Corinthians 6:12-20. Meditate on God's Word and listen to what He has to say to you. Using the text as a guide, spend time in praise, confession and thanksgiving.

Pray for your marriage, that you and your husband would honor God with your bodies by keeping yourselves and your marriage pure: Lord Jesus, it says in Scripture that when my husband and I were married, we became one flesh (Genesis 2:24). And when we united ourselves with You, we became one with You in spirit (I Corinthians 6:17). "Do you not know that your body is a temple of the Holy Spirit, who is in you, whom you received from God? You are not your own; you were bought at a price. Therefore, honor God with your body" (I Corinthians 6:19-20). May we never do anything to blemish Your purity and holiness within us! Our enemy, the devil, would like nothing more than to see us fall captive to impurity, especially through the lure of sexual immorality in our marriage. Please help us, Lord Jesus, to keep ourselves free from bondage in this area. "Marriage should be honored by all, and the marriage bed kept pure, for God will judge the adulterer and all the sexually immoral" (Hebrews 13:4). May my husband and I only have eyes for one another, so as never to incur Your judgment, but only Your blessing!

JOURNAL: _____

_____

_____

———— ∞∞∞ ————

THURSDAY: Read I Peter 1:13-22. Meditate on God's Word and listen to what He has to say to you. Using the text as a guide, spend time in praise, confession and thanksgiving.

Pray for your children to live pure and holy lives, untainted by the sinfulness of this world: Father, I must admit that this is an area where I really struggle to keep from worrying about my children. We live in such a wicked world, full of lust, impurity and immorality, that I despair at times that they can ever survive without becoming contaminated. I so long for my children to be pure – emotionally and physically – so that they can experience Your very best for them! I want my children to be sexually pure – unpolluted by pornography and sex before marriage. Your Word says, "But just as He who called you is holy, so be holy in all you do" (I Peter 1:15). If You call us to holiness, then it must be possible! "How can a young man keep his way pure? By living according to Your Word" (Psalm 119:9). Your Word holds the key to purity, so we as parents must read it, teach it and pray it over our children. No matter how young or old my children are, may they always be convicted to treat the opposite sex "with absolute purity" (I Timothy 5:2), and "keep themselves from being polluted by the world" (James 1:27).

JOURNAL: _____

_____

_____

———— ∞∞∞ ————

FRIDAY: Read Titus 2:11-14. Meditate on God's Word and listen to what He has to say to you. Using the text as a guide, spend time in praise, confession and thanksgiving.

Pray for your church to take a stand for godliness and purity in this world: Oh Lord, I love that You call us "Your very Own" in this passage. Those words make me feel special, valuable, and worthy in Your sight. Thank You for giving Yourself for us to reedem us from all wickedness and to purify us <u>for You</u> (Titus 2:14). May the knowledge that we belong to You motivate the members of my church to be faithful to Your name. We must "say "No" to ungodliness and worldly passions, and live self-controlled, upright and godly lives in this present age" (Titus 2:12). I pray that we would not cower before the worldliness around us, but stand firm for Your Word and speak out against false doctrine. Keep us from hypocrisy - teaching one thing and living another – and equip us to guard our purity. May we be ever mindful that this life is not all there is, but that we are waiting "for the blessed hope – the glorious appearing of our great God and Savior, Jesus Christ!" (Titus 2:13). And as such, we "ought to live holy and godly lives as [we] look forward to the day of God and speed its coming" (II Peter 3:11-12).

JOURNAL: _____

_____

_____

SATURDAY: A Day of Application

Read Ephesians 5:3-18.

Ephesians 5:3 says "But among you there must not be even a hint of sexual immorality, or of any kind of impurity, or of greed, because these are improper for God's holy people." Has the Lord revealed any area of impurity in your life this week?

_____

_____

_____

Confess and repent of this as sin, asking God to create in you a pure heart and renew a steadfast spirit within you (Psalm 51:10). Write out your prayer here and receive God's forgiveness:

_____

_____

_____

Now, "live as children of light" and "find out what pleases the Lord" (Ephesians 5:8-10).

SUNDAY: A Day of Praise

Read Revelation 4:1-11

Praise God that He is Holy – Add your voice to those in heaven who declare in verse 8: "Holy, holy, holy is the Lord God Almighty, who was, and is, and is to come!"

WRITE OUT YOUR PRAYER OF PRAISE HERE:

_____

_____

_____

CHECK YOURSELF! WRITE YOUR MEMORY VERSE HERE:

_____

_____

WEEK TWENTY-EIGHT
Compassion and Mercy

"The Lord is compassionate and gracious, slow to anger, abounding in love. He will not always accuse, nor will He harbor His anger forever; He does not treat us as our sins deserve or repay us according to our iniquities" (Psalm 103:8-10).

WELL, IT'S HIS OWN FAULT!

It seemed like a good idea at the time. Perhaps bored with the monotony of country life and longing for excitement and independence, the boy had asked his father for his share of the estate and set off to "do his own thing". But wild living was expensive, and before long he had spent every last penny of the inheritance his father had given him. Now desperate to fill his empty belly, he took the only job available...feeding pigs. He was so hungry that even the pigs' slop looked good, but no one gave him anything to eat. Realizing his dead-end situation and filled with sorrow for leaving his father and squandering everything he owned, the boy decided to return home in repentance, asking only that his father treat him as one of the hired men.

This well-known account of the Prodigal Son is recorded for us in Luke chapter 15. Scripture tells us that the boy's father feared he was dead and would probably never see his son again. So as his son approached from afar, "his father saw him and was filled with compassion for him; he ran to his son, threw his arms around him and kissed him" (Luke 15:20b). The father treated his long-lost son like royalty, clothing him in his best finery and preparing a huge feast to celebrate his return. But not everyone in the household was as happy to see the boy come home. His older brother, who had remained faithfully by the father's side during the younger brother's absence, was filled with anger. Concerned only with his own situation and what he perceived as neglect in the face of faithful service, the older brother had no compassion for the younger whatsoever.

How many times have I been guilty of similar thoughts toward others? "Well, they brought all this trouble on themselves, and I am NOT going to feel sorry for them!" or "They made their bed, and now they will have to lie in it!" Quick to condemn and cast judgment, compassion is sometimes the last thing on our minds, especially when difficulty has come as a result of sin or disobedience. Worse yet are the times when completely innocent people endure hardship and suffering, and we turn only a blind eye and a hard heart in their direction. So busy with our own lives and our own problems, we don't take the time to listen, let alone care. Or we allow our own hurts to make us callous to what others are going through.

The word "compassion" has been defined as: loving sympathy or empathy; the ability to actually participate in the feelings of another. Simply put, if another person hurts, you hurt. If another person is troubled, you are troubled. Even when the hurts and consequences are a result of disobedience and sin, you reach out in compassion and love. "The Lord is compassionate and gracious, slow to anger, abounding in love. He will not always accuse, nor will He harbor His anger forever; He does not treat us as our sins deserve or repay us according to our iniquities" (Psalm 103:8-10). Thank the Lord that He does not treat us as our sins deserve, but is forever compassionate and merciful toward us. Now, may we go and do likewise.

Memory Verse:
"The Lord is compassionate and gracious, slow to anger, abounding in love" (Psalm 103:8).

MONDAY: Read Zechariah 7:8-14. Meditate on God's Word and listen to what He has to say to you. Using the text as a guide, spend time in praise, confession and thanksgiving.

Pray for yourself, to be compassionate rather than hard-hearted: "This is what the Lord Almighty says: 'Administer true justice; show mercy and compassion to one another'" (Zechariah 7:9). Father, I praise You as the Perfect Judge, the only One who has the completely unbiased ability to condemn or acquit. Please forgive me when I look on others in anger or condemnation, casting judgment rather than compassion, as they incur the consequences of their sin. Please forgive me when I turn my back and stop up my ears...making my heart as hard as flint (Zechariah 7:11-12) to the hurts all around me. Convict me when I reject Your command to be compassionate and loving when others are suffering. Your Word is clear...such apathy makes You angry and turns Your ear from me: "So when they called, I would not listen, says the Lord Almighty" (Zechariah 7:13). Oh Father, I do not want to do anything that would hinder my relationship with You! Please open my eyes to see others as You do and soften my heart to sympathize with those who are hurting.

JOURNAL: _____

_____

_____

———※◈※———

TUESDAY: Read Matthew 14:13-21. Meditate on God's Word and listen to what He has to say to you. Using the text as a guide, spend time in praise, confession and thanksgiving.

Pray for your husband to be a man of compassion like Jesus was: The Bible says, "When He saw the crowds, He had compassion on them, because they were harassed and helpless, like sheep without a shepherd" (Matthew 9:36). How I praise You, Lord Jesus, for Your passionate care and concern for Your creation! You are moved to compassion when you see Your children harassed by the cares of this world, helpless to help even themselves. In like manner, I pray that my husband would be moved to sympathy when he sees those around him struggling. May he be concerned about both the emotional and physical needs of others, taking it upon himself to do what he can to help supply their need. Just as You refused to "send the crowds away" (Matthew 14:15) to fend for themselves, so may my husband look on those You send his way with a personal responsibility to help. If, in judgment or apathy or anger, he realizes that he just does not care, strengthen him to bow the knee in repentance of his hardened heart. May my husband choose to clothe himself with compassion (Colossians 3:12) out of a desire to please You.

JOURNAL: _____

_____

_____

—————

WEDNESDAY: Read Luke 15:11-31. Meditate on God's Word and listen to what He has to say to you. Using the text as a guide, spend time in praise, confession and thanksgiving.

Pray for those in your home, to be especially compassionate with those in their own family: It is sad but true...oftentimes we are the least compassionate and merciful with those we love the most! Maybe it is because our expectations are higher that we are more demanding and critical of family members, but it should not be. I pray, Father God, that as You are "full of compassion and mercy" (James 5:11b), so those in my home would exude love, compassion and mercy. May we each have the same attitude as the father in this story of the prodigal son who was filled with compassion for his flesh and blood, even though he had made poor choices. Rebuke us sternly when our attitude is instead like that of the older brother, full of anger and self-righteousness, uncaring for his brother's welfare. Your Word reminds us that compassion is the test of our love for You: "If anyone has material possessions and sees his brother in need but has no pity on him, how can the love of God be in him?" (I John 3:17). May we prove our love for You, Lord Jesus, as we demonstrate it through our care and concern for those we love.

JOURNAL: _____

_____

_____

—————

THURSDAY: Read Luke 5:17-25. Meditate on God's Word and listen to what He has to say to you. Using the text as a guide, spend time in praise, confession and thanksgiving.

Pray for your children, to have genuine care and concern for others: Father, it says in Scripture: "And what does the Lord require of you? To act justly and to love mercy and to walk humbly with your God" (Micah 6:8). How I pray that my children would walk as You require… in an attitude of humility before You and mercy toward others. If they see a friend going through a difficult time, I pray that compassion would fill their hearts and spur them on to act in kindness. If they see a stranger in need, I pray that they would not turn a blind eye but feel a personal responsibility to reach out in love. Just as the friends of this paralytic man had compassion on him and were determined to get their friend to Jesus *whatever it took*, so may my children be determined in caring for siblings, friends and strangers alike. May they "be kind and compassionate to one another, forgiving each other, just as in Christ God forgave them" (Ephesians 4:32). I praise You, Oh God, that "As a father has compassion on his children, so the Lord has compassion on those who fear Him" (Psalm 103:13).

JOURNAL: _____

_____

_____

———————

FRIDAY: Read II Corinthians 1:3-11. Meditate on God's Word and listen to what He has to say to you. Using the text as a guide, spend time in praise, confession and thanksgiving.

Pray for an attitude of compassion within your church: "Praise be to the God and Father of our Lord Jesus Christ, the Father of compassion and the God of all comfort" (II Corinthians 1:3)! Oh God, out of a heart of gratitude for all that You have done for us, I pray that my church family would be filled with compassion for our brothers and sisters in Christ. Your Word says that You "comfort us in all our troubles, so that we can comfort those in any trouble with the comfort we ourselves have received from God" (II Corinthians 1:4). It is our blessing to receive

Your comfort, and it is our responsibility to offer comfort to others. We can be Your instruments of comfort in so many ways: by extending a dinner invitation to newcomers, by offering to provide childcare for a single mother, or by simply being a companion to the elderly husband struggling to care for his dying spouse. Please show us how to live out Your command to "have equal concern for each other. If one part suffers, every part suffers with it" (I Corinthians 12:25-26). And burden us to help one another by our prayers (II Corinthians 1:11) as You direct.

JOURNAL: _____

_____

_____

SATURDAY: A Day of Application

Read Isaiah 63:7-9.

If someone were to describe you, could they use the words in this passage? Could they tell of your kindnesses, the many good things you have done, your compassion and love for others (Isaiah 63:7)?

_____

Could they say that in all their distress you too were distressed (Isaiah 63:9)?

_____

Has the Lord been dealing with you this week about a lack of compassion towards someone?

_____

If so, confess it here and ask the Lord to give You his love and mercy for that person:

_____

SUNDAY: A Day of Praise

Read Isaiah 54:7-10.

"And when they cried out to You again, You heard from heaven, and in Your compassion You delivered them time after time" (Nehemiah 9:28b).

Praise the Lord for His everlasting kindness and compassion toward us. Thank Him that He is a God who hears our cries for help, even when we sin, and will have compassion on us!

WRITE OUT YOUR PRAYER OF PRAISE HERE:

_____

_____

_____

CHECK YOURSELF! WRITE YOUR MEMORY VERSE HERE:

_____

_____

Whatever You Do, Do It Well!

"Whatever you do, work at it with all your heart,
as working for the Lord, not for men"
(Colossians 3:23).

DO I HAVE TO BE SUPER WOMAN?

If you are feeling the need to evaluate your work, take my advice and do not read the account of "the Proverbs 31 Woman". She makes Mother Theresa seem like a sluggard! All that getting up early and staying up late, cooking and sewing, planting and trading, taking care of the needy...Whew! Anyone out there want to join me on the couch for a cup of coffee? Surely this woman was not that productive ALL of the time. I mean, really? Did she really make the thread before she even set about making the actual clothes?

I appreciate the fact that the footnote in my *Life Application Study Bible* said that this woman "may not be one woman at all – she may be a composite portrait of ideal womanhood."[7] Now, that insight certainly takes the edge off a little bit! Reading Proverbs 31 is not meant to intimidate the ordinary woman or make her feel like she must be Super Woman. We are not expected to imitate her every action; rather, we should allow the portrait of this woman to inspire us to be our best at whatever job we do.

In light of that piece of information, maybe we really can discuss some of the things she does in Proverbs 31:13-24 without stopping for a nap! *She selects wool and flax; she provides food for her family and her servants; she buys a field and plants a vineyard; In her hand she holds the distaff and grasps the spindle with her fingers; she opens her arms to the poor and extends her hands to the needy; she makes coverings for her bed; she is clothed in fine linen and purple. She makes linen garments and sells them, and supplies the merchants with sashes.* No doubt about it… she's a worker! More importantly, look at the way she works: *She works with eager hands; she sets about her work vigorously; her arms are strong for her tasks; she gets up while it is still dark; her lamp does not go out at night.* The Proverbs 31 Woman does not mope about and complain! She works eagerly at her job with a good attitude, giving it 100% all of the time.

It might not be our calling in life to actually plant fields and sew all of the clothing for our household, but it is our calling to work wholeheartedly at whatever task is before us today. "Whatever you do, work at it with all your heart…" (Colossians 3:23). Scripture is clear…we are not to be lazy. We are to work and we are to work hard, ***wherever*** God has us at the current moment. Even if our work is to clean toilets, wash dishes, and pack lunches for school. If the work is boring, unsatisfying, or even downright unpleasant, our Lord's command to "work at it with all your heart" remains the same.

When the grown son of one of my mother's friends complained that his current job wasn't any fun, the mother quickly retorted, "Work isn't supposed to be fun…that's why they call it work!" But work really can be satisfying, fulfilling even, when we get our focus right. The last part of Colossians 3:23 gives the perspective we need: "… as working for the Lord, not for men." That means doing each one of our tasks as if the Lord Himself has asked us to, with a desire to please Him above all else.

Memory Verse:
"Whatever you do, work at it with all your heart, as working for the Lord, not for men" (Colossians 3:23).

MONDAY: Read Proverbs 31:10-31. Meditate on God's Word and listen to what He has to say to you. Using the text as a guide, spend time in praise, confession and thanksgiving.

Pray for yourself, to do all your tasks as if working for the Lord, not for men: Oh Father, I must come to You in an attitude of repentance after reading this passage. Forgive me, Lord, when I go lamely about my work, doing the bare minimum with a resentful heart. May I be ever mindful of the One I am really serving: You, the God Most High. For without You and Your grace upon my life, I would have nothing and I would be nothing. Thank You Lord, for blessing me with the ability to work and with a job to do. May others say of me: "She watches over the affairs of her household and does not eat the bread of idleness" (Proverbs 31:27). Whether I am working at home or outside of the home, I pray that I would be faithful to "work with eager hands" (Proverbs 31:13) and represent You well. No matter what I am doing, I can bring You pleasure if I am obedient to work wholeheartedly. Turn my thoughts toward You throughout the day, and help me find fulfillment in a job well done. I want to be a woman of noble character so that my husband can have "full confidence in [me] and lack nothing of value" (Proverbs 31:11).

JOURNAL: _____

_____

_____

———◦◦◦◦———

TUESDAY: Read Daniel 6:1-5. Meditate on God's Word and listen to what He has to say to you. Using the text as a guide, spend time in praise, confession and thanksgiving.

Pray for your husband, to be known for his exceptional work ethic that results from a desire to please the Lord: Lord Jesus, thank You so much for the job you have given my husband to do. You have been faithful to meet all of our needs (Philippians 4:19), and that includes his need for a job to earn money to pay the bills. As my husband goes to work day after day, year after year, may the responsibility of providing for his family be a blessing to him, not a curse. Like Daniel, may he work hard, doing his very best, and so earn a reputation among his co-workers of distinguishing himself by his exceptional qualities (Daniel 6:3). I pray that when his superiors examine his work, he would be found "trustworthy and neither corrupt nor negligent" (Daniel 6:4). I know that my husband gets weary in his work at times, longing for something more exciting, less routine, more fulfilling, or less demanding. Your Word says, "There is nothing better for a man than to enjoy his work, because that is his lot" (Ecclesiastes 3:22). Please give him a renewed sense of satisfaction in his job as he does it to bring You glory.

JOURNAL: _____

_____

_____

⎯⎯⎯⎯⎯⎯⎯⎯⎯

WEDNESDAY: Read Acts 18:1-3, 24-26. Meditate on God's Word and listen to what He has to say to you. Using the text as a guide, spend time in praise, confession and thanksgiving.

Pray for your marriage, that you and your husband would work well together: Lord Jesus, thank You for sharing this account of Aquila and Priscilla, an ordinary married couple who went about their daily work with hearts focused on You. They were welcoming and invited the Apostle Paul to live in their home. They were hospitable, offering their home as a meeting place for the church (I Corinthians 16:19). They were about the business of teaching others: "They invited [Apollos] to their home and explained to him the way of God more adequately" (Acts 18:26). And they were "fellow workers in Christ Jesus" who "risked their lives" (Romans 16:4) for other believers. You don't call all of us to full-time Christian work, but just as Aquila and Priscilla served You as tentmakers, so my husband and I can serve You in whatever jobs we have. May we strive to be like them...welcoming, hospitable, about the business of training others in godliness, and willing to take risks as Your fellow workers. Whatever our hands find to do, may we do it with all our might (Ecclesiastes 9:10) in service for You.

JOURNAL: _____

_____

_____

⎯⎯⎯⎯⎯⎯⎯⎯⎯

THURSDAY: Read Proverbs 10:1-5. Meditate on God's Word and listen to what He has to say to you. Using the text as a guide, spend time in praise, confession and thanksgiving.

Pray for your children, to honor God's command to work diligently: Father, we do not have to look very far to see a dwindling in the work ethic of those around us. The world says, "just do enough to get by," and "don't put in too much effort – no one will know." How I pray that my children will not be deceived by such misguided opinions! Views like these are in direct opposition to Your Word that says, "The sluggard's craving will be the death of him, because his hands refuse to work" (Proverbs 21:25). My husband and I must teach our children by example that hard work is not only expected of them, it is required. Whether they are doing chores around the house or working at an outside job to earn money, remind them to always give their best effort and even go the extra mile. Teach them quickly that "lazy hands make a man poor, but diligent hands bring wealth. He who gathers crops in summer is a wise son, but he who sleeps during harvest is a disgraceful son" (Proverbs 10:4-5). From a young age I pray that they would earn a reputation for wisdom and hard work, always striving to please You.

JOURNAL: _____

_____

_____

—————————

FRIDAY: Read II Thessalonians 3:6-12. Meditate on God's Word and listen to what He has to say to you. Using the text as a guide, spend time in praise, confession and thanksgiving.

Pray for the people of your nation, to be responsible and hard-working members of society: Father God, I am so thankful to live in a country that looks out for the needs of others. What a blessing that we have a welfare system to care for those individuals who truly are in need or unable to work because of disability or temporary job loss. But may we never take advantage of this system or misuse it for selfish gain! Your Word is clear: if an able-bodied man "will not work, he shall not eat" (II Thessalonians 3:10). Just as Paul and his companions "worked night and day, laboring and toiling so that [they] would not be a burden" (II Thessalonians 3:8), so must we assume responsibility for ourselves. It is up to us as believers to model before others the correct work ethic. May we do all of our work as unto You, and not unto man, being examples of diligent workers who are full of honesty, integrity, and punctuality. And as we do, I pray that others would take notice and follow suit, desiring the satisfaction of a job well done.

JOURNAL: _____

_____

_____

SATURDAY: A Day of Application

Read I Thessalonians 4:11-12.

Are you giving your best effort at home?

_____

If you work outside of the home, are you giving your best effort there?

_____

Do you think your work ethic is worthy of the respect of others?

_____

Are you being unnecessarily dependent on someone else?

_____

Name an area where you realize you have failed to give 100%

Confess it as sin and ask for the Lord's forgiveness. Make a commitment to do your work with all your heart, "as working for the Lord, not for men" (Colossians 3:23). Write out your prayer of commitment here:

_____

_____

SUNDAY: A Day of Praise

Read Philippians 1:6, Philippians 2:13, and Romans 8:28.

Praise God that He is doing a good work in you and for you!

WRITE OUT YOUR PRAYER OF PRAISE HERE:

_____

_____

_____

CHECK YOURSELF! WRITE YOUR MEMORY VERSE HERE:

_____

_____

Contentment

"I know what it is to be in need, and I know what it is to have plenty. I have learned the secret of being content in any and every situation, whether well fed or hungry, whether living in plenty or in want" *(Philippians 4:12).*

JESUS ALONE

I recently bought a new table for my entry hall. After ten years of using an antique piece, I was ready for something new, something different. I guess I was tired of the "old look" and ready for a "new look". But once I got the new table home and in its place, my renovation seemed far from complete. Now everything around it looked old and boring too! I decided that a new picture above the table might help, so I searched the stores for the perfect one. After hanging the picture I stepped back to admire the changes. "You know," I said to myself, "maybe I should replace the lamp and buy some new accessories too." After all, it just didn't seem right to put all that old stuff on my new table! Showing my husband my renovations later that evening, I asked him if I should shop for a few new things to complete the look. After thinking about it for a few seconds he simply said, "Who's to say the new stuff would be any better than the old stuff?"

My husband's simple comment contained much wisdom, not only for my decorating pursuit but for life in general. My desire to replace one piece of furniture had escalated into a much bigger project. Instead of being content with the one new thing, I had become dissatisfied and unhappy about everything else around it. And while I believe there is nothing wrong with redecorating or buying a new piece of furniture when you can afford it, there was much wrong with my attitude in wanting more and more.

A simple definition for the word "contentment" is satisfaction. It doesn't take much to become dissatisfied, does it? Visiting a friend in her new home has the power to send us scurrying back to our own to look around with critical eyes. A bouquet of flowers arriving at the office for a coworker has the potential to ruin our day because we didn't receive the same for ourselves. Monotony or boredom with life in general can make us hungry for something – anything! – new, exciting, or different. The problem is, even if we get what we think we want or need, discontentment rears its ugly head the very next time we become bored or compare what we have with others.

The Apostle Paul said, "I know what it is to be in need, and I know what it is to have plenty. I have learned the secret of being content in any and every situation, whether well fed or hungry, whether living in plenty or in want" (Philippians 4:12). What was Paul's secret? Finding contentment in the daily presence of Christ, *regardless* of his situation! Rather than seeking satisfaction in "things", Paul sought out the Giver of all things. Instead of trying to fill his emptiness with material possessions or pursuits, Paul understood that only a growing relationship with Christ could satisfy his deepest needs for love, acceptance, and fulfillment.

"Therefore, holy brothers, who share in the heavenly calling, fix your thoughts on Jesus" (Hebrews 3:1). As you fix your thoughts on Him – the only true and lasting Source of fulfillment – everything else will fade into the background. So the next time you fall prey to those familiar feelings of discontentment and despair, force your eyes off of your circumstances and back on Jesus where they belong!

Memory Verse:
"I have learned the secret of being content in any and every situation, whether well fed or hungry, whether living in plenty or in want" (Philippians 4:12).

MONDAY: Read Philippians 4:10-13. Meditate on God's Word and listen to what He has to say to you. Using the text as a guide, spend time in praise, confession and thanksgiving.

Pray for yourself, to be content in any and every situation: Father, forgive me. Forgive me when I become disgruntled or dissatisfied. Forgive me for continually grasping for the newest thing. Forgive me when I complain about my "lack" when I truly lack for nothing. Forgive me when I get my eyes off of You and all that You have given me. Forgive me when I covet what others have instead of being thankful for what I have. Lord Jesus, I recognize this behavior as sin. You have given me so much, always meeting all my needs (and so many of my wants!) according to Your glorious riches in Christ Jesus (Philippians 4:19). Please open my eyes to see Your generous abundance all around me and close my eyes to the material things that so easily distract. I pray that I would have an attitude of contentment, not because of the things I have but because of Your Living Presence in my life. May I be able to say like Paul, "I have learned the secret of being content in any and every situation" (Philippians 4:12), because I am seeking fulfillment in You alone.

JOURNAL: _____

_____

_____

———◦◦◦———

TUESDAY: Read Joshua 7:1-13. Meditate on God's Word and listen to what He has to say to you. Using the text as a guide, spend time in praise, confession and thanksgiving.

Pray for your husband, to be content with God's boundaries on his life: Father God, after seeing the Israelites experience great victory at Jericho, we see what happens when we are not satisfied with what You allow us. Not content with Your provision for them, some of the men sinned by wanting more and acting unfaithfully. They took the "devoted things", the plunder from Jericho, as their own possessions instead of following Your command to destroy them (Joshua 7:11). As a result, You refused to go with them into the next battle, and they experienced a humiliating defeat. May it never be so for my husband! I pray that he would carefully stay within Your boundaries of protection, so that he would always prosper and never suffer. Please help him to be content with the things You allow in his life, and "whatever happens, conduct [himself] in a manner worthy of the Gospel of Christ" (Philippians 1:27). May my husband follow You with all of his heart because "the fear of the Lord leads to life: Then one rests content, untouched by trouble" (Proverbs 19:23).

JOURNAL: _____

_____

_____

WEDNESDAY: Read Ecclesiastes 4:8, 5:10-20. Meditate on God's Word and listen to what He has to say to you. Using the text as a guide, spend time in praise, confession and thanksgiving.

Pray for those in your household, to be content with God's provision: Heavenly Father, we see the great contrast in these verses between two men: the one who worked and worked, with "no end to his toil, yet his eyes were not content with his wealth" (Ecclesiastes 4:8); and the other who found "satisfaction in his toilsome labor…for this is his lot" (Ecclesiastes 5:18). Oh Lord, reveal to us any way that we are acting like the first man… always striving, but never content. I pray that we would determine as a family to enjoy the things You give us, accept our lot in this life and be happy in our work – for this is a gift from You! (Ecclesiastes 5:19). Please guide me and my husband in teaching our children the balance between working hard to honor You and working too hard for material gain. May we never put emphasis on wealth and possessions that can disappear in an instant. Rather I pray we would enjoy what You provide and exalt You as the One who provided it! May those in our home not be preoccupied with the pursuit of wealth, but be content in You and "occupied with gladness of heart" (Ecclesiastes 5:20).

JOURNAL: _____

_____

_____

THURSDAY: Read Exodus 15:22-16:8. Meditate on God's Word and listen to what He has to say to you. Using the text as a guide, spend time in praise, confession and thanksgiving.

Pray for your children, not to complain but to be content with what they have: Father God, You once asked Abraham, "Is anything too hard for the Lord?" (Genesis 18:14). Your mighty power to part the Red Sea and allow Your children to cross on dry land proves that You can do anything! But no sooner had You performed this miracle than the Israelites began to grumble when they faced the next obstacle. Instead of being content with the way You were caring for them, they complained to Moses about what they lacked. Just as You must have grown weary when the Israelites grumbled against You (Exodus 16:8), so I grow tired of hearing my children voice complaints to me! I want to teach my children to focus on what You do supply, and not on what we don't have. I know that I cannot expect my children to be content if I am constantly voicing dissatisfaction, so please remind me to display a positive and grateful attitude in all things. Strengthen my children to resist the temptation to covet the possessions of others. And motivate them to do "everything without complaining or arguing" (Philippians 2:14).

JOURNAL: _____

_____

_____

———————

FRIDAY: Read I Timothy 6:6-10. Meditate on God's Word and listen to what He has to say to you. Using the text as a guide, spend time in praise, confession and thanksgiving.

Pray for those in your church to find contentment in the Lord, seeking Him rather than wealth: The Apostle Paul taught Timothy about the danger of desiring riches: "People who want to get rich fall into temptation and a trap and into many foolish and harmful desires that plunge men into ruin and destruction" (I Timothy 6:9). He also advised that, "Some people, eager for money, have wandered from the faith and pierced themselves with many griefs" (I Timothy 6:10b). Lord Jesus, may this never happen to those in my church! I pray that You would protect my church family from a love of money and a spirit of dissatisfaction. Instead of seeking riches, may we be content in seeking You! "But godliness with contentment is great gain" (I Timothy 6:6). May we obey Your command to financially support the church, not to grow it bigger and more luxurious so that we would have a better place to worship; but to grow it into a place where people experience Your Presence and bring You glory! May we never complain about the music or preaching when it fails to suit our individual preferences, but find fulfillment in the act of worshipping You.

JOURNAL: _____

_____

_____

SATURDAY: A Day of Application

Read Hebrews 13:5.

Do you love money?

_____

Are you content with what you have?

_____

When you get something you want are you satisfied, or do you immediately set your sights on getting the next thing?

_____

Do you find fulfillment in things or in the Lord?

Ask the Lord to reveal the true condition of your heart. Confess any area of sin that the Holy Spirit brings to mind:

_____

_____

Only a growing relationship with Christ can truly satisfy! Pray and ask the Lord to help you "learn the secret of being content in any and every situation" (Philippians 4:12):

_____

SUNDAY: A Day of Praise

Read Deuteronomy 32:1-4.

Praise God that He is Perfect and we can find contentment in Him!

WRITE OUT YOUR PRAYER OF PRAISE HERE:

_____

_____

_____

CHECK YOURSELF! WRITE YOUR MEMORY VERSE HERE:

_____

_____

WEEK THIRTY-ONE
Kindness and Hospitality

"Share with God's people who are in need. Practice hospitality"
(Romans 12:13).

A HOME AWAY FROM HOME

Not long after graduating from college, I signed up to serve two years as a Peace Corps Volunteer in Togo, West Africa. Armed with my degree in International Marketing and a minor in French, I was ready to travel the world, see the sites, and hopefully, do some good in a foreign land. I jumped right into the training program and spent the next three months learning the basics of a local language, experiencing new food and customs, and adjusting to another culture. It was all so different and new, just the thing to satisfy my craving for adventure and travel! At the end of the three-month training period, I felt completely equipped to live independently and navigate my way through a foreign city, teaching small business owners basic bookkeeping skills. But while I was prepared with all of the training material and language skills necessary to do the job, I was not prepared for the wave of loneliness that struck as soon as I arrived at my post. Miles away from my fellow volunteers and thousands of miles away from my loved ones, I felt incredibly alone among foreign people in a vastly different culture and environment.

One Saturday not too long after making Kpalime, Togo, my home, I wandered among the marketplace vendors, looking for fresh fruits and vegetables. Across the way I saw a woman and young girl that looked as out of place as I did! Hurrying to meet them I learned that they were missionaries from the United States who lived and worked at a Center for the Blind on the outskirts of town. After greeting me warmly and inviting me over for lunch, they told me about a local church led by another missionary family. L'Eglise Baptiste became my new church home, and those two missionary families, the Washers and the Allstons, welcomed me into their homes with open arms. Psalm 68:6 says, "God sets the lonely in families..." and that is just what He did for this lonely Peace Corps Volunteer. For the next two years they treated me like one of their own. They included me in every Sunday dinner and holiday celebration, and they encouraged me to stop in for a glass of "sweet tea" whenever I was close by (which I made sure was often!) Both families had young children who affectionately called me "Aunt Heather", which added to my sense of belonging. They never once turned me away or were too busy when I showed up on their doorsteps, regardless of the day or hour. I will forever be grateful for the unconditional love and hospitality these dear friends showed me when I so desperately needed it. They lived out the Lord's command to "share with God's people who are in need. Practice hospitality" (Romans 12:13).

Opportunities to be hospitable are all around us...inviting the new neighbors over for dinner, opening our homes for church socials, or allowing our houses to be the neighborhood hangout. My mother taught me by example that hospitality is not just having people in your home. Hospitality is extending warmth and kindness wherever you are – like talking to the chatty stranger at the grocery store or inviting a lonely widow to dine with you at a restaurant. So let's open up our homes and our hearts to the very next person we meet who needs it. After all, God's Word reminds us: "Do not forget to entertain strangers, for by so doing some people have entertained angels without knowing it" (Hebrews 13:2). Now how's that for motivation?

Memory Verse:
"Share with God's people who are in need. Practice hospitality"
(Romans 12:13).

MONDAY: Read II Kings 4:8-17. Meditate on God's Word and listen to what He has to say to you. Using the text as a guide, spend time in praise, confession and thanksgiving.

Pray for yourself, to be willing to offer kindness and hospitality when you see a need: Father, I have been on the receiving end of hospitality, even at the hand of strangers, and I know what a difference even the smallest gesture can make. Please forgive me when I hurry past opportunities to extend warmth and kindness because of my own selfishness or personal agenda. I pray that I would be like the Shunammite woman who opened her home to Elisha, offering him a meal and a place to stay. She didn't just do the bare minimum – she went to much trouble for him (II Kings 4:13). She did everything she could think of to make Elisha feel comfortable. May I delight in showing such hospitality, going the extra mile to make guests feel welcome. At the same time I pray that I would not become "distracted by all the preparations that have to be made" (Luke 10:40), but understand that a welcoming heart is more important than a perfectly clean house! May my willingness to be hospitable never be based on receiving something back – rather, may I do it willingly out of a heart of gratitude for all You have done for me.
JOURNAL: _____

_____

_____

⸻

TUESDAY: Read Genesis 18:1-8. Meditate on God's Word and listen to what He has to say to you. Using the text as a guide, spend time in praise, confession and thanksgiving.

Pray for your husband, to lead his family in showing hospitality to others: Lord, these three men who appeared to Abraham were complete strangers, but he took no shortcuts in providing for their physicals needs and making them feel welcome. He had water brought to wash their feet, gave them a place to rest, asked Sarah to make fresh bread and selected a choice calf for his servant to prepare for their meal. He led his entire household to show kindness and hospitality to these travelers, modeling Your New Testament command to overseers to be hospitable (I Timothy 3:2). If Abraham had chosen to do only the bare minimum for them, those in his household would have followed his lead. So I pray for my dear husband, asking You to help him be hospitable like Abraham was. May he not be overwhelmed at the needs around him, but see each one as an opportunity to serve You. For You say, "Whoever welcomes one of these little children in My name welcomes Me; and whoever welcomes Me does not welcome Me but the one who sent Me" (Mark 9:37).

JOURNAL: _____

_____

_____

———————

WEDNESDAY: Read Matthew 25:31-45. Meditate on God's Word and listen to what He has to say to you. Using the text as a guide, spend time in praise, confession and thanksgiving.

Pray for your household, to be a beacon of warmth and welcome to all who enter: Father, how I praise You that You have had a kingdom prepared for Your children since the creation of the world! Thank You that one day very soon, the Son of Man will come in His glory to gather His flock and grant us an inheritance (Matthew 25:31-34). May this end goal serve to motivate us in being kind and hospitable to those around us. Your Word reminds us that whatever we do for one of the least of the brethren, we do for You (Matthew 25:40). So rebuke us, Lord, when we are tempted to close our doors and focus only on ourselves. May we welcome each visitor to our home as if it was You Who was knocking at the door! Convict us to do whatever we can to extend kindness to others, and to do so "without expecting to get anything back" (Luke 6:35). Please remind us to look for opportunities to show kindness and warmth at home, at school, at work, and wherever we go out in our communities. May we never forget that, "We are therefore Christ's ambassadors, as though God were making His appeal through us" (II Corinthians 5:20).

JOURNAL: _____

_____

_____

———⊰◈⊱———

THURSDAY: Read Luke 10:30-37. Meditate on God's Word and listen to what He has to say to you. Using the text as a guide, spend time in praise, confession and thanksgiving.

Pray for your children, to understand that "loving their neighbor" includes showing kindness and hospitality wherever they are: Thank You Lord, for including the parable of the Good Samaritan in Your Word as a wonderful example of showing kindness to your neighbor. Seeing a complete stranger in need, the Samaritan "took pity on him...bandaged his wounds... took him to an inn and took care of him" (Luke 10:33-35). He even left additional money for further expenses! The Samaritan could have very easily passed on the other side as the Levite and priest did, but he chose the harder thing, the more inconvenient thing, the more costly thing. In like manner, may my children do the right thing, even when it is difficult or inconvenient. If there is a new student at school or a new employee at work, may my child feel a burden to offer a kind word and show them around. When conflict arises at home, may my children choose to "be kind and compassionate to one another" (Ephesians 4:32). In all things may they prove their love for You by acting in kindness and hospitality toward their neighbor.

JOURNAL: _____

_____

_____

———⊰◈⊱———

FRIDAY: Read III John 5-10. Meditate on God's Word and listen to what He has to say to you. Using the text as a guide, spend time in praise, confession and thanksgiving.

Pray for the members of your church, to practice hospitality toward Christian workers: Lord Jesus, I lift my church family up to You today, praying that we would be like Gaius and never like Diotrephes! The apostle John speaks so highly of Gaius in this passage, commending him for what was done "for the brothers, even though they are strangers" (III John 5). In welcoming traveling preachers, missionaries, and fellow believers into his home, Gaius earned a reputation for showing the love of Christ to people he did not know. In like manner, may my church "show hospitality to such men so that we may work together for the truth" (III John 8). I pray that we would never be guilty of "refusing to welcome the brothers" (III John 10), but embrace the common bond we have with fellow believers in Christ. In addition, may we delight in showing hospitality to our fellow church members and visitors by inviting them into our homes. I pray that others could say of us: "Your love has given me great joy and encouragement, because you, brother, have refreshed the hearts of the saints" (Philemon 7).

JOURNAL: _____

_____

_____

SATURDAY: A Day of Application

Read I Peter 4:9. Write it here:

_____

Our memory verse for this week from Romans 12:13 instructs us to: "Share with God's people who are in need. Practice hospitality." Are you in the habit of practicing hospitality?

_____

If so, great! Now, how is your attitude in your hospitality? Do you do it cheerfully and with a willing heart? Or do you grumble and complain about it?

_____

Name one area in particular where you struggle to be hospitable or struggle to have a good attitude about it? (Examples: a certain relative, in-laws, a neighbor who drops by unannounced, strangers who want to strike up conversations):

_____

Pray and ask the Lord to help you be more willing to "practice hospitality" and to do so with a cheerful, loving heart:

_____

List some ways that you will try to show hospitality this week, both with fellow believers and with unbelievers (Maybe a neighbor, acquaintance at school, etc.):

_____

SUNDAY: A Day of Praise

Read II Peter 1:10-11.

Praise God that a "rich welcome into the eternal kingdom" awaits those who have trusted Jesus Christ as Lord and Savior.

WRITE OUT YOUR PRAYER OF PRAISE HERE:

_____

_____

CHECK YOURSELF! WRITE YOUR MEMORY VERSE HERE:

_____

_____

Obedience

"Whoever has My commands and obeys them, he is the one who loves Me. He who loves Me will be loved by My Father, and I too will love him and show Myself to him" (John 14:21).

EVEN IN THE LITTLE THINGS

Dinner was ready and the table was set. Opening the refrigerator in search of the tea pitcher, I called my family to come to the table. I pushed aside the milk jug and orange juice container to find the tea pitcher – sitting empty – on the back of the shelf. "How many times have I told you boys not to put the empty tea pitcher back into the refrigerator?" I asked. With no time left to brew more tea, we had only one option left. "I guess we're just going to have to drink water with our meal tonight," I complained to my husband.

Later that evening as I put the kettle on to boil water for more tea, I muttered to myself: "Why can't those boys just listen to me and obey my instructions?" As soon as the words were out of my mouth, the Lord turned them around and spoke them to me. "Well, how about you, Heather? How well do you listen to Me and obey what I ask of you?" The familiar words hit home, bringing to mind a lesson the Lord had taught me several years before....

I had been asking the Lord for a closer walk with Him. After weeks of praying, I came across this verse one morning in my daily quiet time: "Whoever has My commands and obeys them, he is the one who loves Me. He who loves Me will be loved by My Father, and I too will love him and show Myself to him" (John 14:21). Two things dawned on me as I allowed God's Words to sink in my head. First, I prove my love for the Lord through my obedience. Second, I cannot grow in my relationship with the Lord without obedience. When we obey God, we prove our love for Him. When we prove our love for Him, He reveals Himself to us!

It didn't take long for the Lord to bring some very specific things to my mind that were hindering my intimacy with Him. By my lack of obedience in the "small things," I was virtually closing the door on our fellowship. Telling a little white lie, exerting my independence, acting out of selfishness, sharing a juicy tidbit of gossip about someone else…in each of these things I was being disobedient to God's Word. Just because these were "little things" in my eyes, didn't mean they were not sin. If obedience is the way we prove our love for the Lord, I was basically saying that I didn't love Him by my lack of obedience. And because of this disobedience, the Lord was not willing to "show Himself to me" any further.

In his book, <u>My Utmost for His Highest</u>, Oswald Chambers says, "All God's revelations are sealed until they are opened to us by obedience... Obey God in the thing He shows you, and instantly the next thing is opened up... God will never reveal more truth about Himself until you have obeyed what you know already."[8] Slowly, and a bit painfully, I began to bring each little area of disobedience before the Lord, to confess it as sin and turn away from it. As I did, God began to reveal Himself to me (truly speaking directly to me through His Word) in a way I had never experienced before, with such clarity and realness that I longed for more!

God wants our complete obedience – just going part of the way is not enough. Even if they seem insignificant to us, the "little things" are not insignificant to the Lord. As difficult as it may be, our willingness to obey Him in everything proves our love and opens the door to a closer walk with Him. "And this is love: that we walk in obedience to His commands" (II John 1:6).

Memory Verse:
"Whoever has My commands and obeys them, he is the one who loves Me. He who loves Me will be loved by My Father, and I too will love him and show Myself to him" (John 14:21).

MONDAY: Read John 14:15-24. Meditate on God's Word and listen to what He has to say to you. Using the text as a guide, spend time in praise, confession and thanksgiving.

Pray for yourself, to be willing to obey God in all things, thus proving your love for Him: As I read this passage I want to yell out, "Of course I love You, Lord Jesus!" But I understand that You are teaching me that just saying "I love you" is not enough…You say that I must prove it by my actions: "If you love me, you will obey what I command" (John 14:15). Forgive me Lord, when I pick and choose from Your Word, selecting only the easiest or most convenient commands to obey. Forgive me, Lord Jesus, when by my actions I declare that I do not love You enough to do what You ask of me. I realize now that both my closeness to You and my spiritual growth are contingent upon my obedience. "Whoever has My commands and obeys them, he is the one who loves Me. He who loves Me will be loved by My Father, and I too will love him and show Myself to him" (John 14:21). How I long for You to "show Yourself to me," speaking directly to me in a very real way. May my complete obedience give You the desire to make Your home with me (John 14:23) each and every day.

JOURNAL: _____

_____

_____

TUESDAY: Read Genesis 12:1-5 & Hebrews 11:8. Meditate on God's Word and listen to what He has to say to you. Using the text as a guide, spend time in praise, confession and thanksgiving.

Pray for your husband, to have faith to obey God completely: Lord Jesus, You have made my husband the head of our household. As such, he is responsible for leading us in the way we should go. I pray that he would be like Abraham, who did exactly as You directed when You called him to leave everything behind and follow You. "By faith Abraham, when called to go....obeyed and went, even though he did not know where he was going" (Hebrews 11:8). When You lead my husband to do something irrational or unusual by the world's standards, give him the courage to "obey God rather than men" (Acts 5:29). When his flesh rises up against him, please give him the strength to obey. Remind him that Your "commands are not burdensome" (I John 5:3), because You ask only the things that will be in our ultimate best interest. May I be his faithful partner, trusting him to lead our family as You command and following even when I do not understand or agree. In all things, I pray that my husband would "be careful to obey all the law"...may he "not turn from it to the right or to the left" (Joshua 1:7).

JOURNAL: _____

_____

_____

—————=◦◦◦=—————

WEDNESDAY: Read Deuteronomy 6:1-12. Meditate on God's Word and listen to what He has to say to you. Using the text as a guide, spend time in praise, confession and thanksgiving.

Pray for those in your household, to keep God's commandments upon your hearts and carefully obey Him in all things: Father, I praise You today as the One True God! May You alone be exalted in our home as we love You with our hearts, souls and strength (Deuteronomy 6:5). May my husband and I teach our children that our love for You is proven by the things we do. I pray that we would be careful to give great attention to Your commandments, impressing them on our children at every opportunity...when we sit at home and when we walk along the road, when we lie down and when we get up (Deuteronomy 6:7). Any time is a good time to talk to our kids about You and the consequences of obedience and disobedience! In an age where we have so many material possessions – cars, electronics, clothes, and "houses filled with all kinds of good things" – it is easy to get our eyes off of You and onto this world. Your Word teaches: "When you eat and are satisfied, be careful that you do not forget the Lord" (Deuteronomy 6:11-12). I pray we would never forget, but "serve the Lord our God and obey Him" (Joshua 24:24).

JOURNAL: _____

_____

_____

━━━━━━

THURSDAY: Read Ephesians 6:1-6 & Colossians 3:20-22. Meditate on God's Word and listen to what He has to say to you. Using the text as a guide, spend time in praise, confession and thanksgiving.

Pray for your children, to obey you and to obey the Lord: Father, thank You so much that Your Word addresses this issue of a child's obedience to his parents. Thank You that You don't leave us to guess and even doubt the correct thing to do...children are to obey and parents are to instruct in the Lord. Your Word says, "Children, obey your parents in everything, for this pleases the Lord" (Colossians 3:20). May our children understand that they cannot please You unless they obey us! Please help them to realize that their attitude in obedience is key...it requires respect and humility. At the same time, we as parents must continually look to You for guidance in setting rules and boundaries in our home. You tell us clearly not to exasperate or "embitter [our] children, or they will become discouraged" (Colossians 3:21). So please give me and my husband the wisdom to institute rules that are reasonable and in accordance with Your Word. May our children choose to obey and do the right thing whether or not we are present, "but like slaves of Christ, doing the will of God from [their] hearts" (Ephesians 6:6).

JOURNAL: _____

_____

_____

━━━━━━

FRIDAY: Read Jeremiah 7:21-28. Meditate on God's Word and listen to what He has to say to you. Using the text as a guide, spend time in praise, confession and thanksgiving.

Pray for your country, to repent and turn back to the Lord in obedience: Oh Father, forgive us! Forgive us when we do "not listen or pay attention;" instead, following "the stubborn inclinations of [our] evil hearts" (Jeremiah 7:24). Forgive us when we reject Your servants with messages of correction, choosing our own way over Your way. It is so easy to point the finger at disobedience in the lives of others, while ignoring the lack of obedience in ourselves. May we as a nation open our hearts to Your examination and be willing to answer when You call us to repentance. You said in Jeremiah 7:23, "Obey Me, and I will be your God and you will be my people. Walk in all the ways I command you, that it may go well with you." I pray that even if it requires discipline or correction, "whether it is favorable or unfavorable, we will obey the Lord our God" (Jeremiah 42:6). We must reverse the downward trend in our land. Help us move forward in obedience toward a closer relationship with You, rather than backward toward sin and all the consequences of disobedience.

JOURNAL: _____

_____

_____

SATURDAY: A Day of Application

Read I Samuel 15:22-23. Are you guilty of substituting some type of "offering or sacrifice" in place of complete obedience?

_____

(Example: Giving extra money, doing deeds to try to "atone" for disobedience to God's Word).

Has the Lord convicted you this week of partial obedience (which is the same as complete disobedience) in any areas? If so, list them here:

_____

_____

Write out your prayer of commitment to prove your love for the Lord through your obedience to Him, so that He will reveal Himself to you in new ways:

_____

_____

SUNDAY: A Day of Praise

Read Matthew 8:23-27.

Praise the Lord as the One Who must be obeyed by all of creation.

WRITE OUT YOUR PRAYER OF PRAISE HERE:

_____

_____

_____

CHECK YOURSELF! WRITE YOUR MEMORY VERSE HERE:

_____

_____

Humility

"Your attitude should be the same as that of Christ Jesus: Who, being in very nature God, did not consider equality with God some-thing to be grasped, but made Himself nothing, taking the very nature of a servant, being made in human likeness. And being found in appearance as a man, He humbled himself and became obedient to death – even death on a cross!"
(Philippians 2:5-8).

HOW LOW CAN YOU GO?

In the game of limbo, contestants take turns passing under a horizontal stick. The stick starts out high, but with each turn the stick is lowered an inch or two. Players are forced to lower their entire bodies in order to pass, and it gets harder and harder to get under the stick without touching it on each subsequent turn. The players continue to compete amid calls of, "How low can you go?" often contorting themselves in some pretty unusual positions. The player who passes under the stick at the lowest point is the winner.

Imagine for a few minutes, what it would be like if we lived out our lives in the same way people play the game of limbo? If we acted out of humility rather than pride, ever striving to "go lower" than others? If, for example, a wife choosing to put her husband's need for rest above her own desire to go out, might persuade him to willingly keep the kids the next day so she could go shopping? If, as one child graciously offered to be last in line, another child might gladly accept the smaller piece of pie after dinner? If, as upper management went out of their way to appreciate and value those who worked for them, employees might be motivated to look for ways to improve productivity and punctuality?

If one person giving up his seat for someone else in a crowded waiting room might encourage onlookers to seek out similar opportunities? The trickle-down effect would be enormous!

Unfortunately, it usually goes against human nature to voluntarily lower self and elevate others. Our flesh tells us that we are better than others, that our opinion matters most, and that we deserve to get what we want! Our pride keeps us from wanting to take second place or deny our "rights" in submission to another. But God's Word tells us: "Your attitude should be the same as that of Christ Jesus: Who, being in very nature God, did not consider equality with God something to be grasped, but made Himself nothing, taking the very nature of a servant, being made in human likeness. And being found in appearance as a man, He humbled himself and became obedient to death – even death on a cross!" (Philippians 2:5-8). If our Lord Jesus did not proudly hold to His position as God, but was willing to humble Himself for the sake of others, shouldn't we be willing to have the same kind of attitude?

Definitions for the word "humble" include: not proud or haughty, not arrogant or assertive, expressing a spirit of deference, ranking low in a hierarchy. Feelings of superiority or excessive self-esteem should be blaring warning lights to us. "Pride goes before destruction, a haughty spirit before a fall" (Proverbs 16:18). May we look for ways to deny self and exalt others, avoiding the pitfalls that accompany selfish pride. For when we determine to humble ourselves before the Lord, He will lift us up! (James 4:10).

Memory Verse:
"Your attitude should be the same as that of Christ Jesus...He humbled himself and became obedient to death – even death on a cross!" (Philippians 2:5, 8).

MONDAY: Read Philippians 2:3-11. Meditate on God's Word and listen to what He has to say to you. Using the text as a guide, spend time in praise, confession and thanksgiving.

Pray for yourself, to have an attitude of humility: Oh Lord Jesus, I stand in awe of You! "Who, being in very nature God, did not consider equality with God something to be grasped, but made [Yourself] nothing" (Philippians 2:6-7). At the same time, I stand ashamed before You. How many times have I demanded my own way, proudly thinking that my opinion, my needs, or my place was superior to others? Father, forgive me. Your Word says, "Do nothing out of selfish ambition or vain conceit, but in humility consider others better than yourselves. Each of you should look not only to your own interests, but also to the interests of others" (Philippians 2:3-4). Show me, Lord Jesus, where I need to change my attitude....both of how I view myself and how I am treating others. Bring Your knife of conviction to slice away my pride and arrogance. The next time I am tempted to look to my own interests, open my eyes to see others from Your perspective. "This is what the Lord says: "This is the one I esteem: he who is humble and contrite in spirit, and who trembles at My Word" (Isaiah 66:2). Instead of taking pride in myself, may I strive to make You proud of me!

JOURNAL: _____

_____

_____

——=◦◦◦=——

TUESDAY: Read Numbers 12:1-11. Meditate on God's Word and listen to what He has to say to you. Using the text as a guide, spend time in praise, confession and thanksgiving.

Pray for your husband, to seek to be humble and receive the Lord's blessing: This passage reminds us, dear Lord, of our fleshly struggles with jealousy and pride. Envious of the popularity and influence Moses had over the people and jealous of his intimacy with You, Miriam and Aaron began to look for ways to discredit him. Scripture tells us that You not only heard their accusations against Moses, Your anger burned against them. As a result, Miriam was struck with leprosy. "When pride comes, then comes disgrace" (Proverbs 11:2), and what could have been more disgraceful at the time than leprosy? In sharp contrast was Moses, "a very humble man, more humble than anyone else on the face of the earth" (Numbers 12:3). How I pray that my husband would be like Moses. I long for him to experience the blessings of humility – things like intimacy with You, guidance and contentment. Please protect him from the consequences of jealousy and pride –Your anger, public disgrace and destruction! You promise to guide the humble in what is right and teach them Your way (Psalm 25:9), so rebuke my husband before he goes astray. In all things remind him to keep his focus on You.

JOURNAL: _____

_____

_____

―――――♦♦♦――――

WEDNESDAY: Read Romans 12:3-16. Meditate on God's Word and listen to what He has to say to you. Using the text as a guide, spend time in praise, confession and thanksgiving.

Pray for those in your household, to be more concerned with honoring one another than elevating self: Oh Father, I cannot think of a better passage to pray for those in my home! May none of us think of ourselves more highly than we ought, but in humility consider others better than ourselves (Romans 12:3). Open our eyes to see that each one of us has different gifts, abilities, and roles, but each is a valuable and important part of the household. I pray we would be "devoted to one another in brotherly love" and honor one another above ourselves (Romans 12:10). Even when it seems unfair, even when it's not really "their turn", may we choose to deny self in order to put the needs of someone else ahead of our own. As we do, may an unbroken cycle of humility, honor and compassion circulate through our home. When frustrating circumstances threaten to disrupt family unity, remind us to "be joyful in hope, patient in affliction, faithful in prayer" (Romans 12:12). May we make it our goal to be "peaceable and considerate, and to show true humility toward all men" (Titus 3:2).

JOURNAL: _____

_____

_____

―――――♦♦♦――――

THURSDAY: Read Matthew 23:1-12. Meditate on God's Word and listen to what He has to say to you. Using the text as a guide, spend time in praise, confession and thanksgiving.

Pray for your children, to understand that humility is not just a "show" but a condition of the heart: Father, thank You for this reminder to examine our motives in what we do. Jesus was clear in His rebuke of the Pharisees, saying that "everything they do is done for men to see" (Matthew 23:5). In making a display of their "godliness" and thriving on receiving places of honor, the Pharisees revealed that the accolades of man were more important to them than worshipping You. Your evaluation was clear: "Woe to you, teachers of the law and Pharisees, you hypocrites! You clean the outside of the cup and dish, but inside they are full of greed and self-indulgence" (Matthew 23:25). Oh Lord, how I pray that my children exhibit true humility. May they not just "play the part" when others are around to notice, but be willing to humble themselves even when You are the only One Who sees it. If they are struggling with an attitude of pride or selfishness, please convict them and help them to see the error of their ways. May they understand that it is the one who humbles himself who will be exalted (Matthew 23:12).

JOURNAL: _____

_____

_____

FRIDAY: Read I Peter 5:1-7. Meditate on God's Word and listen to what He has to say to you. Using the text as a guide, spend time in praise, confession and thanksgiving.

Pray for your pastor and church members to have a reputation of humility: Lord, first I want to pray for my pastor, thanking You for his service and his love for the people under his care. I pray that You would protect him, teach him, and equip him in his day-to-day service to us. Give him a heart that is willing to lead us and is "eager to serve; not lording it over those entrusted to [him], but being an example to the flock" (I Peter 5:2-3). May he have a humble spirit and an "others-centered" outlook, both at home, at church, and in the community. Likewise, I lift up the members of my church, praying that we would clothe ourselves "with humility toward one another, because, "God opposes the proud but gives grace to the humble" (I Peter 5:5). As we walk amongst unbelievers in our daily activities, may Your love shine through us. Please give us the grace to treat strangers with consideration, deference, and humility. I pray that You would empower us to follow Your example of being "gentle and humble in heart" (Matthew 11:29) as a witness before a lost world.

JOURNAL: _____

_____

_____

SATURDAY: A Day of Application

Read Luke 18:9-14.

Do you take confidence in your own righteousness? (Luke 18:9)

_____

Are you guilty of looking down on others? (Luke 18:9)

_____

Do you compare yourself to others as a way of feeding your pride?

_____

If so, confess your attitude of pride here. Make the prayer of the tax collector your own: "God, have mercy on me, a sinner" (Luke 18:13):

_____

Using Philippians 2:3-4 as a guide, ask the Lord to help you have an attitude of humility. Write out your prayer here:

_____

SUNDAY: A Day of Praise

Read Job 38:1-18. (If time permits, read all the way through 40:4).

Dwell on all that our God has done and is able to do. Humbly remember your position before the eternal, all-mighty, incomprehensible God.

PRAISE HIM OUT OF A SPIRIT OF HUMILITY AND AWE FOR WHO HE IS! WRITE OUT YOUR PRAYER OF PRAISE HERE:

_____

_____

_____

CHECK YOURSELF! WRITE YOUR MEMORY VERSE HERE:

_____

_____

Turning Your Back on Sin

"But if you fail to do this, you will be sinning against the Lord; and you may be sure that your sin will find you out" (Numbers 32:23).

WHAT ARE YOU HIDING?

Why is it, that when we decide to break our diet and eat that forbidden piece of chocolate that is calling out to us, we sneak into the pantry to eat it where no one can see us? As if perhaps eating it in secret nullifies the fact that it happened, and it won't show up on the scales! What kind of twisted rationale is that? In like fashion, we sometimes try to hide things from the Lord...things in our lives that we know He disapproves of, but we are unwilling to give up. For example, we know we should not gossip, but sometimes we think we just have to share a juicy tidbit with a friend so we lower our voices and whisper behind closed doors. Or we secretly destroy the evidence of a mistake at work by shredding any paperwork that might cast us in an unfavorable light before the boss. Ashamed to let anyone know about a momentary lapse in good judgment, or just determined to do what we want regardless of what God may think, we convince ourselves that if we conceal the matter, no one will find out. But just as that forbidden chocolate will reveal itself on "weigh-in" day, so any sin we are trying to conceal from the Lord will eventually be exposed. "You may be sure that your sin will find you out" (Numbers 32:23).

II Samuel chapter 11 gives us an account of someone else who thought he could conceal his sin from God and others. This passage tells us that one night while King David was walking around on the roof of his palace, he saw a very beautiful woman bathing. He sent someone to find out about this woman and learned that she was Bathsheba, the wife of Uriah the Hittite, one of his soldiers away at battle. Full of lust for her, David sent for Bathsheba and slept with her. When David heard that Bathsheba had conceived a child as a result of their night together, he devised a plan to hide their secret sin. He sent for Uriah under the guise of receiving a report about the war, intending for Uriah to spend the night with his wife and later assume that the child was his own. But Uriah refused to even go up to his house while his fellow soldiers were on the battlefield. The next night David invited Uriah to his palace to get him drunk, thinking surely then he would go and sleep with his wife! But again, Uriah refused to go home. Out of options for covering up his adultery with Bathsheba, David instructed Joab, his commanding officer, to put Uriah on the front lines of battle and then withdraw surrounding support so that Uriah would be killed. Uriah did indeed die, and thinking his sin had been covered up, David took Bathsheba as his wife, and she bore him a son. It wasn't until the Lord sent the prophet Nathan to confront David that he became convicted of what he had done. Finally accepting the gravity of his sin, David repented saying, "I have sinned against the Lord" (II Samuel 12:13). But the consequences for both him and his family were inescapable. The child died, and there was much turmoil in David's family for years to come.

I doubt King David ever gave much thought to the ripple effect his one night of pleasure would cause. I've heard it said: Sin will always take you farther than you wanted to go, keep you longer than you wanted to stay, and cost you more than you wanted to pay. May we not fool ourselves into thinking that we can hold on to one or two "hidden sins" that won't hurt anyone. Sin has a way of catching up with us.

Memory Verse:
"But if you fail to do this, you will be sinning against the Lord; and you may be sure that your sin will find you out" (Numbers 32:23).

MONDAY: Read Psalm 36:1-4 & II Samuel 22:21-25. Meditate on God's Word and listen to what He has to say to you. Using the text as a guide, spend time in praise, confession and thanksgiving.

Pray for yourself, to turn from sin and stand blameless before God: Oh Father, I see in these two passages the great contrast between two men: the prideful man who "flatters himself too much to detect or hate his sin" (Psalm 36:2); and the righteous man who is blameless before You and has kept himself from sin (II Samuel 22:24). I know that every day I stand before you a sinner, presented with the choice to either keep Your way or turn away from You. Please give me the strength I need to stand strong in the face of temptation. Humble me quickly when I begin to rationalize away any sinful behavior. Rebuke me when on my bed I plot evil and commit myself to a sinful course, refusing to reject what is wrong (Psalm 36:4). I am ever thankful that "Christ Jesus came into the world to save sinners—of whom I am the worst" (I Timothy 1:15b). I pray that one day I will be able to stand before Your throne in heaven with clean hands and receive Your reward (II Samuel 22:21)!

JOURNAL: _____

_____

_____

———

TUESDAY: Read Job 11:13-20. Meditate on God's Word and listen to what He has to say to you. Using the text as a guide, spend time in praise, confession and thanksgiving.

Pray for your husband, to flee from sin and have a heart devoted to the Lord: "O righteous God, who searches minds and hearts" (Psalm 7:9), we truly have no secrets from You. May my husband be constantly aware of this fact, never forgetting that "a man's ways are in full view of the Lord, and He examines all his paths" (Proverbs 5:21). In the book of Genesis when Joseph faced the temptation to sin with Potiphar's wife, he asked her this question: "How then could I do such a wicked thing and sin against God?" (Genesis 39:9). Joseph fled the scene as quickly as he could, literally running away. May my husband RUN, not walk, when tempted to sin. I would never want You to turn a deaf ear to his prayers because he has cherished sin in his heart (Psalm 66:18). So this is my fervent prayer: please help my husband devote his heart to You and stretch out his hands to You; may he put away the sin that is in his hand and allow no evil to dwell in his tent; then he can lift up his face without shame, standing firm and without fear (Job 11:13-15). Amen!

JOURNAL: _____

_____

_____

WEDNESDAY: Read Psalm 101:1-8. Meditate on God's Word and listen to what He has to say to you. Using the text as a guide, spend time in praise, confession and thanksgiving.

Pray for those in your household, to carefully guard against the sin that so easily infiltrates our homes: Heavenly Father, in the very beginning You warned: "Sin is crouching at your door; it desires to have you, but you must master it" (Genesis 4:7). In a world where so much sin is tolerated or dismissed as harmless, it would be very easy to allow "little things" to slip in the door. Please give us the discipline to "throw off everything that hinders and the sin that so easily entangles" (Hebrews 12:1) before it enters our home. With television and computers, access to virtually any type of sin is available at the click of a button, and we must carefully guard ourselves against it. May we each be willing to declare: "I will walk in my house with blameless heart. I will set before my eyes no vile thing" (Psalm 101:2b-3b). It is up to my husband and me to set a godly example, refusing to tolerate inappropriate material in our home. May it be our testimony that "we have renounced secret and shameful ways" (II Corinthians 4:2), determined to live each day in great anticipation of Your second coming!

JOURNAL: _____

_____

_____

THURSDAY: Read Psalm 19:7-14. Meditate on God's Word and listen to what He has to say to you. Using the text as a guide, spend time in praise, confession and thanksgiving.

Pray for your children, to heed the warnings in God's Word to steer clear of sin: Father, this passage reminds us just how important Your Word is in our lives! Your commands are perfect, trustworthy, right, radiant, pure, sure and precious. They revive the soul, make wise the simple, give joy to the heart, and give light to the eyes. "By them is your servant warned" (Psalm 19:11) of so many sins that threaten to entice and entrap. How I pray that my children would listen to Your warnings and humbly bow before You to say: "Direct my footsteps according to Your Word; let no sin rule over me" (Psalm 119:133). Please keep them from willful sins, Lord Jesus, and may their sins never rule over them (Psalm 19:13). When sinners entice my children may they not give in to them (Proverbs 1:10), but boldly stand firm in the faith. If my child is involved in some type of secret sin, I pray You would bring it to light so that he will not be able to continue in it. And please give my husband and me the wisdom and discernment to know how to deal with the sin and help our child turn away from it.

JOURNAL: _____

_____

_____

———◦◦◦◦———

FRIDAY: Read Romans 6:1-14. Meditate on God's Word and listen to what He has to say to you. Using the text as a guide, spend time in praise, confession and thanksgiving.

Pray for the members of your church, to carefully guard their hearts from sin's deceitfulness: Father, thank You that Your children already have victory over sin! "For we know that our old self was crucified with Him so that the body of sin might be done away with, that we should no longer be slaves to sin" (Romans 6:6). How I praise You that sin is no longer our master....You are our Master! So by the power of Your Holy Spirit within us, I pray that the members of our church would refuse to offer the parts of our bodies to sin, as instruments of wickedness, but rather offer our bodies to You as instruments of righteousness (Romans 6:13). Remind us that as one body of believers, "If one part suffers, every part suffers with it" (I Corinthians 12:26). So when one of us struggles with the temptation to sin, the rest of us should rally around him in love and support. May we never be a church that sweeps sin under the carpet and refuses to deal with it. Rather, help us be diligent to "encourage one another daily…so that none of [us] may be hardened by sin's deceitfulness" (Hebrews 3:13).

JOURNAL: _____

_____

_____

SATURDAY: A Day of Application

Read I Peter 4:1-6.

Are you currently living your life for God or for "evil human desires"?

Are you struggling with some type of sin in your life?

_____

If Jesus were to come back today, would you be ready "to give account to Him who is ready to judge the living and the dead" (I Peter 4:5)?

_____

If the Lord has convicted you of sin in your life, confess it here and ask for forgiveness:

_____

_____

Now, hear the precious words of I John 2:1a - "But if anybody does sin, we have One Who speaks to the Father in our defense – Jesus Christ, the Righteous One. He is the atoning sacrifice for our sins, and not only for ours but also for the sins of the whole world." Write out your prayer of thanksgiving that Jesus Christ intercedes on your behalf:

_____

_____

SUNDAY: A Day of Praise

Read Hebrews 4:14-16.

Praise the Lord that He is our Great High Priest – He is able to sympathize with our weaknesses, for He has been tempted in every way, just as we are – yet was without sin!

WRITE OUT YOUR PRAYER OF PRAISE HERE:

_____

_____

_____

CHECK YOURSELF! WRITE YOUR MEMORY VERSE HERE:

_____

_____

Unity, Not Division

"I appeal to you, brothers, in the name of our Lord Jesus Christ, that all of you agree with one another so that there may be no divisions among you and that you may be perfectly united in mind and thought" (I Corinthians 1:10).

DIVIDING WALLS

We had been anticipating the trip for weeks. My husband longed for a diversion from the routine of work, my boys were weary from the long school year, and I was definitely ready for a break from the monotony of housework. Summer vacation had finally arrived, and we were ready for a week at the beach! Free from the cares of the world and responsible only for building sand castles and working on our tans, the days stretched gloriously before us. I looked forward to being together as a family – playing in the waves of the ocean, laughing over inside jokes, and simply spending quality time together that seemed harder to come by as our children grew up.

But before we had spent our first night in the condo that feeling of excitement for what the week would bring came crashing down like waves against the sea shore. Maybe it was the combination of the packing, the early wake time, and the close quarters of being cooped up for eleven hours during the long drive that made us all a little irritable. But whatever the reason, what started out as a quick trip to stock up on provisions for the week ended with a car full of silence and hurt feelings. My husband and I had a disagreement over something trivial that quickly erected walls of division between us, and the tension was felt by every member of the family. Although we worked through it before going to bed that night, that one little incident robbed us of the harmony and togetherness we had been longing for.

I woke early the next morning with a heavy heart and poured out my regret to the Lord that our long-awaited trip had started off so badly. Seeking solace from God's Word, I found it no coincidence that my Bible reading for that day included this verse from I Corinthians 1:10: "I appeal to you, brothers, in the name of our Lord Jesus Christ, that all of you agree with one another so that there may be no divisions among you and that you may be perfectly united in mind and thought." The Lord knew I needed just the right words to pray over my situation, and I love Him still for giving them to me that morning! I prayed that verse back to the Lord for the duration of our trip, asking Him to remove any division and reunite us in mind and thought. God used His Word to heal my hurt and restore the unity in my family that I desperately needed.

Such a spirit of unity has become my desire in all areas of life. Nothing steals my joy more than a little (or a lot) of conflict with others! Whether it is a small clash of opinion over a trivial matter, or a huge disagreement over something important, our differences can erect walls of division that seem impenetrable. These walls hinder our ability to see clearly, they stand in the way of much-needed communication, and they block the path to reconciliation. And most importantly, they destroy the sense of unity that Christ desires for His children. Jesus said to God the Father in His prayer for His believers, "I in them and You in Me. May they be brought to complete unity to let the world know that You sent Me and have loved them even as You have loved Me" (John 17:23). May we base our lives on Him and His Word, allowing His Spirit to tear down the dividing walls and bring us into complete unity with one another.

———=•:•=———

Memory Verse:
"I appeal to you, brothers, by the name of our Lord Jesus Christ, that all of you agree with one another so that there may be no divisions among you and that you may be perfectly united in mind and thought" (I Corinthians 1:10).

———=•:•=———

MONDAY: Read John 17:20-26. Meditate on God's Word and listen to what He has to say to you. Using the text as a guide, spend time in praise, confession and thanksgiving.

Pray for yourself, to live in unity with the Lord and with others: Father, what an amazing privilege that You would allow Your believers to share in the very relationship that You enjoy with Your Son! Jesus summed it up simply by saying, "I in them and You in Me" (John 17:23). Thank You that as Your child, I have died to sin and my "life is now hidden with Christ in God" (Colossians 3:3). I know that if I am to live in a spirit of unity with others, I must be willing to put to death anything that causes division and strife in my relationships. "What cause fights and quarrels among you? Don't they come from your desires that battle within you? You want something but don't get it" (James 4:1-2a). Please rebuke me, dear God, when I stubbornly hold on to my supposed rights instead of letting go of bitterness and hurt feelings. Whenever I am tempted to nag or complain remind me that, "A quarrelsome wife is like a constant dripping on a rainy day" (Proverbs 27:15)! May my words only be used to build others up, and may I be diligent to tear down any dividing walls that have been erected in selfishness and unforgiveness.

JOURNAL: _____

_____

_____

———⊰◈⊱———

TUESDAY: Read Romans 16:17-19. Meditate on God's Word and listen to what He has to say to you. Using the text as a guide, spend time in praise, confession and thanksgiving.

Pray for your husband, to be alert to anything that might hinder his unity with the Lord or with others: Father, we are aware that we live in a fallen world with a fallen enemy who "comes only to steal and kill and destroy" (John 10:10). Our adversary the devil enjoys nothing more than stealing our spirit of unity with others, killing our closest relationships and destroying our sense of peace. For this reason the apostle Paul urged the brethren "to watch out for those who cause divisions and put obstacles in your way that are contrary to the teaching you have learned. Keep away from them" (Romans 16:17). So I pray for my husband, that he would be on the alert for Satan, his flesh, or any others who try to stir up division, suspicion and animosity. May he not be deceived "by smooth talk and flattery" (Romans 16:18), but be grounded in the truth of Your Word that promotes unity. Even in the midst of disagreements, I pray that he would strive to maintain unity with his wife (Genesis 2:24), pursue reconciliation with his children, and be willing to keep the lines of communication open with others until resolution takes place.

JOURNAL: _____

_____

_____

WEDNESDAY: Read Acts 2:42-47. Meditate on God's Word and listen to what He has to say to you. Using the text as a guide, spend time in praise, confession and thanksgiving.

Pray for those in your household, to live together in unity: Lord Jesus, what a beautiful picture this passage is of people living together in unity! "All the believers were together and had everything in common" (Acts 2:44). They ate together, prayed together, worshipped together, and enjoyed one another. How I desire for this to be the description of my own home! May it be said of us that we are "one in heart and mind. No one claimed that any of his possessions was his own, but they shared everything they had" (Acts 4:32). Your Word is clear, "Every kingdom divided against itself will be ruined, and every city or household divided against itself will not stand" (Matthew 12:25). So I pray that we would be diligent to maintain a united front against the distractions that threaten to tear us apart and the sin that so easily divides. You warned believers that families would be divided as some members choose to live for You while others do not (Luke 12:52). May each member of my family bow the knee to Your Lordship, protecting us from such division. Please bless our home, Oh Lord!

JOURNAL: _____

_____

_____

———◦◦◦———

THURSDAY: Read Psalm 133:1-3 and I Peter 3:8-12. Meditate on God's Word and listen to what He has to say to you. Using the text as a guide, spend time in praise, confession and thanksgiving.

Pray for your children to live together in unity and peace: Father, Your Word says, "How good and pleasant it is when brothers live together in unity!" (Psalm 133:1). I know from personal experience just how true these words are. When my children get along, choosing pleasant words and caring actions, our home is a joyous and peaceful place. But when my children have differences of opinion that escalate into self-willed division, joy and harmony go out the front door. So I pray that my children would not "have anything to do with foolish and stupid arguments, because...they produce quarrels" (II Timothy 2:23). May they understand that, "It is to a man's honor to avoid strife, but every fool is quick to quarrel" (Proverbs 20:3). Rebuke them Lord, when short tempers lead to selfish attitudes and prideful hearts. Give my children the desire to "live in harmony with one another; be sympathetic, love as brothers, be compassionate and humble" (I Peter 3:8). If one is having a bad day, may the others be sensitive to this and not "repay evil with evil or insult with insult, but with blessing" (I Peter 3:9).

JOURNAL: _____

_____

_____

———◦◦◦———

FRIDAY: Read I Corinthians 12:12-25. Meditate on God's Word and listen to what He has to say to you. Using the text as a guide, spend time in praise, confession and thanksgiving.

Pray for your church, the very body of Christ, to come together as one: "The body is a unit, though it is made up of many parts; and though all its parts are many, they form one body" (I Corinthians 12:12). Lord, thank You for this reminder that just as the many different parts of a physical body are all needed to make up one person, so all the members of our church are needed to make up the body of Christ! May we never allow our varying roles or abilities to divide us because of jealousy, or to separate us because of pride. Rather, I pray that our different gifts and talents would serve to unite us as we realize our need for one another. "There should be no division in the body" (I Corinthians 12:25), so use Your Holy Spirit to unite us so strongly that unbelievers would have a desire for fellowship with us too! May the church staff, the governing committees, the teachers, and the lay people all come together for the common purpose of reaching a lost world with the Gospel. We daily cling to Your promise: "If we have been united with Him like this in His death, we will certainly also be united with Him in His resurrection" (Romans 6:5).

JOURNAL: _____

_____

_____

SATURDAY: A Day of Application

Read Ephesians 4:1-6.

Are you currently struggling with a lack of unity in one of your relationships?

What is the source of your division?

_____

_____

_____

Are you making "every effort to keep the unity of the Spirit through the bond of peace" (Ephesians 4:3)? _____ Or have you actually fallen into sin by being unwilling to forgive and restore the relationship? "He who loves a quarrel loves sin" (Proverbs 17:19).

Write out your prayer here, confessing any sin on your part and asking the Lord to do whatever it takes to bring reconciliation:

_____

_____

Now, be willing to do as He directs!

SUNDAY: A Day of Praise

Read Ephesians 2:11-22.

Praise God that we are no longer separate from Christ. He has "destroyed the barrier, the dividing wall of hostility" through His blood shed on the cross. Praise Him that we now have "access to the Father by one Spirit".

WRITE OUT YOUR PRAYER OF PRAISE HERE:

_____

_____

_____

CHECK YOURSELF! WRITE YOUR MEMORY VERSE HERE:

_____

_____

WEEK THIRTY-SIX
Being Thankful

"Always giving thanks to God the Father for everything, in the name of our Lord Jesus Christ" (Ephesians 5:20).

A GENTLE REMINDER

It wasn't just any old box, it was my grandmother's sewing box. She had passed away a few months before, and now my mother brought the box of sewing notions to me since I had taken an interest in sewing myself. The box was full of old wooden spools of thread, delicate lace yellowed with age, and assorted zippers, thimbles, and straight pins. Each item was a reminder of my dear grandmother, but it was the smell that overwhelmed me as I opened it... that wood-burning stove smell that filled my grandparents' home year round and permeated everything within the walls. Instantly my mind was flooded with memories of childhood. Long summer days filled with trips to the Tasty Queen and dime store with my sister and grandpa in his dust-covered truck; making homemade peach pies and drinking "milk-coffee" in bed with my grandmother; and going swimming at the river with cousins, aunts and uncles. I was transported to another time, a past way of life where you could go to the local grocery store and buy afternoon treats "on credit" (truth be told I don't think we ever said a word to the owner...he knew to whom we belonged and charged my grandparents' account accordingly!) The memories washed over me as I took in the smell...to others, the smell of a wood-burning stove might be disagreeable, but to me it was the aroma of unconditional love, of grandparents who spoiled me, and the simplicity of youth.

What a joy it was for me to open that old sewing box, full of reminders of so many special childhood memories. And when we open God's

Word it has many precious reminders for us as well. Ephesians 5:20 holds one of the most important ones...a reminder to be thankful. "Always giving thanks to God the Father for everything, in the name of our Lord Jesus Christ." We are to give thanks <u>always</u> and we are to give thanks <u>for everything</u>. In fact, Colossians 2:7 tells us to take our thanksgiving one step further...we are to be "<u>overflowing</u> with thankfulness!" Now, I am willing to admit that an attitude of thankfulness is not always the first thing on my mind. Especially when the days are long and difficult, full of problems, disappointments, and dashed hopes. But I've found that the way to changing my attitude is to begin to give thanks, even when I don't feel like it! Irritability at being stuck in traffic turns into thankfulness that it doesn't happen every day. Disappointment that plans with friends are dashed because of problems at work are transformed by thankfulness that my husband has a job in this difficult economy. The simple act of finding something to be thankful for gets my focus back on the Lord Jesus Christ, Who gave His everything for us.

There are still times that I purposely seek out that old sewing box just to inhale the scent. After five years now the smell is beginning to fade, but the reminder of days gone by still lingers. May the reminder in God's Word to be thankful linger in our minds too. We must determine to do it at times, but once we get a "whiff" of something we have to be thankful for, the other reasons tend to flood our minds as well. Amazing, isn't it, how a little smell can conjure up so much!

Memory Verse:

"Always giving thanks to God the Father for everything, in the name of our Lord Jesus Christ" (Ephesians 5:20).

MONDAY: Read Colossians 3:15-17. Meditate on God's Word and listen to what He has to say to you. Using the text as a guide, spend time in praise, confession and thanksgiving.

Pray for yourself, to have an attitude of thankfulness: Father, forgive me when I choose to dwell on the negative. I am so very blessed, and I never want to appear ungrateful or take a single one of Your blessings for granted. Please help me to follow Your command to <u>always</u> give thanks to You for <u>everything</u>, in the name of my Lord Jesus Christ (Ephesians 5:20). At the first sign of irritability or displeasure, use Your Holy Spirit to whisper words of correction to my heart. Remind me of something for which I can be thankful, even in difficult situations, so that I can bring glory to Your Name. I know from experience that a thankful spirit can change my entire outlook, so give me the determination to "give thanks in all circumstances, for this is God's will for [me] in Christ Jesus" (I Thessalonians 5:18). In fact, may I overflow with thankfulness and be a testimony of Your Spirit within me to those I spend time with every day. Whatever I do, whether in word or deed, may I do it all in the name of the Lord Jesus, giving thanks to God the Father through Him (Colossians 3:17).

JOURNAL: _____

_____

_____

TUESDAY: Read I Chronicles 16:1-13. Meditate on God's Word and listen to what He has to say to you. Using the text as a guide, spend time in praise, confession and thanksgiving.

Pray for your husband, to lead your family in giving thanks to God: Lord Jesus, King David was so excited to have the ark of God back in Jerusalem that he led the people in a time of great celebration and thanksgiving! He gave the people these words to pray: "Give thanks to the Lord, call on His name; make known among the nations what He has done" (I Chronicles 16:8). In much the same way, I pray that my husband would lead our family in giving thanks to You. May praise and thanksgiving be part of his regular routine, shining forth as a testimony of Your goodness before others. As he gives You thanks, I pray that You would draw him close and allow him glimpses of Your glory. Remind him to make a conscious effort to remember what You have done in the past, especially when life is difficult in the present. Help him maintain that attitude of thankfulness at all times and never miss an opportunity to speak of Your faithful provision. Like King David, give him boldness to "give You thanks in the great assembly; among throngs of people" to praise You (Psalm 35:18).

JOURNAL: _____

_____

_____

WEDNESDAY: Read Psalm 118:19-29. Meditate on God's Word and listen to what He has to say to you. Using the text as a guide, spend time in praise, confession and thanksgiving.

Pray for those in your household, to be thankful and to give God credit for all the prayers He has answered: Oh Father, "I thank my God every time I remember" those in my family (Philippians 1:3). You are so good to give me a husband and children to love and care for! May I never take them for granted. It is my prayer that those in my home will begin and end each day in thanksgiving to You. As we awake every morning may we say like the psalmist, "This is the day the Lord has made; let us rejoice and be glad in it" (Psalm 118:24). As we return home each night, overwhelm us with the knowledge of how greatly we are blessed! May we "enter and give thanks to the Lord" (Psalm 118:19) every time we cross the threshold of the home You have provided for us. Forgive us when we pray about various things, asking You to work in our lives, and then fail to give You thanks when You work on our behalf! May we never attribute answered prayers to coincidence or the work of anyone but You. "You are my God, and I will give you thanks; You are my God, and I will exalt you" (Psalm 118:28).

JOURNAL: _____

_____

_____

THURSDAY: Read Psalm 100:1-5. Meditate on God's Word and listen to what He has to say to you. Using the text as a guide, spend time in praise, confession and thanksgiving.

Pray that your children will grow up in an attitude of thankfulness: Lord, as I see my children grow and see Your power at work in their lives, it confirms that Your "faithfulness continues through all generations" (Psalm 100:5). How grateful I am that long after I am gone, You will continue to be with my children, my grandchildren, and the generations that follow! I pray that they will comprehend that everything they have is a gift from You Who made them and care for them as sheep of Your pasture (Psalm 100:3). When our children are young, may my husband and I teach them to be thankful for the basic necessities like food, clothing, a home and family. As they grow into teenagers and young adults, use us to remind them that every privilege, friendship, accomplishment and blessing comes from Your hand. Then, when they are fully grown and responsible for their own families, they will exhibit an attitude of thanksgiving in front of their children. May they understand the joy that comes in giving thanks to You and praising Your name (Psalm 100:4) no matter what comes across their paths.

JOURNAL: _____

_____

_____

FRIDAY: Read Romans 1:18-23. Meditate on God's Word and listen to what He has to say to you. Using the text as a guide, spend time in praise, confession and thanksgiving.

Pray for your country, to acknowledge the One true God and give Him the glory and thanks due His holy name: Father God, Your Word says, "For since the creation of the world God's invisible qualities – His eternal power and divine nature – have been clearly seen, being understood from what has been made, so that men are without excuse" (Romans 1:20). Your very creation shouts out Your majesty! "The heavens declare the glory of God; the skies proclaim the work of His hands" (Psalm 19:1).

And yet, many neither glorify You as God or give thanks to You (Romans 1:21). How it must grieve You that so many choose not to believe. Oh Father, do whatever it takes to open their minds to the truth! Remove the blinders from their eyes and the foolishness from their hearts, so that they may see themselves as they really are: sinners in need of a Savior. I pray that my country would experience revival, turning to You in repentance and recognition of Who You are! May "we give thanks to you, O God, we give thanks, for your Name is near"; may we "tell of your wonderful deeds" (Psalm 75:1).

JOURNAL: _____

_____

_____

SATURDAY: A Day of Application

Read Psalm 136:1-9, 23-26.

"Give thanks to the Lord, for He is good. His love endures forever."

Have you needed the reminder this week to "give thanks in all circumstances, for this is God's will for you in Christ Jesus" (I Thessalonians 5:18)?

_____

Determine to have an attitude of thankfulness today! List at least five things for which you are thankful:

1) _____

2) _____

3) _____

4) _____

5) _____

Write out your prayer of thanksgiving to the Lord here:

_____

_____

SUNDAY: A Day of Praise

Read I Corinthians 15:50-57.

Praise God for victory through our Lord Jesus Christ and thank Him for the certainty of heaven! "Therefore, since we are receiving a kingdom that cannot be shaken, let us be thankful, and so worship God acceptably with reverence and awe" (Hebrews 12:28).

WRITE OUT YOUR PRAYER OF PRAISE HERE:

_____

_____

_____

CHECK YOURSELF! WRITE YOUR MEMORY VERSE HERE:

_____

_____

_____

Faith

"Now faith is being sure of what we hope for and certain of what we do not see. This is what the ancients were commended for"
(Hebrews 11:1-2).

HANGING BY A THREAD

I almost ran right into it. Exiting the back door of my house and turning to walk down the steps, I was startled to see a spider's web just inches from my nose. I stepped back quickly, reluctant to ruin what surely had taken a great deal of time to create. The spider's web was nothing less than a masterpiece! Silk threads were sewn in and out, spiraling away from the center. The pattern was not perfect, but the result seemed perfect anyway. Stepping closer to examine the spider's handiwork, I was amazed at how big the web was. I noticed the bottom of the web was attached by a few slender threads to bushes on each side of the walkway. But it was up so high, I wondered what could possibly be supporting it! My eyes scanned the perimeter of the web, seeing nothing. Finally, the sun shone down through the trees, and I caught a glimpse of one single thread stretching from the top of the web heavenward. I had to step backward to see that the thread continued more than 30 feet up, attaching to a tree limb overhead. How strong that little thread must be, I thought, in order to support the entire web! If it were to break, the entire web would collapse! And I had almost missed seeing it, camouflaged as it was by everything else in the background.

We can learn so much from that spider web! A spider goes about his God-given role, in determined pursuit of his goal: creating a web in order to catch his next meal. Relying on that one strand of support from above, he weaves from one task to the next. From time to time he attaches a few strands to the bushes below for balance, but his confidence is in the strength of the one strand above him. In keeping himself and his work firmly attached to that source of strength, he completes his web. Now he need only sit back and await his next meal.

How fully do we rely on God, our "support from above," as we go about our daily duties? How strong is our faith in Him to hold us up under the weight of our circumstances? Are we certain that He is there for us, that He is at work on our behalf, even when we cannot see Him for the distractions around us? "Now faith is being sure of what we hope for and certain of what we do not see" (Hebrews 11:1). That spider was sure that the strand overhead would support his work, and he was certain that he could build his web in reliance on it. In much the same way, we can be sure that God will support us in the work He has ordained for us, and we can be certain that we can rely on Him, no matter how difficult the road before us appears. We must have faith in His character – He is Who He claims to be! We must have faith in His promises – He will do what He says in His Word! And we must have faith in His continual Presence, even when we cannot see Him there.

"And without faith it is impossible to please God because anyone who comes to Him must believe that he exists and that He rewards those who earnestly seek Him" (Hebrews 11:6). May we not fail to please Him because of a lack of faith. Rather, may we exhibit faith in our God at every twist and turn in the road ahead of us, because He who promises is faithful!

Memory Verse:

"Now faith is being sure of what we hope for and certain of what we do not see" (Hebrews 11:1).

MONDAY: Read Mark 5:25-34. Meditate on God's Word and listen to what He has to say to you. Using the text as a guide, spend time in praise, confession and thanksgiving.

Pray for yourself, asking God to grow your faith in Him and in the reliability of His Word: Thank You, Lord Jesus, that I do not have to hide anything from You! You know the flood of responsibilities and problems that make up my days. You know my struggle to keep my head above water, fearing that at any moment I might drown in worry, fear, and helplessness. Forgive me, Lord, when I get my eyes off of You and onto my surroundings. I know that I must purposely "fix my eyes on You" (Hebrews 12:2) alone, seeking You out with great persistence and diligence. Oh Father, may I be like the woman in this story who reached out to Jesus, confident that a mere touch would bring healing to her body. May You be able to say of me, "Daughter, your faith has healed you" (Mark 5:34)... whether it is a healing from past hurts, from the bondage of present sin, from anxiety over future uncertainty, or from a spirit of unbelief. I know that You alone are the answer to my needs, so help me "live by faith, not by sight" (II Corinthians 5:7).

JOURNAL: _____

_____

_____

TUESDAY: Read Genesis 6:9-22 and Hebrews 11:7. Meditate on God's Word and listen to what He has to say to you. Using the text as a guide, spend time in praise, confession and thanksgiving.

Pray for your husband to walk step by step in faith as Noah did: Lord, Your Word says, "By faith Noah, when warned about things not yet seen, in holy fear built an ark to save his family" (Hebrews 11:7). We never read that Noah resisted Your leading or questioned Your authority. Rather, it is recorded that, "Noah did everything just as God commanded him" (Genesis 6:22). Oh, how I pray for such a faith for my dear husband! Like Noah, may he be known as a "righteous man, blameless among the people of his time, and he walked with God" (Genesis 6:9). May my husband focus on You as his top priority, making it his goal to please You in every way, especially by his unwavering faith. May he obey You out of "holy fear", knowing that You truly do know what is best and that You have his best in mind. As Noah led his family to follow God, therefore receiving Your blessing, so I pray that my husband would lead our family by faith in Your Word.

JOURNAL: _____

_____

_____

WEDNESDAY: Read Matthew 8:5-13. Meditate on God's Word and listen to what He has to say to you. Using the text as a guide, spend time in praise, confession and thanksgiving.

Pray for those in your household, that you would demonstrate faith in God by your words and actions: Father God, I love this account of the Roman centurion and his total confidence in Jesus. "Just say the word, and my servant will be healed" (Matthew 8:8), declared the centurion! He neither asked nor desired Jesus to come to his home in Person to heal his servant....rather, he had such faith in the authority of Jesus that His Word alone was enough! We often think, "If I could just see Jesus in Person, if I could just feel His physical touch, it would be so much easier to believe." Father, forgive our lack of faith! And thank You that our lack of faith can never nullify Your faithfulness (Romans 3:3). We echo the words of the father who asked Jesus to heal his demon-possessed boy, declaring, "I do believe; help me overcome my unbelief!" (Mark 9:24). May my husband and I determine to stand firm in our faith, trusting in You to take care of us and believing in You to provide every need of our household (Philippians 4:19).

JOURNAL: _____

_____

_____

THURSDAY: Read I Thessalonians 3:1-10. Meditate on God's Word and listen to what He has to say to you. Using the text as a guide, spend time in praise, confession and thanksgiving.

Pray for your children, to stand firm in the Lord and grow in their faith: Oh Father, how can we thank You enough for our children "in return for all the joy we have in the presence of our God" because of them (I Thessalonians 3:9)? It is both a blessing and a privilege to be their parents and to share in each of their lives. How we long to see them grow in their faith, being conformed a little more each day into the image of Your Precious Son! Knowing that we are all destined for trials in some form or another, we pray that You would equip our children to stand firm in their faith. When they come under attack, may they remember "to take up the shield of faith, with which [they] can extinguish all the flaming arrows of the evil one" (Ephesians 6:16). As they grow older and leave our circle of influence, we pray that You would send other believers to strengthen and encourage our children in their faith (I Thessalonians 3:2). Please bring them continually to our minds, that we may be faithful night and day to pray most earnestly for our children (I Thessalonians 3:10).

JOURNAL: _____

_____

_____

_____

FRIDAY: Read Hebrews 10:32-39. Meditate on God's Word and listen to what He has to say to you. Using the text as a guide, spend time in praise, confession and thanksgiving.

Pray for your church, to persevere in faith in the midst of adversity: Oh Father, in these compromising days of "political correctness" and a growing animosity toward Your church, it is becoming increasingly difficult to stand firm in the faith. We do well to remember those saints of old who stood their ground in the face of suffering, insult and persecution. They "joyfully accepted the confiscation of [their] property," because they knew that they had "better and lasting possessions" (Hebrews 10:34). We praise You, Lord Jesus, that You are at this moment preparing for us that place of lasting possessions, full of unspeakable beauty and riches! May we not throw away our confidence in You, for "it will be richly rewarded" (Hebrews 10:35). I pray that our testimony on the last day will be: "But we are not of those who shrink back and are destroyed, but of those who believe and are saved" (Hebrews 10:39). Please strengthen us to "hold unswervingly to the hope we profess, for He who promised is faithful" (Hebrews 10:23).

JOURNAL: _____

_____

_____

SATURDAY: A Day of Application

Read Matthew 17:14-21.

Confess your lack of faith before the Lord:

_____

_____

_____

Jesus said, "I tell you the truth, if you have faith as small as a mustard seed, you can say to this mountain, 'Move from here to there' and it will move. Nothing will be impossible for you" (Matthew 17:20-21).

Will you have faith in the Lord today for the "impossible" in your life? Write out your prayer of faith here:

_____

_____

SUNDAY: A Day of Praise

Read Hebrews 11:1-6. (If time permits, read the entire chapter for a wonderful reminder of those who have walked by faith!)

Praise God that like these "heroes of the faith," we can have faith in Him because He is faithful to do what He promises.

WRITE OUT YOUR PRAYER OF PRAISE HERE:

_____

_____

_____

CHECK YOURSELF! WRITE YOUR MEMORY VERSE HERE:

_____

_____

WEEK THIRTY-EIGHT
Yielding to God's Plan

*"For it is God who works in you to will and to
act according to His good purpose"
(Philippians 2:13).*

SITTING IN YOUR POUTING CORNER

When my middle son Mitchell was little, he was very determined and independent. He was constantly wandering away from me to get into something he shouldn't. He was the one I would find eating mulch out of the flower beds, digging all the moss out of my ficus tree, or tearing into the presents under the Christmas tree. At the same time, he was a very sweet and loving child, and I would affectionately call him my "sugar booger"... completely adorable and full of charm, but quite the booger when he set his mind on something. Mitchell was very inventive at getting his way, and he would try different approaches if we told him no. But once he knew that we meant business and he could not have what he wanted, he would go and sit in what we called his "pouting corner". Down on his knees, facing the corner in our foyer, Mitchell would sit and pout, waiting for us to coax him away.

There are many days when I am just as tempted as Mitchell to go and sit in my own "pouting corner". Things have not gone the way I wanted, so I am just going to pout, and I want to make sure that everyone knows about it! Whether my plan for the day was interrupted, or my husband disagreed with something I wanted to do, or someone has made me mad, I am not happy and feel like pouting. When well-meaning friends or family members try to make me feel better I refuse to be consoled and, as my father says, make everyone else miserable too!

If we are honest, I think we can all identify such times in our lives. We set out on our own course, determined to get what we want, only to have those perfect plans come to a screeching halt. Sometimes we do remember to stop and actually pray about the matter first. Humbly we go to God, telling Him what we want, asking Him to grant our heart's desire, and then if He doesn't give us what we want we pout! "I've done my best to serve Him, I've done my best to obey Him, I've done my best to have my quiet time, etc... So why isn't He giving me what I want?" we wonder. All of a sudden those sweet prayers are forgotten and we turn into little "boogers" demanding our own way. But what God desires more than attempts to work for Him is a willingness to yield to Him. More often than not, God will eventually allow us to see that He "had planned something better for us..." (Hebrews 11:40a). We might not realize it at the moment, but someday we will be able to see that His plan was the better plan.

The best way that I have found to help myself yield to God's plan is by praying His Word in Philippians 2:13: "For it is God who works in you to will and to act according to His good purpose." I must ask God to change me and my desires so that they line up with Him and His plan. Then I can yield wholeheartedly to what He is doing in my life. So I continually pray, "Lord, please work in me to will and act according to Your good purpose," not my own. It is a daily dying to self and to what I want, in order to live for Christ and what He wants.

So the next time God's plan doesn't quite line up with mine, may I stop short of sitting in my pouting corner. Instead, may I be willing to declare, "I desire to do your will, O my God" (Psalm 40:8), yielding to His way rather than demanding my own.

Memory Verse:
"For it is God who works in you to will and to act according to His good purpose" (Philippians 2:13).

MONDAY: Read Luke 1:26-38. Meditate on God's Word and listen to what He has to say to you. Using the text as a guide, spend time in praise, confession and thanksgiving.

Pray for yourself, to be yielded to God's plan: Oh Father, when I read this account of Mary I am amazed by her response to Your plan for her life! Here she was, a virgin pledged to be married, facing a future that she had anticipated since childhood. Then all of a sudden, Your angel reveals a very different plan to her...that Your Holy Spirit would come upon her and she would bear the Son of God, Jesus Christ. In humble obedience Mary answered, "I am the Lord's servant. May it be to me as you have said" (Luke 1:38). Wow... that I would be so willing, that I would so quickly yield to You that I could respond as Mary did. Not in selfishness, not in anger, not in pride, or even in fear, but in trusting acceptance of Your will for me. Lord, I pray that You would "work in me to will and to act according to [Your] good purpose" (Philippians 2:13). Even when You reveal a plan that fills me with uncertainty or dread, please "grant me a willing spirit, to sustain me" (Psalm 51:12b). And thank You that no matter where this life takes me, You promise to be with me every step of the way.

JOURNAL: _____

_____

_____

TUESDAY: Read Matt 26:36-46. Meditate on God's Word and listen to what He has to say to you. Using the text as a guide, spend time in praise, confession and thanksgiving.

Pray for your husband, to yield to God's will for his life: What a Perfect Example we have in Jesus Christ! He, Who was fully God, humbled Himself to become fully man, yielding completely to God the Father's will for Him. Then, when He faced death in order to pay the penalty for our sin, He prayed and asked the Father, "If it is possible, may this cup be taken from Me. Yet not as I will, but as You will" (Matthew 26:39). Jesus had complete and total deference to You, Father God, in spite of His own desire to flee the pain and discomfort of Your will. In the same way, I pray that my husband would yield to Your plan for his life when it proves contrary to his own desires. May he humbly accept that "many are the plans in a man's heart, but it is the Lord's purpose that prevails" (Proverbs 19:21). If it is not Your will for him to have something that his heart desires, may he be willing to let it go. Thank You that he can rest in Your plans for him, trusting that they are plans to prosper him and not to harm him, plans to give him hope and a future (Jeremiah 29:11).

JOURNAL: _____

_____

_____

WEDNESDAY: Read Isaiah 29:13-16. Meditate on God's Word and listen to what He has to say to you. Using the text as a guide, spend time in praise, confession and thanksgiving.

Pray for your marriage, that you and your husband would be true to the Lord and yield to His plan for your family: Oh Lord Jesus, thank You for this reminder of Your omniscience... You know, You see and You hear everything that goes on in our home. Please forgive us when we only give "lip service" to You, coming near You with our mouths and honoring You with our lips (Isaiah 29:13), while keeping our hearts far from You. Your Word says, "Woe to those who go to great depths to hide their plans from the Lord" (Isaiah 29:15). How ridiculous we are to think we can choose our own way and hide our plans from You! So I pray that my husband and I would willingly come before You with every decision, seeking Your plan for us, and yielding to You even when that plan differs from our own. Forgive us for any feelings of resentment we may have over discontentment with the way things have worked out – whether with a job, or where we live, or the amount of money we make. Please equip us with everything good for doing Your will, and work in us what is pleasing to You (Hebrews 13:21).

JOURNAL: _____

_____

_____

———◦◦◦◦◦———

THURSDAY: Read Jeremiah 18:1-12. Meditate on God's Word and listen to what He has to say to you. Using the text as a guide, spend time in praise, confession and thanksgiving.

Pray for your children, to yield to the Lord as He forms them: I acknowledge afresh that You are the Potter, Lord Jesus, and that my children are the clay in Your hands. It is up to You, not me, to decide what is best for them. So often I want to take control, I want to shield them from difficult things, I want to determine the path they will follow....but only You in Your perfect wisdom can know what will be best for them. So I surrender them, one by one, trusting You to shape them as seems best to You (Jeremiah 18:4). I pray that my children would quickly learn that it is always better to yield to You than to fight against You. Help me teach them by example to trust You even when they do not understand, thereby avoiding the mistake of following the stubbornness of their evil hearts (Jeremiah 18:12). May they not be like obstinate children who carry out plans that are not Yours...who go down without consulting You (Isaiah 30:1-2). I would never want them to miss out on all You want to do in their lives because they "were not willing" (Matthew 23:37b).

JOURNAL: _____

_____

_____

———◦◦◦◦◦———

FRIDAY: Read Hebrews 10:1-10. Meditate on God's Word and listen to what He has to say to you. Using the text as a guide, spend time in praise, confession and thanksgiving.

Pray for your church, to trust in Christ alone and yield to His work in you: Lord Jesus, thank You that You came to do the Father's will. "And by that will, we have been made holy through the sacrifice of the body of Jesus Christ once for all" (Hebrews 10:10). What a gift! How freeing that we no longer must live under the law, offering sacrifices and burnt offerings and sin offerings to atone for our sins... You were the Perfect Sacrifice and the Only One needed for all eternity. May my church never lose sight of the fact that we have "been cleansed once for all" (Hebrews 10:2). We do not have to live under the burden of guilt and working endlessly for our salvation. As believers in You our salvation is secure and we are FREE! Now, Lord, instead of trying to do enough <u>for You</u>, may we seek instead to yield completely <u>to You</u> and to what You want to do through us. May each and every member of our congregation willingly put aside any personal agendas to follow Your leading. And may unbelievers see the freedom of the Christ-filled life in us and long to experience You for themselves.

JOURNAL: _____

_____

_____

SATURDAY: A Day of Application

Read Luke 9:23-26.

In Luke 9:23 Jesus said, "If anyone would come after Me, he must deny himself and take up his cross daily and follow Me." In what ways do you need to deny yourself and yield to the Father?

_____

_____

_____

Your "cross" has been defined as "anything you must sacrifice in order to get in on the redemption of others." Is there something God is asking you to sacrifice to Him so that others will come to know Him? (Examples: money, time, a spirit of pride, etc.)

_____

_____

Write out a prayer of commitment to yield to God's plan rather than demanding Your own way:

_____

_____

SUNDAY: A Day of Praise

Read II Samuel 22:31-37.

Praise God that His way is perfect: entirely without fault, certain, complete, pure, lacking in no essential detail.

WRITE OUT YOUR PRAYER OF PRAISE HERE:

_____

_____

_____

CHECK YOURSELF! WRITE YOUR MEMORY VERSE HERE:

_____

_____

WEEK THIRTY-NINE
Doing the Right Thing

"Speak up for those who cannot speak for themselves, for the rights of all who are destitute. Speak up and judge fairly; defend the rights of the poor and needy" (Proverbs 31:8-9).

WE CAN'T HEAR YOU!

Years ago when I was in my early twenties, I was in line at the bank when I realized that a customer being served ahead of me was someone I knew. A fellow employee at my workplace at the time, I had seen this lady fairly often as she went about her duties cleaning hallways and offices with the custodial staff. We had never exchanged more than general greetings, but I knew her name and recognized her voice. She was a gentle, soft-spoken lady, and while I couldn't hear what she was saying, everyone in the bank could hear what the teller had to say. "I just can't understand you, ma'am. What is it that you want?" the teller raised her voice impatiently. My coworker attempted to explain again what she needed, but the teller was in no mood to try to help. With a wave of her hand in a final gesture of dismissal, the teller called another bank employee over to handle the matter, stating, "I just can't understand these people." My skin bristled at her uncaring words, her lack of compassion, and her generalization regarding my coworker. Whether the teller's statement about "these people" indicated the color of her skin, her lack of education, or simply the way she was dressed, the teller had absolutely no right to sit in judgment of her or to treat her in such manner. "Maybe I should do something," I thought to myself, "but what? And all these people are around, what would they think? Well, it's really none of my business," I rationalized and simply looked away.

279

I will go to my grave regretting my lack of action that day at the bank. I knew what I should have done....I should have intervened, I should have asked my coworker how I could help her explain what she needed, and I should have reported the impertinent teller to her supervisor! But I did nothing, except turn my head and pretend like I wasn't there. I can try to blame it on my young age at the time or my lack of experience in confronting someone older than I was, but I really have no one to blame but myself.

Since that incident some twenty years ago, the Lord has convicted me that it is not enough just to make sure that I treat others fairly. It is also my responsibility to speak up in defense of someone else who is being treated unjustly. God's Word says, "Speak up for those who cannot speak for themselves, for the rights of all who are destitute. Speak up and judge fairly; defend the rights of the poor and needy" (Proverbs 31:8-9.) So whether we witness an injustice being done to a virtual stranger, or are in the position to take a stand for God's Word in our community, or are simply privy to an unflattering conversation about an absent friend, the choice is ours. Will we stand up for what is right, or will we choose to do nothing?

It is easy to be dismayed by the injustices we encounter all around us, even outraged by them at times. We shake our heads and wonder, "Why does God allow this? Why doesn't God do something?" Maybe the better question to ask is, "Why don't we?" So the next time the Holy Spirit whispers, "Are you just going to sit there and do nothing?" may we strive to please God rather than man (Galatians 1:10) and take a stand for what is right.

Memory Verse:
"Speak up for those who cannot speak for themselves, for the rights of all who are destitute. Speak up and judge fairly; defend the rights of the poor and needy"
(Proverbs 31:8-9).

MONDAY: Read Esther 3:8-4:14. Meditate on God's Word and listen to what He has to say to you. Using the text as a guide, spend time in praise, confession and thanksgiving.

Pray for yourself, to be willing to speak up in defense of others: How terribly afraid Queen Esther must have been! A law had been passed to annihilate every single Jew in King Xerxes' kingdom, and Esther was the one called upon to "go into the king's presence to beg for mercy and plead with him for her people" (Esther 4:8). Knowing that approaching the king without a summons could result in death, Esther was hesitant to intervene. But the wise words from her uncle Mordecai spurred her on to action! "Do not think that because you are in the king's house you alone of all the Jews will escape...and who knows but that you have come to royal position for such a time as this?" (Esther 4:13-14). Oh Father, in like manner You put me in position at times to intervene, to speak up, or to act on behalf of another. Forgive me, Lord, when I neglect such responsibilities. Please give me Your strength and Your boldness to do the right thing even when it may put me at a personal disadvantage. May I refuse to turn away and ignore the injustices I see, waiting for someone else to act or show they care. It is up to me.

JOURNAL: _____

_____

_____

TUESDAY: Read Job 31:13-23. Meditate on God's Word and listen to what He has to say to you. Using the text as a guide, spend time in praise, confession and thanksgiving.

Pray for your husband, to act justly and to pursue justice for others: Father God, this passage reminds us that we are all equal. "Did not He who made me in the womb make them? Did not the same one form us both within our mothers" (Job 31:15). As such, we all have value in Your eyes and should treat one another with mutual respect and justice. So I pray that my husband would see it as his personal responsibility to not only act justly toward others, but to pursue justice for those who are being mistreated. If he falls short in either way, confront him with the truth of Your Word. Give him a heart that is always ready to respond to You humbly and obediently "when called to account" (Job 31:14). Thank you for the times I have personally seen him speak out in defense of me or the children. I pray that he would be willing to use whatever influence he has to help others in need (Job 31:21), boldly speaking on their behalf. May my husband be counted among those who are blessed because they "maintain justice, who constantly do what is right" (Psalm 106:3).

JOURNAL: _____

_____

_____

⸻⸻

WEDNESDAY: Isaiah 1:10-17. Meditate on God's Word and listen to what He has to say to you. Using the text as a guide, spend time in praise, confession and thanksgiving.

Pray for those in your household, to stop doing wrong and learn to do right: Lord Jesus, Your Word says, "To do what is right and just is more acceptable to the Lord than sacrifice" (Proverbs 21:3). Forgive us when we substitute "meaningless sacrifices" (Isaiah 1:13) for heartfelt obedience to Your command to do the right thing. We must stop doing wrong, and we must stop doing nothing at all! Please remind my husband and me that such behavior begins at home! As our children see us speak on their behalf in the face of injustice, it will encourage them to do the same for others. As we choose to do the right thing, even when it is hard or uncomfortable, it will motivate them to do so also. Please Lord, use Your Holy Spirit to guide us as parents to "seek justice" within our home. I pray that we never be guilty of turning a blind eye when one child mistreats another, but diligently defend the cause of all of our children equally. May it be our goal each day to do our small part to "seek justice, encourage the oppressed. Defend the cause of the fatherless, plead the case of the widow" (Isaiah 1:17).

JOURNAL: _____

_____

_____

———◦◦◦◦———

THURSDAY: Read I Samuel 19:1-6. Meditate on God's Word and listen to what He has to say to you. Using the text as a guide, spend time in praise, confession and thanksgiving.

Pray for your children, to speak up when they witness an injustice: Heavenly Father, how I pray that my children will have the courage and the desire to speak up when they see another being mistreated. When Jonathan learned that his father, King Saul, intended to kill David, even though he had done nothing wrong, Jonathan did not stand back and do nothing. He boldly approached his father, spoke well of David in his defense, and as a result, King Saul changed his mind about killing him. In like manner, I pray that my children would "not withhold good from those who deserve it, when it is in [their] power to act" (Proverbs 3:27). May they not turn aside in apathy, lacking compassion, or shrink back in fear, afraid that any intervention might bring negative consequences on themselves. For Your Word says, "But even if you should suffer for what is right, you are blessed" (I Peter 3:14). I pray that they would yield to Your Holy Spirit when You direct them to action, especially when You call them to speak up in defense of one another. Convict them to always treat others as they would want to be treated.

JOURNAL: _____

_____

_____

———◦◦◦◦———

FRIDAY: Read Exodus 23:1-9. Meditate on God's Word and listen to what He has to say to you. Using the text as a guide, spend time in praise, confession and thanksgiving.

Pray for your country, to follow the laws of justice and proper living established in God's Word: Father, as I read through this passage of Scripture, I notice that each verse contains the words "do not." Thank You that You give us very specific guidelines on how to live, making it easier to establish laws and govern fairly. I pray that our citizens and lawmakers alike would follow Your Word and do what is right. May we deal with one another in honesty and compassion, treating others as we want to be treated. May we judge fairly, without regard to wealth, position or nationality. God forbid that if we see the majority going astray, we give in to the temptation to just stand back and do nothing! You clearly say, "Do not follow the crowd in doing wrong...do not pervert justice...do not show favoritism" (Exodus 23:2-3). We as individuals are called to take a stand, and as believers we must take a stand for the truth of Your Word! May our judges and officials be diligent to "judge the people fairly" and not "pervert justice or show partiality" (Deuteronomy 16:18b-19a), knowing that they must answer to You.

JOURNAL: _____

_____

_____

SATURDAY: A Day of Application

Read Proverbs 21:3, 13, 15.

Has the Lord convicted you this week of failing to do what is right in a certain matter? Have you refused to speak up, pursue justice, offer help to someone in need?

_____

If so, confess it as sin and accept the Lord's forgiveness. "If we confess our sins, He is faithful and just and will forgive us our sins and purify us from all unrighteousness" (I John 1:9).

Pray and ask the Lord to help you yield to His Holy Spirit when He directs you to do the right thing, even if it is difficult or uncomfortable. Write out your prayer here:

_____

_____

"God is not unjust; He will not forget your work and the love you have shown Him as you have helped his people and continue to help them" (Hebrews 6:10). Never forget that you are showing your love for the Lord when you help someone else!

SUNDAY: A Day of Praise

Read Deuteronomy 10:17-22.

Praise God as your Defender! He is "God of gods and Lord of lords, the great God, mighty and awesome, who shows no partiality and accepts no bribes" (Deuteronomy 10:17).

WRITE OUT YOUR PRAYER OF PRAISE HERE:

_____

_____

_____

CHECK YOURSELF! WRITE YOUR MEMORY VERSE HERE:

_____

_____

Anger

"In your anger do not sin: Do not let the sun go down while you are still angry, and do not give the devil a foothold" (Ephesians 4:26-27).

AN ANGRY AND CONTENTIOUS WOMAN, WHO CAN STAND?

"Stop wrestling," I warned my two older sons as they laughingly threw each other on the couch and jumped on top of their willing victim. They settled down briefly, but moments later they were at it again. "If you're not careful, you're going to break something!" I shouted. Sure enough, their peals of laughter turned to silence when they accidently knocked over a side table, sending the lamp crashing to the floor. "Go to your rooms," I yelled angrily, "and don't come out until I tell you!" I glared at them as they disappeared up the stairway, fuming about the crack in the lamp and their persistent rough-housing. It was the second time in just a few weeks that my lamp had been broken because of their wrestling, and this time, I didn't think I could repair the damage too easily.

For the next thirty minutes I stomped around the kitchen preparing dinner, making sure they could hear my disapproval in every slammed cabinet door. When my sons were called to dinner they came down chastened and apologetic, but my lingering anger made the meal a less than enjoyable experience. Truth be told the entire evening was ruined by my angry attitude. The rest of the family became sullen and short with one another, scattering to separate corners as soon as dinner was over. And who could blame them? After all, Proverbs 21:19 (KJV) says, "It is better to dwell in the wilderness, than with a contentious and an <u>angry</u> woman." I finally went to bed in a bad mood, just ready for the day to end and to put the episode behind me.

But as soon as I awoke the next morning, the Lord quickly informed me that the incident was far from over. Shame washed over me as the Holy Spirit brought my angry words and attitude to the forefront of my mind, and God used His knife of conviction on my heart. The Bible says, "In your anger do not sin: Do not let the sun go down while you are still angry, and do not give the devil a foothold" (Ephesians 4:26-27). By allowing my initial anger over my sons' disobedience to fester and grow instead of dealing with it and letting it go, I had defiantly gone to bed angry. The devil had certainly gained a foothold, not only in my heart but also in my home. Strife and discord had replaced the peace and harmony for which I continually pray as I intentionally focused on my anger. I might not have gone to bed happy, but I think the devil did!

Feelings of anger come naturally. In fact, the Lord Himself repeatedly became angry with the Israelites for their rebellion, disobedience, and idol worship. When I began to think of all the things that can anger me, it took just a few seconds to compile a long list: my children's disobedience, God's discipline in my life, my plans going awry, my needs going unmet, the injustices around me, why even traffic jams can bring out my anger in lightening speed! Anger is natural, but it is how we handle those angry feelings that matter. The Lord says, "You must rid yourselves of all such things as these: anger, rage, malice…" (Colossians 3:8). We must deal with these issues as soon as they arise, hand out/accept punishment as needed, extend forgiveness and love, pray for patience, and then by all means, get rid of our anger! If anyone is going to be angry, let it be our adversary the devil because we refuse to allow him into our lives.

Memory Verse:
"In your anger do not sin: Do not let the sun go down while you are still angry" (Ephesians 4:26).

MONDAY: Read Ephesians 4:26-27 & James 1:19-21. Meditate on God's Word and listen to what He has to say to you. Using the text as a guide, spend time in praise, confession and thanksgiving.

Pray for yourself, that in your anger you will not sin: Father, I understand from these two passages that my unresolved anger does two things: it "gives the devil a foothold" (Ephesians 4:27); and it "does not bring about the righteous life that God desires" (James 1:20). Please open my eyes to these truths from Your Word the next time I become angry. Remind me that when I hold on to my anger I am giving the devil an open door to wreak havoc in my life – "The thief comes only to steal and kill and destroy" (John 10:10a). Satan will use my anger against me to steal my joy, kill my witness before others and destroy my relationships. I don't want to be that "contentious and angry woman" (Proverbs 21:19) that no one can stand to be around! But You "have come that they may have life, and have it to the full" (John 10:10b). I want the kind of life You offer that is full of peace, forgiveness, unity and love. I pray for the cleansing work of Your Holy Spirit to convict me to "get rid of all bitterness, rage and anger, brawling and slander, along with every form of malice" (Ephesians 4:31). And may I refuse to sin by going to bed angry.

JOURNAL: _____

_____

_____

———⊷∘⊶———

TUESDAY: Read I Samuel 20:28-34. Meditate on God's Word and listen to what He has to say to you. Using the text as a guide, spend time in praise, confession and thanksgiving.

Pray for your husband, to control his anger in all circumstances: In this tragic account we see King Saul become so furious with another person that he turns his anger on his own son Jonathan. As a result, Jonathan develops a fierce anger toward his father. It is clear from this passage that anger left unchecked can have drastic consequences – even on those we love and never intended to harm. So Father I pray for my husband, asking You to give him wisdom in handling his anger. When something goes wrong and his temper flares, may he not give "full vent to his anger," but be like the wise man who "keeps himself under control" (Proverbs 29:11). Enable my husband to deal with difficult situations calmly, with clarity of thought, and with an even-temper. "A man's wisdom gives him patience; it is to his glory to overlook an offense" (Proverbs 19:11), so enlarge his capacity to forgive when wronged. May he not make the same mistake as King Saul, but heed Your strong warning: "Fathers, do no embitter your children, or they will become discouraged" (Colossians 3:21).

JOURNAL: _____

_____

_____

WEDNESDAY: Read Genesis 4:1-12. Meditate on God's Word and listen to what He has to say to you. Using the text as a guide, spend time in praise, confession and thanksgiving.

Pray for those in your household to master any sin caused by anger: What a tragic account of the quick succession of sin that anger can cause. God's disapproval of Cain's offering made him angry, so he did the unthinkable and murdered his own brother Abel. I doubt Cain, blinded by rage, ever thought through his actions to foresee the terrible cost of his anger. He was cursed by God to be a restless wanderer on the earth, and he was forced to leave his parents and his home. Oh Father, protect my family from such disastrous consequences! May those in my household heed Your strong words of warning: "If you do not do what is right, sin is crouching at your door; it desires to have you, but you must master it" (Genesis 4:7b). I pray that we would never open the door to sin by allowing jealousy, petty arguments, or hurt feelings to escalate out of control. "For as churning the milk produces butter, and as twisting the nose produces blood, so stirring up anger produces strife" (Proverbs 30:33). Please enable us to do everything possible to dispel anger and live in the peace that You desire for us.

JOURNAL: _____

_____

_____

———— ❧ ————

THURSDAY: Read II Kings 5:1-14. Meditate on God's Word and listen to what He has to say to you. Using the text as a guide, spend time in praise, confession and thanksgiving.

Pray for your children, to turn from anger and follow godly advice: Oh Lord, Naaman almost missed it! In his anger he almost missed Your healing, Your blessing, and Your provision for him because his pride rebelled at Your command. Naaman thought he was "too good" to follow Your directions, and he became angry at the thought of debasing himself with such a simple act. The Bible reminds us that, "Pride goes before destruction and a haughty spirit before a fall" (Proverbs 16:18). Leprosy would have destroyed Naaman had it not been for Your healing power and the godly advice of his faithful servants to do as You directed. How I pray for my dear children to listen to godly advice when they are tempted to give in to their anger! May they never miss Your best for them because they listened to lies of the flesh and stubbornly held on to anger and pride. Rather, may they listen to the truth of Your Word and its warnings about anger. And may they "not make friends with a hot-tempered man" or "associate with one easily angered" or they may learn his ways and get themselves ensnared (Proverbs 22:24-25).

JOURNAL: _____

_____

_____

———— ❧ ————

FRIDAY: Read Matthew 5:21-24. Meditate on God's Word and listen to what He has to say to you. Using the text as a guide, spend time in praise, confession and thanksgiving.

Pray for the members of your church, to obey God's commands about anger and reconciliation: Lord Jesus, in these verses You teach the truth about anger. We will be held accountable not only for acting in anger, but also for attitudes of anger. "Anyone who is angry with his brother will be subject to judgment" (Matthew 5:22). Not only do we sin when we hold on to our anger and allow it to fester, we are also hurting ourselves. So please help those in my church to be willing to let go of their anger, choosing reconciliation and forgiveness over division and pride. Open our eyes to see that our anger not only affects our relationships with others, it affects our worship of You. "Therefore, if you are offering your gift at the altar and there remember that your brother has something against you, leave your gift there in front of the altar. First go and be reconciled to your brother; then come and offer your gift" (Matthew 5:23-24). May those in my church family be able to worship You in Spirit and in Truth, as they "lift up holy hands in prayer, without anger or disputing" (I Timothy 2:8).

JOURNAL: _____

_____

_____

SATURDAY: A Day of Application

Read Ecclesiastes 7:9 & Jonah 4:1-4.

Are you quick to become angry with others or in difficult situations?

_____

Are you guilty of holding on to your anger and allowing it to fester?

_____

Has this lesson on anger struck a nerve with you this week because you are angry about something right now? If so what is it?

_____

Think through the Lord's words in Jonah 4:4: "Have you any right to be angry?" Ask the Lord to reveal to you if your anger has caused you to sin (Ephesians 4:26). If so, confess it here:

_____

_____

Pray and ask the Lord to help you be "gracious and compassionate, slow to anger and abounding in love" (Nehemiah 9:17):

_____

_____

SUNDAY: A Day of Praise

Read Psalm 30:4-5 & Psalm 103:8-9.

Praise God that He is slow to anger, abounding in love.

WRITE OUT YOUR PRAYER OF PRAISE HERE:

_____

_____

CHECK YOURSELF! WRITE YOUR MEMORY VERSE HERE:

_____

_____

Being Honest and Trustworthy

"Their wives are to be women worthy of respect, not malicious talk-
ers but temperate and trustworthy in everything"
(I Timothy 3:11).

POISON IVY

It was a beautiful sunny morning, and I was delighted for the excuse to spend the day outside. As a chaperone for my son's class field trip, I was responsible for leading a small group of first-grade children through a nature center in our city. One of the first things we were told upon our arrival was that we should be careful to stay on the path and not touch anything with which we were unfamiliar. The woods were full of poison ivy, the instructor warned, and then she taught us three little rhymes to help us identify the plant so we could steer clear of it. "Leaves of three, leave them be! Berries white, run in fright! Hairy vine, no friend of mine." I had heard the first rhyme before, but the last two were new, so I listened carefully and committed the rhymes to memory. I was no stranger to the misery of an outbreak of poison ivy, and I wanted to be sure I never got it again!

Three years earlier my family had moved into a new home in a highly wooded area, and we loved all the old trees and verdant yard. My husband and I were anxious to clear out an overgrown flowerbed in a sunny area of the yard to make way for rose bushes and tomato plants. I dug into the task enthusiastically, pulling up weeds by the fistful with my bare hands, unaware that some of those weeds might not be as innocent looking as they seemed! Completely unfamiliar with poison ivy, I had no idea what the plant looked like or that the flower bed was full of it. So a few days later when I noticed some itchy spots on the inside of my wrists and on one of my shins, I didn't think too much about them. But it didn't take long for the itchiness to intensify, especially after I shaved my legs and spread the rash from the poison ivy all over both legs. Once I realized what it was, I tried over-the-counter medications like calamine lotion and itch-relief cream, but those were worthless. After several miserable days I finally went to the doctor for some professional help. I was so grateful for the steroid shot and prescription ointment that finally made the horrible rash from that poisonous plant subside!

The Apostle Paul is quite blunt in his description of something else that is full of poison...the lying and deceitful words from our own mouths. In describing man's sinfulness by using quotes from the Old Testament, Paul said "Their throats are open graves; their tongues practice deceit. The poison of vipers is on their lips" (Romans 3:13). Poison by definition is a substance that can injure, taint or kill; affect destructively or corrupt. Just as surely as poison ivy can cause a terrible allergic reaction and a snake bite can injure or even kill, so our dishonest words can cause incredible harm to others. Furthermore, we corrupt ourselves through our trickery and deceit, as we align ourselves with Satan who is "a liar and the father of lies" (John 8:44). Act dishonestly just once or twice and others will lose all trust in you.

May we never poison those we come in contact with through lies, deception or a betrayal of trust. Rather, may our mouths be full of truth, earning us reputations as "women worthy of respect, not malicious talkers but temperate and trustworthy in <u>everything</u>" (I Timothy 3:11).

———❖———

Memory Verse:
"Their wives are to be women worthy of respect, not malicious talkers but temperate and trustworthy in everything" (I Timothy 3:11).

———❖———

MONDAY: Read Proverbs 11:1-13. Meditate on God's Word and listen to what He has to say to you. Using the text as a guide, spend time in praise, confession and thanksgiving.

Pray for yourself, to be honest and trustworthy in everything: Lord from the beginning, You set the standard in this matter of honesty. "You shall not give false testimony against your neighbor" (Exodus 20:16). And while it is tempting to dismiss little lies as insignificant or harmless, You see them as destructive. "The integrity of the upright guides them, but the unfaithful are destroyed by their duplicity" (Proverbs 11:3). May I never say one thing, intending to do something else, but make every effort to let my 'yes' be 'yes' and my 'no' be 'no' (Matthew 5:37). I know that You abhor dishonesty, so I open my heart to Your examination in the desire to correct any misbehavior. I want to delight You by my honesty and be found trustworthy by those around me. I pray that my children and my husband will have full confidence in me (Proverbs 31:11), because they can count on me to tell the truth. The Bible says, "A gossip betrays a confidence, but a trustworthy man keeps a secret" (Proverbs 11:13). May I prove myself trustworthy to anyone who confides in me.

JOURNAL: _____

_____

_____

TUESDAY: Read Job 2:1-10. Meditate on God's Word and listen to what He has to say to you. Using the text as a guide, spend time in praise, confession and thanksgiving.

Pray for your husband, to maintain his integrity at all times: Father God, what a godly example Job is for us! In absolute misery, Job held on to his integrity (Job 2:9). Even when his wife suggested that he "Curse God and die!" he adamantly refused. Oh Father, how I pray that my husband would have the strength and devotion to do the same. When trouble strikes, please use me to come alongside him in encouragement and prayer. I would never want to be like Job's wife and advise him to turn away from You! May he determine as Job did, "My lips will not speak wickedness, and my tongue will utter no deceit....till I die, I will not deny my integrity" (Job 27:4-5). Your Word tells us that there is protection in an honest life, for "the man of integrity walks securely, but he who takes crooked paths will be found out" (Proverbs 10:9). So please keep my husband off the crooked paths of lying, twisting words, misrepresentation, and stretching the truth. Convict him to be above reproach at work, even if his coworkers act dishonestly and the boss is not present. May he earn the reputation that "he was a man of integrity [who] feared God more than most men do" (Nehemiah 7:2).

JOURNAL: _____

_____

_____

WEDNESDAY: Read Luke 16:1-13. Meditate on God's Word and listen to what He has to say to you. Using the text as a guide, spend time in praise, confession and thanksgiving.

Pray for those in your household to act responsibly and prove themselves trustworthy: Father God, integrity is something that must be taught, and it should begin at home. My husband and I must take our responsibilities seriously, demonstrating honesty and trustworthiness before our children on every occasion. Then, as they begin to assume duties of their own, they will have the correct example to follow. I want them to understand that, "Whoever can be trusted with very little can also be trusted with much, and whoever is dishonest with very little will also be dishonest with much" (Luke 16:10). As they prove themselves to be honest and responsible in the small things, we can entrust them with more. But if they act irresponsibly or deceitfully, it shows us that they cannot be trusted. Please help us teach them these truths. As our children grow up and begin to take on responsibilities outside the home, I pray that they would not lie, deceive, or slander. And may they never steal, but show that they can be fully trusted (Titus 2:10)! At all times, may the members of my family be above reproach and completely honest.

JOURNAL: _____

_____

_____

THURSDAY: Read Proverbs 12:13-22. Meditate on God's Word and listen to what He has to say to you. Using the text as a guide, spend time in praise, confession and thanksgiving.

Pray for your children, to be completely truthful and bring the Lord delight: Father God, honesty is such a difficult thing to maintain in our world today. In a culture filled with lying, cheating and doing whatever it takes to get ahead, it is hard to teach the value of complete truthfulness. Even so, Your Word declares, "The Lord detests lying lips, but He delights in men who are truthful" (Proverbs 12:22). So I pray that my children would keep their tongues from evil and their lips from speaking lies (Psalm 34:13). As parents we must require absolute honesty from our children, being very careful not to undermine our words with contradictory behavior. If they do act dishonestly, I pray that we would take it seriously. We must teach them that, "A false witness will not go unpunished, and he who pours out lies will not go free" (Proverbs 19:5). Please show my children that it is never worth it to lie! "A fortune made by a lying tongue is a fleeting vapor and a deadly snare" (Proverbs 21:6). Finally, I ask You to deliver them from those "whose mouths are full of lies, whose right hands are deceitful" (Psalm 144:11).

JOURNAL: _____

_____

_____

———— ✦ ————

FRIDAY: Read II Kings 22:1-7. Meditate on God's Word and listen to what He has to say to you. Using the text as a guide, spend time in praise, confession and thanksgiving.

Pray for your pastor and church staff, to act faithfully and with complete honesty: Lord Jesus, thank You so much for the men and women You have placed in leadership positions in my church. I pray Your blessings and protection on each one of them, asking You to equip them to fulfill their duties in complete honesty. May my pastor be a man like Josiah, who "did what was right in the eyes of the Lord...

not turning aside to the right or to the left" (II Kings 22:2). May our church staff have such a solid reputation for honesty that "they need not account for the money entrusted to them, because they are acting faithfully" (II Kings 22:7). I pray that we as a congregation would be found trustworthy as well, living up to the same standards of honesty that we expect of our leaders. The Bible says, "You must have accurate and honest weights and measures, so that you may live long in the land the Lord your God is giving you. For the Lord your God...detests anyone who deals dishonestly" (Deuteronomy 25:15-16). May we use accurate standards and deal truthfully with one another, both in church and in the community.

JOURNAL: _____

_____

_____

SATURDAY: A Day of Application

Read Proverbs 6:16-19. The Bible says that the Lord hates "a lying tongue" and "a false witness who pours out lies." These things are detestable to Him.

Are you guilty of having a lying tongue?

_____

Are you guilty of telling little whites lies? (Asking your kids to tell a phone caller you are not home, calling in "sick" to work when you are really not, making up a story for the police officer who stops you for speeding in hopes that he doesn't give you a ticket?) .

_____

If so, confess this as sin and ask the Lord to forgive you for your dishonesty:

_____

God wants us to be completely honest and trustworthy. "Surely you desire truth in the inner parts" (Psalm 51:6). Make a commitment to be truthful in all things: Lord, I renounce secret and shameful ways; I will not use deception (II Corinthians 4:2). Write out your prayer here:

_____

_____

SUNDAY: A Day of Praise

Read Numbers 23:19 and Psalm 119:86.

Praise God that He never lies. Praise God that His commands are completely trustworthy. He always does what He says He will do!

WRITE OUT YOUR PRAYER OF PRAISE HERE:

_____

_____

_____

CHECK YOURSELF! WRITE YOUR MEMORY VERSE HERE:

_____

_____

Wholehearted Love and Devotion to God

"And that you may love the Lord your God, listen to His voice, and hold fast to Him. For the Lord is your life..." (Deuteronomy 30:20).

HOLD ON AS IF YOUR LIFE DEPENDS ON IT

My son and I were at the airport, anxiously anticipating my husband's return home from a business trip. As we waited for the plane to land and pull up to the gate, I happened to notice two young ladies sitting nearby. When the door to the terminal finally swung open and the passengers began to emerge, one of the ladies quickly got up from her seat and stood as close as possible to the doorway. One of the first people to walk through the door was a young man, and he had barely crossed the threshold when the lady threw her arms around his neck and began to cry. She held tightly to the man, never saying a word. As other passengers began to come up behind them, the man eased the two of them over to the side where they would not block the flow of traffic. All the while, the lady maintained her strong grip around his neck. My husband came through a moment later, and I turned my attention to greet him. After visiting for a few minutes we were ready to leave. As I glanced behind me to gather my belongings I was surprised to see the young lady still clinging to the man! It did not look like either of them had moved from their embrace, and I began to wonder about their situation... was the lady crying tears of sadness at some bad news, clinging to the man for comfort? Was she weeping with joy because she was finally reunited with her loved one? Or was she crying with relief, knowing that someone else was there to support her? I will never know the reason, but the picture of that young lady clinging to her man remains embedded in my mind. Whatever the reason, she held on to him as if her life depended on it.

Deuteronomy 30:20 says, "And that you may love the Lord your God, listen to His voice, and hold fast to Him. For the Lord is your life…" This verse brings to mind another young woman who was "holding fast" to Someone…the Lord Jesus Christ. In chapter seven of the book of Luke, we find the account of the woman who anointed Jesus' feet with some expensive perfume. Scripture tells us that this woman had led a sinful life, and when she heard that Jesus was in town she deliberately sought Him out. This woman wept at the Lord's feet until they were wet with her tears. She wiped His feet with her hair, kissed them over and over again, and poured perfume on them. Overwhelmed by her sinfulness and supremely grateful for the Lord's forgiveness, this woman unashamedly lavished her love on her Lord without a single care for what anyone else thought. He had changed her life – He <u>was</u> her life – and her devotion to Him was obvious!

So what about me? Is my love for the Lord obvious to those around me? Or are those I come in contact with on a daily basis even aware that I know His name? Do I hold fast to Him as the lady at the airport clung to her man, as if my next breath depends on His touch? Or do I merely give Him a brief nod in the morning as I start my day? Do I lavish my attention on Him as did the sinful woman who anointed His feet, seemingly unaware of anyone else around me? Or am I too concerned with the opinions of others to possibly draw attention to myself or create a scene that shows my love and devotion for the One Who loved me first? What, then, about me?

Memory Verse:
"That you may love the Lord your God, listen to His voice, and hold fast to Him. For the Lord is your life…" (Deuteronomy 30:20).

MONDAY: Read Luke 7:36-50. Meditate on God's Word and listen to what He has to say to you. Using the text as a guide, spend time in praise, confession and thanksgiving.

Pray for yourself, to love the Lord your God with all your heart and never be ashamed to show it: Lord Jesus, I never fail to read this story and be touched by the woman's display of affection for You. Your Word tells us why she did it…"she loved much", overwhelmed at Your forgiveness of her sins (Luke 7:47). Oh Father, I stand ashamed for taking Your forgiveness for granted. And how many times have I failed to give You thanks or lavish my love on You in praise? Forgive me when I do not love You as I should, when I give other people or things more attention than I give You. May I be like this woman who kissed Your feet, wiped them with her hair, and anointed them with expensive perfume out of a heart of pure devotion. I do not want to be ashamed to pour out my love for You – not to make a "display" before men, but because my love for You is so great that I cannot contain myself. I know that I have been forgiven much, so may I love much in return. Show me what it means to love You with all my heart and with all my soul and with all my strength (Deuteronomy 6:5).

JOURNAL: _____

_____

_____

TUESDAY: Read Psalm 86:1-13. Meditate on God's Word and listen to what He has to say to you. Using the text as a guide, spend time in praise, confession and thanksgiving.

Pray for your husband, to love the Lord and be deeply devoted to Him: Father God, when I think of someone who loved You supremely my thoughts turn instantly toward King David. You sought him out as a man after Your own heart and appointed him leader of his people (I Samuel 13:14). David loved You, and we see many places in Scripture where he spoke boldly of that love for You. May my husband be such a man. I pray David's own prayers for himself from this Psalm over my husband...may he be "devoted to You" (verse 2), keeping You as his main priority; may he "call to You all day long" (verse 3), constantly seeking Your face for direction at work and at home; may he lead others to worship and bring glory to Your name (verse 9), proclaiming that "You are great and do marvelous deeds; You alone are God" (verse 10). When the temptations of this world pull him in every direction, please give my dear husband "an undivided heart, that [he] may fear Your name" (verse 11). And when the storms of this life assault him, may he still declare, "I love You, O Lord, my strength" (Psalm 18:1).

JOURNAL: _____

_____

_____

—————◦◦◦◦————

WEDNESDAY: Read Jeremiah 32:38-41. Meditate on God's Word and listen to what He has to say to you. Using the text as a guide, spend time in praise, confession and thanksgiving.

Pray for those in your household, that your love for the Lord would motivate you to live boldly for Him: Father I am so thankful that we are Your people and You are our God (Jeremiah 32:38). I praise You for the salvation of each one under our roof who has opened his heart to a relationship with You. If there are any who have not yet trusted in You as Lord and Savior, I beg You to open their eyes to the truth of the Gospel very soon! As You have entrusted my husband and me with this family, please give us "singleness of heart and action" (Jeremiah 32:39) in all our ways. We must fear You for our own good and for the good of our children after us! If there is any sin – any thought that denies You or any action that rebels against Your authority – please circumcise our hearts and the hearts of our descendants, so that we may love You with all our hearts and with all our souls (Deuteronomy 30:6). May we never attribute Your goodness and blessings to any other; rather, may these things inspire us to fear You, so that we will never turn away from You (Jeremiah 32:40).

JOURNAL: _____

_____

_____

———⊶∘⊷———

THURSDAY: Read Joshua 22:1-5. Meditate on God's Word and listen to what He has to say to you. Using the text as a guide, spend time in praise, confession and thanksgiving.

Pray for your children, to be devoted in their love for the Lord till the end: Father, You know my fears for my children. This world we live in seems to become more and more evil all the time, and it frightens me to think of the things they will have to face as they grow up. So I pray that from a very young age, my children would learn to love You, the Lord their God, walk in all Your ways, obey Your commands, hold fast to You and serve You with all their hearts and all their souls (Joshua 22:5). I pray that they would "not love the world or anything in the world" (I John 2:15a), but be totally sold out to You. May my children be like Caleb, who had a "different spirit and followed [You] whole-heartedly" (Numbers 14:24). It is not easy to choose to be "different" in a culture of conformity and ridicule for anyone who doesn't follow the latest beliefs. Please help them to be more concerned with what You think than what others think. I pray that their love for You would guide their every decision and influence their every action. Use me to "encourage them all to remain true to the Lord with all their hearts" (Acts 11:23).

JOURNAL: _____

_____

_____

———⊶∘⊷———

FRIDAY: Read Ezekiel 11:16-21. Meditate on God's Word and listen to what He has to say to you. Using the text as a guide, spend time in praise, confession and thanksgiving.

Pray for your country, to remember their "first love" and return to the Lord and His commands on which this nation was founded: Lord Jesus, You rebuked the church in Ephesus in Revelation 2:4 saying, "You have forsaken your first love." As I look around my country today I know that the same sad truth can be said of us! We have constructed idols of fame, wealth, sex, and success. We have become addicted to work, pleasure and self-gratification. Your Word warns that those "whose hearts are devoted to their vile images and detestable idols" (Ezekiel 11:21) will be brought down. So I pray, Lord Jesus, that You would give us "undivided hearts and put a new spirit" in us…remove from us our hearts of stone and give us hearts of flesh (Ezekiel 11:19). May unbelievers fall at Your feet for the first time, and may believers renew their dedication to You and You alone. May we love You with all our hearts, follow Your decrees and be careful to keep Your laws (Ezekiel 11:20). Then we can declare, "We are His people, and He is our God!" and take refuge in Your unfailing love for us!

JOURNAL: _____

_____

_____

SATURDAY: A Day of Application

Read Revelation 3:15-16 and I Samuel 7:3-4.

Are you guilty of being "lukewarm" in your devotion to the Lord?

_____

Do you want to "return to the Lord with all your heart"?

_____

If so, confess your complacency and worship of others "gods" as sin, and ask the Lord for forgiveness:

_____

Think back to the moment of your salvation and ask the Lord to remind you of that "first love" you had for Him. Recommit yourself to Him, praying that you would "love the Lord your God, listen to His voice, and hold fast to Him. For the Lord is your life!" (Deuteronomy 30:20).

Write out your prayer here:

_____

_____

If you realize that you have never experienced salvation and accepted Jesus as Lord and Savior, today would be the perfect day to begin that "love relationship" with Him! See Week 21 for help on how to do it.

SUNDAY: A Day of Praise

Read Romans 8:35-39.

Praise God that nothing can separate you from His love!

WRITE OUT YOUR PRAYER OF PRAISE HERE:

_____

_____

_____

CHECK YOURSELF! WRITE YOUR MEMORY VERSE HERE:

_____

_____

Standing Up to Satan

"Be self-controlled and alert. Your enemy the devil prowls around like a roaring lion looking for someone to devour. Resist him, standing firm in the faith, because you know that your brothers throughout the world are undergoing the same kind of sufferings"
(I Peter 5:8-9).

THE WRESTLING MATCH

My boys love wrestling with their daddy. Now, as a female who does not enjoy getting punched or thrown on the sofa, I truly don't see the appeal. In fact, when the wrestling ensues I usually retreat to a corner of the den, watching nervously for the first "accident" to happen. Because now that the boys are bigger, someone is going to end up getting hurt. They always do... it's just part of the game. But when they were little, before they were strong enough to do too much harm to each other, it was actually quite amusing to watch their play. The boys would take places along the sectional couch, waiting for their turn and watching for an opportunity to attack. My husband would stand with his feet firmly planted, and when they threw their little bodies against his chest, they would literally bounce off as if they had hit a wall, giggling endlessly as they fell to the padded ottoman below. My husband rarely wavered as they tirelessly hurled themselves against him again and again. Standing firm and prepared for their attack, he was ready for whatever the boys had in mind.

God's Word gives us this strong warning: "Be self-controlled and alert. Your enemy the devil prowls around like a roaring lion looking for someone to devour. Resist him, standing firm in the faith, because you know that your brothers throughout the world are undergoing the same kind of sufferings" (I Peter 5:8-9). It honestly terrifies me to think that my enemy is walking around, seeking to devour me, my husband, or my children. But praise the Lord that greater is He that is in me, "than the one who is in the world" (I John 4:4)! As a child of God I do not have to be afraid of the enemy, but I do need to be prepared so that <u>when</u> he attacks, I will be able to stand firm. The keys to victory are contained in this passage from I Peter: self-control, being alert, resistance, and standing firmly in the faith.

My husband and I play around with each other sometimes when we do not like what the other person is saying. We will put our hands over our ears and start humming or making some type of noise, thereby blocking out the words we do not want to hear. Usually done in jest, we are still giving a very clear signal that we don't want to hear what the other person has to say! In the same way, we must resist the lies, taunts, and accusations of the enemy. We can refuse to listen to him or allow him to knock us down by standing firm like a brick wall in the truth of God's Word. We must not allow anything to dull our consciousness or steal control of our minds, but be fully yielded to the control of the Holy Spirit within us. And we must stand firm in the faith, trusting God's promises and drawing on the prayers and support of fellow believers to keep us strong.

"Submit yourselves, then, to God. Resist the devil, and he will flee from you" (James 4:7). May we force our enemy to "tuck tail and run" because we are standing firm in the Lord!

Memory Verse:
"Be self-controlled and alert. Your enemy the devil prowls around like a roaring lion looking for someone to devour. Resist him, standing firm in the faith"
(I Peter 5:8-9b).

MONDAY: Read Ephesians 6:10-18. Meditate on God's Word and listen to what He has to say to you. Using the text as a guide, spend time in praise, confession and thanksgiving.

Pray for yourself, to be fully armed so that you can stand firmly against the devil's schemes: Father God, this passage reminds us that when we face difficulty in this world, our struggle is not against other people, "but against the rulers...authorities...powers of this dark world and against the spiritual forces of evil in the heavenly realms" (Ephesians 6:12). The devil may attack, but he is no match for <u>You</u> – the all-powerful, all-mighty God! Thank you for providing your children with the armor necessary to fight back and stand our ground when the day of evil comes. Please help me to stand firm with the belt of truth buckled around my waist, the breastplate of righteousness in place, and my feet fitted with the readiness that comes from the Gospel of peace. When the evil one shoots his flaming arrows at me, trying to injure me with lies, persecution, and even attacks from other people, may I be ready to extinguish them with my shield of faith. And after putting on all of my protective armor, remind me to fight back with my sword of the Spirit, striking my adversary with the truth of Your Word (Ephesians 6:14-18)!

JOURNAL: _____

_____

_____

TUESDAY: Read Revelation 12:7-12. Meditate on God's Word and listen to what He has to say to you. Using the text as a guide, spend time in praise, confession and thanksgiving.

Pray for your husband, to firmly resist when Satan attacks: Lord Jesus, I am so thankful that the last chapter of Your book has already been written and we know how it will all end. "For the accuser of our brothers, who accuses them before our God day and night, has been hurled down" (Revelation 12:10b). Never to accuse again, Satan will be defeated and the heavens will rejoice! I pray that this certainty will give my husband the strength and fortitude he needs to stand strong in the face of opposition today. May he remember that he can overcome his enemy "by the blood of the Lamb and by the word of [his] testimony" (Revelation 12:11a). I pray that he will clearly see Your saving power in his own life and testify before his accuser of Your goodness and grace. When he is weak and no longer able to fight his enemy alone, please bring seasoned saints across his path to encourage him and remind him of truth. Whenever he senses the enemy creeping in on his thoughts with lies and deception, urge my husband to rebuke him just as You did: "Get behind me, Satan!" (Mark 8:33).

JOURNAL: _____

_____

_____

WEDNESDAY: Read Psalm 20:1-9. Meditate on God's Word and listen to what He has to say to you. Using the text as a guide, spend time in praise, confession and thanksgiving.

Pray for those in your household, to call out to the Lord for strength to stand firm in the faith: Father God, in addition to daily arming ourselves for battle and claiming the blood of Jesus when Satan attacks, this passage reminds us that we must ask You for help. When we do, You <u>will</u> answer from Your holy heaven with the saving power of Your right hand (Psalm 20:6)! When we call out to You it proves that we trust You. "Some trust in chariots and some in horses, but we trust in the name of the Lord our God" (Psalm 20:7). Please forgive us when we look elsewhere for help. Show us clearly when we are trusting in our own forms of "chariots and horses" in order to resist our enemy. I pray that we would never allow our own self-sufficiency, human effort, and even denial to bring us to our knees and fall, but that we would "rise up and stand firm" (Psalm 20:8) in You. How grateful I am that I need not fear: "For the Lord your God moves about in your [household] to protect you and to deliver your enemies to you" (Deuteronomy 23:14a).

JOURNAL: _____

_____

_____

THURSDAY: Read I Corinthians 10:1-13. Meditate on God's Word and listen to what He has to say to you. Using the text as a guide, spend time in praise, confession and thanksgiving.

Pray for your children, to listen to instruction and stand firm in the faith: Lord, there is so much truth in the saying, "With age, comes wisdom." How many times did I strike out on my own in my youth, truly believing that I didn't need help or advice from anyone else, only to fall flat on my face? Scripture says, "So, if you think you are standing firm, be careful that you don't fall!" (I Corinthians 10:12). I'm so thankful that no matter how the enemy attacks my children – whether through temptation, internal struggles with their own flesh, or the external struggles with other people – You promise to provide a way out so that they can stand up under it (I Corinthians 10:13). But they must be receptive to teaching in order to stand strong and avoid failure. Oh Father, impress it on my heart that praying for my children is serious business! I must fight back against the enemy for my children, just as a lion would fight for her cubs! May You find me "always wrestling in prayer" for them, so that they "may stand firm in all the will of God, mature and fully assured" (Colossians 4:12).

JOURNAL: _____

_____

_____

———≈◊≈———

FRIDAY: Read II Thessalonians 2:13-3:5. Meditate on God's Word and listen to what He has to say to you. Using the text as a guide, spend time in praise, confession and thanksgiving.

Pray for your pastor and the members of your church, to stand firmly united against the evil one: Father God, thank you for choosing just the right pastor to lead my church and for hand-picking each and every member. Thank you for allowing each one of us to "share in the glory of our Lord Jesus Christ" (II Thessalonians 2:14) and be an active member of Your church. May we be found faithful to "stand firm and hold to the teachings" (II Thessalonians 2:15) of Your Word, for by them we

311

find our Source of strength. When others see our church may they see a united body "standing firm in one spirit, contending as one man for the faith of the gospel without being frightened in any way by those who oppose us" (Philippians 1:27-28). In times of trouble, remind us by Your Spirit that we serve the One Who is faithful, and He will strengthen and protect us from the evil one (II Thessalonians 3:3). No matter what happens, may we give ourselves fully to the work of the Lord, because we know that our labor in the Lord is not in vain (I Corinthians 15:58).

JOURNAL: _____

_____

_____

SATURDAY: A Day of Application

Read Ephesians 6:10-18 again.

Name one area where you feel like you are struggling to stand firm and resist your enemy:

_____

Make this area of struggle a matter of prayer. Whenever it surfaces, "pray in the Spirit on all occasions with all kinds of prayers and requests" (Ephesians 6:18).

Using this passage from Ephesians as a guide, mentally put on each piece of your armor:

- Belt of truth
- Breastplate of righteousness
- Feet fitted with the readiness that comes from the gospel of peace
- Shield of faith
- Helmet of salvation

Now, take up your sword of the Spirit, which is the Word of God, and fight back!

Write out your prayer here:

_____

_____

_____

_____

SUNDAY: A Day of Praise

Read Psalm 93:1-5.

Praise God that His throne is firmly established and His statues will stand firm forever!

WRITE OUT YOUR PRAYER OF PRAISE HERE:

_____

_____

_____

CHECK YOURSELF! WRITE OUT YOUR MEMORY VERSE HERE:

_____

_____

313

Generosity

"No man should appear before the Lord empty-handed: Each of you must bring a gift in proportion to the way the Lord your God has blessed you" (Deuteronomy 16:16b-17).

TO WHOM MUCH IS GIVEN, MUCH IS TO BE REQUIRED

I am blessed to come from a long line of generous givers. My grandfather was one such man. He always picked up the bill when we went out to dinner, passed out generous checks at Christmas time, and every time I went to visit he would press a $20 bill in my hand for "gas money." But he wasn't just generous with those in our family....he was known all over town for his generosity, and from the time I was a young girl I can remember people coming to his doorstep asking for help. My grandfather was always ready to give out a loan, often times with the full understanding that the money would never be repaid. He owned a good bit of land in the small Mississippi town where they lived, and he allowed others to build houses or put mobile homes on his land, completely free of charge.

My parents have upheld this example of giving. They taught my sister and me to tithe as soon as we started earning money of our own, and they are always willing to support the efforts of their church and community. A giver to countless philanthropic organizations, my mother seems to have an "open wallet" policy, the first in line to buy anything anyone is selling to raise money for a good cause. My father works part-time in his retirement, and my mother says there are times that his earnings never make it in their bank account because my father just signs his check over to someone in need. A self taught mechanic and certified in air conditioning, he often spends hours repairing whatever is broken for friends and needy members of his church, refusing to accept payment for his services.

My parents and my grandparents all lived out God's command in Deuteronomy 16:16b-17: "No man should appear before the Lord empty-handed: Each of you must bring a gift in proportion to the way the Lord your God has blessed you." They knew they had been blessed by God and wanted to give back – both to the Lord through their tithes and offerings and also to those less fortunate than they were. I am thankful for these models of generosity that have spurred me on in my own giving. But a recent encounter challenged me to examine just how "proportionate" my gifts actually were! I was on a mission trip working in a church located in a trailer park community in the poorest county of our state. The pastor of that church had recently lost his regular job and his family of four was going through a hard time, living off of his wife's salary from working in a local factory. But seeing the need of a father and daughter in his church, the pastor went to the store and probably spent $10 or so to get them some food: a loaf of bread, a package of ham, a bag of chips, and even a large bottle of soda for the young girl. When I saw what he had done, all I could think was, "$10 would have been nothing for me to spend on lunch for someone in need, but it was a great act of sacrifice and love for that pastor." Out of his lack, he had given an abundance. What am I giving out of my plenty?

May I never appear before the Lord empty-handed, but always seek to be as generous to others as the Lord has been to me. After all, everything I have is His anyway. "Everything comes from You, and we have given You only what comes from Your hand" (I Chronicles 29:14b).

―――――――

Memory Verse:
"No man should appear before the Lord empty-handed: Each of you must bring a gift in proportion to the way the Lord your God has blessed you" (Deuteronomy 16:16b-17).

―――――――

MONDAY: Read Mark 12:41-44. Meditate on God's Word and listen to what He has to say to you. Using the text as a guide, spend time in praise, confession and thanksgiving.

315

Pray for yourself, to be a generous giver in proportion to the way you have been blessed: Father, I want to be the kind of "giver" who pleases You. I want to give as You direct me, not out of an unwilling heart, but out of a heart that is full of gratitude for all You have done for me. This story of the poor widow makes me wonder…what are You thinking as You watch me give, both to You and to those around me? Am I like those who only give "out of their wealth" (Mark 12:44)? Or am I willing to give even when there is little to spare? Shed Your revealing light on the conditions of my giving, showing me clearly what needs to change. Open my eyes to see the needs all around me, and prick my heart to give as you direct. Thank You for the examples of sacrificial giving that I have witnessed in others, which often spur me on toward love and good deeds (Hebrews 10:24). May the gifts I send to others be a "fragrant offering, an acceptable sacrifice, pleasing to God" (Philippians 4:18b) because they are sent out of a willing and generous heart.

JOURNAL: _____

_____

_____

———<><>———

TUESDAY: Read Deuteronomy 15:7-11. Meditate on God's Word and listen to what He has to say to you. Using the text as a guide, spend time in praise, confession and thanksgiving.

Pray for your husband, to be willing to give as the Lord directs and receive His blessings: Lord Jesus, my husband works so hard to earn a living for our family. Thank you for the work he does for us, day in and day out. As he receives his paycheck every week, may he not cling too tightly to his wages, but remember that "good will come to him who is generous and lends freely" (Psalm 112:5). You say in Your Word: "There will always be poor people in the land. Therefore I command you to be openhanded toward your brothers and toward the poor and needy" (Deuteronomy 15:11). This might be hard for my husband to do at times when he has worked tirelessly for his money, but remind him never to be "hardhearted or tightfisted toward a poor brother. Rather to be openhanded and freely lend him whatever he needs" (Deuteronomy

15:7b-8). May he listen to Your voice, and when You tell him to give, strengthen him to give generously and without a grudging heart. Then because of this, You Oh Lord, will bless him in all his work and in everything he puts his hand to (Deuteronomy 15:10).

JOURNAL: _____

_____

_____

WEDNESDAY: Read II Corinthians 9:6-15. Meditate on God's Word and listen to what He has to say to you. Using the text as a guide, spend time in praise, confession and thanksgiving.

Pray for those in your household, to be cheerful and generous givers: Heavenly Father, as my husband and I lead our family in this matter of giving, help us be examples of willingness and generosity. Your Word says, "Whoever sows sparingly will also reap sparingly, and whoever sows generously will also reap generously" (II Corinthians 9:6). Please give my husband and me the confidence in Your Word to "sow generously" so that our children can see Your Word fulfilled! They need to see us reach into our wallets and give to the needy around us, so remind us to involve them in the next opportunity. May we teach them that we cannot out-give You, so there is no reason to be stingy or selfish with our money. Forgive us if we ever give "reluctantly or under compulsion, for God loves a cheerful giver" (II Corinthians 9:7). May we live our lives before men so that they will testify that all our family "were devout and God-fearing; [we] gave generously to those in need and prayed to God regularly" (Acts 10:2). I pray that our generosity to others will always result in thanksgiving to You (II Corinthians 9:11).

JOURNAL: _____

_____

_____

THURSDAY: Read II Corinthians 8:1-15. Meditate on God's Word and listen to what He has to say to you. Using the text as a guide, spend time in praise, confession and thanksgiving.

Pray for your children to excel in the grace of giving: Lord Jesus, You are the Ultimate Giver, and I thank You for the gift of each one of my children! But I pray that my love and gratitude for them would not cause me to overindulge them where they develop an "entitlement attitude". Rather may I often remind them that every single blessing we have is a gift from Your hand and that Your generosity toward us is to be returned. I realize sometimes they think, "I don't have much, so how can I give anything?" Help me to teach them that just as You multiplied the offering of the little boy who was willing to share his two fish and five loaves, so You can multiply any offering they give. You are not nearly as impressed with the amount they give, but that they "give as much as they were able" (II Corinthians 8:3). "For if the willingness is there, the gift is acceptable according to what one has, not according to what he does not have" (II Corinthians 8:12). I pray that my children would view sharing with those in need as a privilege (II Corinthians 8:4), desiring to be Your instruments of giving in this hurting world.
JOURNAL: _____

_____

_____

FRIDAY: Read Malachi 3:6-12. Meditate on God's Word and listen to what He has to say to you. Using the text as a guide, spend time in praise, confession and thanksgiving.

Pray for those in your church, to be obedient to the Lord's command to tithe: Father God, Your command is crystal clear: "Be sure to set aside a tenth of all that your fields produce each year" (Deuteronomy 14:22). Not just when we have extra after the bills are paid, not just when we feel especially grateful for one of Your many blessings on our lives, but every time we receive a paycheck, the first 10% should be returned to You. After all, You are the One Who gave it to us in the first place. And when we do not, we literally "rob You". Your Word tells us: "Bring the whole tithe into the storehouse" (Malachi 3:10a)... not 1% or 5%, but **at least** 10% off the gross of what we are paid. "Test me in this," says the Lord Almighty, "and see if I will not throw open the floodgates of heaven and pour out so much blessing that you will not have room enough for it" (Malachi 3:10b). So I pray that my church family would be obedient to this command. May we faithfully give You the first and very best of what we have earned and willingly provide for our pastor and those who work in our church.

JOURNAL: _____

_____

_____

SATURDAY: A Day of Application

Read Matthew 6:1-4.

Are you obeying the Lord's command to tithe?

_____

Are you obeying the Lord's command to be openhanded toward the poor and needy?

_____

When you give do you give willingly, out of a thankful heart, or reluctantly, out of compulsion?

_____

If you have been disobedient in the area of giving, both back to the Lord and also to others, confess it as sin and ask the Lord's forgiveness:

_____

Thank God that you can never outgive Him! "Give, and it will be given to you. A good measure, pressed down, shaken together and running over, will be poured into your lap. For with the measure you use, it will be measured to you" (Luke 6:38). Ask the Lord to help you trust Him in this area of giving:

_____

_____

SUNDAY: A Day of Praise

Read John 3:16-18.

Praise God as the Ultimate Giver! He gave the most precious gift of all...He gave His one and only Son so that we may have eternal life.

WRITE OUT YOUR PRAYER OF PRAISE HERE:

_____

_____

_____

CHECK YOURSELF! WRITE OUT YOUR MEMORY VERSE HERE:

_____

_____

Respect for Authority

"Everyone must submit himself to the governing authorities, for there is no authority except that which God has established. The authorities that exist have been established by God"
(Romans 13:1).

"YOU'RE NOT THE BOSS OF ME!"

When my sister and I were young children, we would often try to tell the other one what to do. My mother said she could hear us arguing back and forth until one of us would finally announce, "You're not the boss of me!" Only two years apart in age, we both knew who was really in charge (mom and dad), and that we did not have to take orders from each other. But from that young age we understood the idea of authority – of having rule or power over someone else – and believe me, both of us wanted to have some. I was reminded of this fact when I had my own children, and one of them asked my husband and me if he could be "in charge of the bugs." At the tender age of 3 or 4, he already had the desire to be in command of something, even if it was only the fly swatter!

In this day and age, the idea of authority has gotten a bad rap. Understood as something to bucked and pushed against, young people are taught that they should not let anyone rule over them. Certainly, historical misuse of authority contributes to many of the reasons why people rebel against it. But when authority follows biblical guidelines it is meant to provide organization and a chain of command that ensure protection and well-being for those under its power. God's Word has much to say about the lines of authority and how they are to be played out in the home, the workplace, the church, and our government. Scripture clearly teaches that we are not to undermine or rebel against those in authority over us, but willingly subject ourselves to them. "Everyone must submit himself to the governing authorities, for there is no authority except that which God has established. The authorities that exist have been established by God" (Romans 13:1).

Our chief authority is Jesus Christ, Who is seated at God's "right hand in the heavenly realms, far above all rule and authority, power and dominion, and every title that can be given, not only in the present age but also in the one to come. And God placed all things under His feet and appointed Him to be head over everything for the church" (Ephesians 1:20b-22). As believers in Jesus Christ, we are under His authority. The question is, are we submitting to that authority in every area of our lives? In our personal relationships with the Lord, He is to be the one in charge, directing our every move. In our households, we are to be following the chain of command that He has set forth in His Word: children submitting to the authority of their parents, wives looking to their husbands as head of the household, and husbands answering for their households before the Lord. In the community, students are to respect those in authority over them at school, employees are to submit to bosses in the workplace, and constituents are to obey the law and follow the rules set forth by our government.

Huge disagreements revolve around these issues of authority today, but as God's people we must use His Word as our measuring stick in all things, including lines of authority. After all, "The authorities that exist have been established by God" (Romans 13:1b), and who are we to tell God what to do?

Memory Verse:
"Everyone must submit himself to the governing authorities, for there is no authority except that which God has established. The authorities that exist have been established by God" (Romans 13:1).

MONDAY: Read Colossians 1:15-20. Meditate on God's Word and listen to what He has to say to you. Using the text as a guide, spend time in praise, confession and thanksgiving.

Pray for yourself, to live in submission to the authority of Christ: I praise You, Lord Jesus, for You are supreme! The very image of the invisible God, all things were created by You and for You. You are before all things, and in You all things hold together (Colossians 1:16-17). What power, what authority, what reverence is due Your name! Rebuke me Lord, when I try to live outside of Your rightful authority on my life. Your Word is clear: "He is the head of the body, the church... so that in everything He might have the supremacy" (Colossians 1:18). You deserve to have first place in every single area of my life. In order to do that I must yield to Your authority and the authorities You have established for me. Show me where my flesh is getting in the way, demanding my rights and my desires at the expense of total submission to You. Forgive me, Lord Jesus, when as the old hymn says, "prone to wander, Lord I feel it; prone to leave the God I love." Out of love for You may I willingly submit to my husband, my boss, my government officials, or any other person You place in authority over me.

JOURNAL: _____

_____

_____

TUESDAY: Read I Peter 2:18-23. Meditate on God's Word and listen to what He has to say to you. Using the text as a guide, spend time in praise, confession and thanksgiving.

Pray for your husband, to submit to and respect the authorities God has placed over his life: Lord Jesus, You are our Perfect Example in all things. Even though "power and might are in Your hand, and no one can withstand You" (II Chronicles 20:6b), You willingly chose to submit to the Father's plan and entrust Yourself "to Him who judges justly" (I Peter 2:23b). How I pray that my husband would follow Your

Example and Your Word in submitting to those in authority over him. May he "realize that the head of every man is Christ" (I Corinthians 11:3) and yield to Your direction and leading for him and his family. May he submit himself to his bosses with all respect, "not only to those who are good and considerate, but also to those who are harsh" (I Peter 2:18). Help him to follow orders completely, deferring to their wishes even when he does not agree or benefit from doing so. For Your Word teaches, "But if you suffer for doing good and you endure it, this is commendable before God" (I Peter 2:20b). As he honors and respects Your authority may he be a model for his coworkers and family to follow.

JOURNAL: _____

_____

_____

WEDNESDAY: Read Ephesians 5:22-31. Meditate on God's Word and listen to what He has to say to you. Using the text as a guide, spend time in praise, confession and thanksgiving.

Pray for your marriage, that you would each do the work God has for you in your roles of husband and wife: Lord Jesus, how can I ever sufficiently thank You for loving me so much that You would give Yourself up for me? The only possible response to such a sacrificial gift is complete adoration and total surrender. So I submit myself afresh to Your will and Your direction in my life. As I read this much disputed text about submission, I am fully aware that it is my will, my pride, and my independence that sometimes hinder me from obeying You in this area. If my husband follows Your command to love his wife, "just as Christ loved the church and *gave Himself up for her*" (Ephesians 5:25), then his every action toward me will be honorable and trustworthy! Why would I not want to respect and "submit to my husband in everything" (Ephesians 5:24) if he only wants the best for me? Forgive us both when we follow the ways of this world, choosing selfishness and pride over love and submission. May I do my part to submit, and may my husband do his part to love, so that Your perfect plan can be accomplished in the life of our family.

JOURNAL: _____

_____

_____

———◦◦◦◦———

THURSDAY: Read I Peter 2:13-17. Meditate on God's Word and listen to what He has to say to you. Using the text as a guide, spend time in praise, confession and thanksgiving.

Pray for your children, to show proper respect to those in authority over them: Father God, I remember as a child how I disliked being told what to do! But as a parent, I can see that there is much safety and protection in being under the authority of another who has greater wisdom and experience. So please help my children understand that authority is not meant to "hold them back" but rather to "help them along". I pray that my children would be willing to submit themselves "for the Lord's sake to every authority instituted among men" (I Peter 2:13): first to You, and then to their parents, their teachers, their employers, their church leaders, and their government officials. May they heed Your command to: "Obey your leaders and submit to their authority...obey them so that their work will be a joy, not a burden, for that would be of no advantage to you" (Hebrews 13:17). As they submit, may they not do it critically or dishonorably but with an attitude of respect. "Show proper respect for everyone: love the brotherhood of believers, fear God, honor the king" (I Peter 2:17).

JOURNAL: _____

_____

_____

———◦◦◦◦———

FRIDAY: Read Romans 13:1-7. Meditate on God's Word and listen to what He has to say to you. Using the text as a guide, spend time in praise, confession and thanksgiving.

Pray for those in your country, to have a renewed sense of respect for and submission to authority: Father, it troubles me to see such a lack of respect for authority today. This is certainly a learned behavior, acquired over years of false teaching that promotes "do what you want and to heck with anybody who doesn't like it!" Your Word teaches that anyone "who rebels against the authority is rebelling against what God has instituted, and those who do so will bring judgment on themselves" (Romans 13:2). How I pray that we would not rebel against authority and incur Your judgment, but pray for those "in authority so that we may live peaceful and quiet lives in all godliness and holiness" (I Timothy 2:2). Oh Father, give us a renewed sense of right and wrong in this nation. We must obey the law, drive the speed limit, pay taxes, follow the rules established for us by our elected officials, etc, with honor and respect at all times. Impress on each one of us that it is for our own good that we "submit to the authorities, not only because of possible punishment but also because of conscience" (Romans 13:5).

JOURNAL: _____

_____

_____

SATURDAY: A Day of Application

Read Titus 3:1-2.

Has the Lord convicted you this week of refusing to submit to His authority?

Of refusing to submit to any of the authorities He has established for you? At home, at work, out in the community?

As you deal with those in authority over you, are you disrespectful in any way?

_____

If so, confess these as sin, and ask the Lord's forgiveness:

_____

Aren't you glad that the Lord has "authority on earth to forgive sins" (Matthew 9:6)?!

Thank the Lord for the authorities He has placed in your life. Make a renewed commitment to respectfully submit to those authorities and to pray for them. Write out your prayer here:

_____

SUNDAY: A Day of Praise

Read Matthew 28:18 & I Peter 3:22.

Praise the Lord that He is Supreme in authority – everyone and everything else is in submission to Him!

WRITE OUT YOUR PRAYER OF PRAISE HERE:

_____

_____

CHECK YOURSELF! WRITE YOUR MEMORY VERSE HERE:

_____

_____

WEEK FORTY-SIX
Transformed, Not Conformed

"Therefore, I urge you, brothers, in view of God's mercy, to offer your bodies as living sacrifices, holy and pleasing to God – this is your spiritual act of worship. Do not conform any longer to the pattern of this world, but be transformed by the renewing of your mind. Then you will be able to test and approve what God's will is – His good, pleasing and perfect will" (Romans 12:1-2).

OUT WITH THE OLD, IN WITH THE NEW!

I am a different person now that I am saved than I was before I gave my heart to Christ. I have different desires, different thoughts, different actions, and different reactions. Was a complete transformation immediate? No, but a new creation was. II Corinthians 5:17 says, "Therefore, if anyone is in Christ, he is a new creation; the old has gone, the new has come!" When I asked Jesus to be Lord and Savior of my life, He made me a new creation, but He also gave me a new mandate: refuse to be like this world any longer and strive to be like Him instead. Romans 12:1-2 says, "Therefore, I urge you, brothers, in view of God's mercy, to offer your bodies as living sacrifices, holy and pleasing to God – this is your spiritual act of worship. Do not conform any longer to the pattern of this world, but be transformed by the renewing of your mind. Then you will be able to test and approve what God's will is – His good, pleasing and perfect will." I must refuse to conform to the world, choosing instead the path of continual transformation to look more and more like Christ. In order to do that I must give the Lord complete access to my life, allowing the Holy Spirit to renew my mind, day by day, by the transforming power of His Word.

As much as I long for the transforming power of God's Word in my own life, I desire it all the more in the lives of my children. As the parents, we are the ones who are responsible for teaching God's Word to our children….not the pastor, not the Sunday School teacher, and not the Vacation Bible School worker. Sure, it is wonderful to have these godly Christian workers come along side us, but Scripture is clear: "Fix these words of mine in your hearts and minds; tie them as symbols on your hands and bind them on your foreheads. Teach them to your children, talking about them when you sit at home and when you walk along the road, when you lie down and when you get up" (Deuteronomy 11:18-19). The text says, "Teach them to your children"... that is speaking to you, fellow parent. It is your responsibility to teach your child to hide God's Word in his heart so that he will not sin against Him (Psalm 119:11). This passage in Deuteronomy tells us to make God's Word part of our ongoing daily conversation with our children. Then, as we "walk along the road of life," we can deal with worldly issues as they arise. We can tell our children about our own struggles with worldliness and testify to God's transforming power in us. We can lovingly point out sinful areas in their lives and pray with our children, asking God to help them turn their backs on the pull of this world. As we set aside some time every day to read Scripture with our children, they will grow up seeing God's Word as not only important but necessary for their lives. And all the while, we can cling to God's promise in Isaiah 55:11 that His Word "will not return empty," but will accomplish what He desires in transforming both us and our children.

To look less like this old sinful world and more like our Lord Jesus Christ…it really can happen with the transforming power of the Word of God!

———⊷∞⊶———

Memory Verse:
"Do not conform any longer to the pattern of this world, but be transformed by the renewing of your mind. Then you will be able to test and approve what God's will is – His good, pleasing and perfect will" (Romans 12:2).

———⊷∞⊶———

MONDAY: Read Romans 12:1-2. Meditate on God's Word and listen to what He has to say to you. Using the text as a guide, spend time in praise, confession and thanksgiving.

Pray for yourself, to welcome God's transforming power on your life: Father, in reading this passage I understand that just as Jesus offered His body as a Living Sacrifice in obedience to You, so You want me to offer my body as a living sacrifice in obedience to You. Daily You ask that I choose to die to self, and as an act of my will refuse to "conform any longer to the pattern of this world" (Romans 12:2). But it is up to me to allow You to "renew my mind" by getting in Your Word every day. Oh, how I want to be transformed more and more into the image of Your precious Son, Jesus! When Your transforming work in my body makes me uncomfortable, may I not resist, knowing that "inwardly [I am] being renewed day by day" (II Corinthians 4:16). I don't want to be fooled by the materialism and "me-first" attitude of this world, so please help me to truly understand that "godliness with contentment is great gain" (I Timothy 6:6). May the lures of this world with all of its temptations lose their attractiveness to me, and may Your righteousness be my goal.

JOURNAL: _____

_____

_____

TUESDAY: Read Matthew 16:21-28. Meditate on God's Word and listen to what He has to say to you. Using the text as a guide, spend time in praise, confession and thanksgiving.

Pray for your husband, to follow God and deny himself: Oh Lord Jesus, may my husband recognize when Satan and this world mean to be a stumbling block to him. This world we live in is full of Satan's lies that say money, fame, and self-gratification will bring happiness and peace. How I pray that my husband would not be deceived by these empty promises! "What good will it be for a man if he gains the whole world, yet forfeits his soul?" (Matthew 16:26). Please help him, Lord, any time he struggles with the temptations of this world. May the things of God be heavy on his mind and not the things of men (Matthew 16:23). I pray that he will learn to "take captive every thought to make it obedient to Christ" (II Corinthians 10:5), so that Your Holy Spirit can show him when he has gotten his eyes off of You and onto this world. May he put to death any fleshly tendency that challenges Your rightful authority on his life and respond to Your call to "deny himself and take up his cross and follow [You]" (Matthew 16:24).

JOURNAL: _____

_____

_____

WEDNESDAY: Read Deuteronomy 11:16-21. Meditate on God's Word and listen to what He has to say to you. Using the text as a guide, spend time in praise, confession and thanksgiving.

Pray for those in your household, to worship God and Him alone: Heavenly Father, this passage begins with a warning: "Be careful, or you will be enticed to turn away and worship other gods and bow down before them" (Deuteronomy 11:16). The other gods of this world are endless, and the god of "self" tops the list: living for self, pleasing self, and putting self before others. But if we make it our goal to concentrate on You, our focus will become less on self and what we want, and more on You and what You want. That is why You instruct us to fix Your Words in our hearts and minds, to teach them to our children, and to talk about them continually (Deuteronomy 11:18-19). May my husband and I take this command very seriously, embracing our responsibility as parents and being careful in teaching our children. Please open our eyes to opportunities to share Your Word in everyday matters. May our home always be a safe haven where our children and our guests can "come out from (this world) and be separate" (II Corinthians 6:17).

JOURNAL: _____

_____

_____

THURSDAY: Read Colossians 3:1-11. Meditate on God's Word and listen to what He has to say to you. Using the text as a guide, spend time in praise, confession and thanksgiving.

Pray for your children, to look like Christ rather than the world: Lord Jesus, thank You for these children that You have given me to raise up for Your kingdom. I have such a desire for them to be godly individuals, not just as adults, but even now in childhood and adolescence. The lure of this world is so strong that they often resist any attempts to shelter them from ungodly things, seeing the things of this world as more fun and inviting. How I pray that You would give them the desire to "set [their] minds on things above, not on earthly things" (Colossians 3:2). May they choose to look like You, rather than this world, and "put to death" whatever belongs to the earthly nature: sexual immorality, impurity, lust, evil desires and greed (Colossians 3:5). My children have a choice to make every day, just as I do, to take off the old self with its practices and "put on the new self, which is being renewed in knowledge in the image of its Creator" (Colossians 3:10). Please strengthen them for this task, and let not their hearts "be drawn to what is evil, to take part in wicked deeds with men who are evildoers" (Psalm 141:4).
JOURNAL: _____

_____

_____

FRIDAY: Read II Corinthians 3:18-4:7. Meditate on God's Word and listen to what He has to say to you. Using the text as a guide, spend time in praise, confession and thanksgiving.

Pray for your church, to not lose heart in the face of worldliness, but to reflect the Lord's glory all the more: Father God, it is so disheartening at times to see the wicked world in which we live. Sometimes we are tempted to just give up, seeing that "the god of this age has blinded the minds of unbelievers, so that they cannot see the light of the gospel of the glory of Christ" (II Corinthians 4:4). Father, help us not to give in to this ungodliness, but to stand up for the Gospel. May we, Your church, renounce "secret and shameful ways," never using deception or distorting Your Word (II Corinthians 4:2), but speaking the truth in love. By the power of Your Holy Spirit in us, transform us into Your likeness with ever increasing glory (II Corinthians 3:18) so that we might be lights that shine for You in this dark world. Please open the eyes that Satan has blinded and turn unbelievers "from darkness to light, and from the power of Satan to God, so that they may receive forgiveness of sins and a place among those who are sanctified by faith" in Christ Jesus (Acts 26:18).

JOURNAL: _____

_____

_____

SATURDAY: A Day of Application

Read Ephesians 4:22-24.

Ask God to reveal to you any way that you are still choosing to be "conformed to the pattern of this world":

_____

Repent of this as sin. As an act of your will, turn away from this area of worldliness, and "put off your old self, which is being corrupted by its deceitful desires; to be made new in the attitude of your minds; and to put on the new self, created to be like God in true righteousness and holiness" (Ephesians 4:24).

Write out your prayer of confession here, and ask God to transform your life in this area:

_____

_____

SUNDAY: A Day of Praise

Read I Peter 1:3-9.

Praise God that He is your Hope! Praise Him that He has given you "new birth into a living hope" (v.3) and He has the power to transform your life!

WRITE OUT YOUR PRAYER OF PRAISE HERE:

_____

_____

_____

CHECK YOURSELF! WRITE YOUR MEMORY VERSE HERE:

_____

_____

WEEK FORTY-SEVEN
Freedom from Fear

"So do not fear, for I am with you; do not be dismayed, for I am your God. I will strengthen you and help you; I will uphold you with my righteous right hand" (Isaiah 41:10).

GRASP HOLD OF HIS HAND

Fears. They come in all shapes and sizes, they can be rational or irrational, natural or unnatural, but they affect each and every one of us. Sometimes our fears are based on our own insecurities...we have been asked to do something, and the mere thought of it leaves us shaking in our shoes! Sometimes our fears center on the unknown...we cannot see what is ahead of us, and we are scared to take that first step of faith. And sometimes our fears center on something that is so big and so over-whelming that we literally feel incapacitated. I cannot imagine a more fearful situation than the one this woman faced in II Kings chapter 4...

The woman's husband was dead, and she was left alone to care for her two sons. Still fresh in her grief over her husband's death, this woman learned that her husband owed a creditor a large sum of money. Since she had no money to pay off her husband's debt, his creditor intended to come and take her two boys as his slaves. Afraid of losing her children in addition to her husband, the Bible tells us that the woman cried out to the prophet Elisha for help. Learning that the woman had nothing "except a little oil," Elisha told her to go around and ask the neighbors for all their empty jars. Once these had been gathered, Elisha instructed the woman to go inside her house, shut the door, and begin pouring her little bit of oil into all the jars she had collected. She followed his instructions, and only as the very last jar was filled did the oil stop flowing. Elisha then told the woman to sell the oil and pay her debts, and she and her sons would be able to live on what was left.

This story always makes me want to stand up and cheer over the incredible power and provision of our Lord! He took a seemingly impossible situation and provided an answer for this desperate woman in her time of fear. The Bible says, "For God hath not given us the spirit of fear; but of power, and of love, and of a sound mind" (II Timothy 1:7 KJV). The One Who loves us has the power to protect us, equip us, and take care of us. We do not have to succumb to our fears! Instead, we can reach out to God Almighty and accept the direction and peace He freely offers as we cast every care upon Him. And then we can stand back and watch His mighty power at work in each of our lives!

Since I married, I have noticed that on my husband's arm I don't give nearly as much thought to those things that would seem scary on my own. When I know that my husband is right there beside me, holding me by the hand, I feel much more safe and protected than I do alone. But sometimes he is not there...sometimes he is out-of-town, or away at work. And you know what? Even then I am not alone! My God is right there beside me... "So do not fear, for I am with you; do not be dismayed, for I am your God. I will strengthen you and help you; I will uphold you with my righteous right hand" (Isaiah 41:10). What precious promises are contained in this verse!

We have no reason to fear if the God of the Universe is at our side. And we have no reason to be afraid with His righteous right hand grasping our own for support and strength. So take hold, dear friend, and don't let go!

Memory Verse:
"So do not fear, for I am with you; do not be dismayed, for I am your God. I will strengthen you and help you; I will uphold you with my righteous right hand"
(Isaiah 41:10).

MONDAY: Read Psalm 34:1-7. Meditate on God's Word and listen to what He has to say to you. Using the text as a guide, spend time in praise, confession and thanksgiving.

Pray for yourself, to not succumb to your fears but to give them all to God: Oh Father, I come to You confessing the many times I have focused on my fears rather than on You. Forgive me when I refuse the peace You freely offer, clinging instead to my insecurities about myself or to fear of what might happen in the future. Truly, I want to "extol the Lord at all times" so that Your "praise will always be on my lips" (Psalm 34:1). As I focus on praise and thanksgiving, my fears just naturally subside in the reality of Your Presence and power! I claim Your Word that says, "I sought the Lord, and He answered me; He delivered me from all my fears" (Psalm 34:4). May my face be radiant with Your peace because I have looked to You rather than dwelling on my fears. Thank You for Your constant Presence and Your promise to uphold me with Your righteous right hand (Isaiah 41:10b). The next time something surfaces and I feel fear rising in my chest, may I boldly proclaim, "In God I trust; I will not be afraid. What can man do to me?" (Psalm 56:11).

JOURNAL: _____

_____

_____

⸺◦◦◦⸺

TUESDAY: Read Deuteronomy 1:19-36. Meditate on God's Word and listen to what He has to say to you. Using the text as a guide, spend time in praise, confession and thanksgiving.

Pray for your husband, to fearlessly follow the Lord and lead his family as God directs: Father God, what a living example we see in Caleb of someone who "followed the Lord wholeheartedly" (Deuteronomy 1:36). Because he was unafraid to obey You, even if it meant facing enemies and obstacles much greater and stronger than he, You declared that he would be allowed to enter the "good land" You had promised. How I pray that my husband would be a man like Caleb. May he never allow fear or discouragement to hold him back from following You, or be unwilling to go where You have directed and rebel against Your commands. Rather may he cling to Your Word that says, "Do not be terrified; do not be afraid of them. The Lord your God, who is going before you, will fight for you" (Deuteronomy 1:29-30). Thank You, Lord, that You will never lead my husband down the wrong pathway or abandon him when things get hard. Instead, You promise to do his fighting for him and even carry him "as a father carries his son" (Deuteronomy 1:31) when he is unable to stand on his own!

JOURNAL: _____

_____

_____

WEDNESDAY: Read II Chronicles 20:14-27. Meditate on God's Word and listen to what He has to say to you. Using the text as a guide, spend time in praise, confession and thanksgiving.

Pray for those in your household to live in joy, not fear, trusting in God to work on your behalf: Lord Jesus, sometimes it seems like everything is going wrong. There are problems at work, troubles at school, and even our home is not always the sanctuary I desire it to be! The "battle" we face on every side threatens to overwhelm us, drowning us in fear, worry and sleepless nights. In such times of anxiety and stress may we remember that it is through our praise and thanksgiving that You begin to work on our behalf. "As they began to sing and praise, the Lord set ambushes..." (II Chronicles 20:22). Instead of being paralyzed by fear we must choose to remember Your goodness and proclaim Your deliverance, even when we cannot see how things will turn out. Thank You that we can trust in You to "set ambushes" to protect the members of our family from attack and defeat. Thank you that we do not have to be afraid or discouraged. We can go out and face our enemies tomorrow, and You will be with us (II Chronicles 20:17b). I pray that each night when we lie down, we will not be afraid; when we lie down, our sleep will be sweet (Proverbs 3:24).

JOURNAL: _____

_____

_____

THURSDAY: Read Deuteronomy 31:1-8. Meditate on God's Word and listen to what He has to say to you. Using the text as a guide, spend time in praise, confession and thanksgiving.

Pray for your children, to experience freedom from their fears: Oh Father, there are so many scary things out there for a child! Being separated from mom and dad, facing a bully at school, and simple "fear of the unknown" can sometimes render a child completely helpless! I know that it is not Your will for my child to be afraid, so help me teach them to "say with confidence, "The Lord is my helper; I will not be afraid. What can man do to me?" (Hebrews 13:6). As they see me face my fears and run to You for help, it will set an example for them to do likewise. In this passage we see Joshua grow up to take Moses' place of leadership. In much the same way my children are growing up and taking on more responsibilities of their own. While this can be a liberating and growing experience, I know firsthand that it can also be quite scary and intimidating. I ask You to help them be strong and courageous, not afraid or terrified. May they take full confidence in Your Word which says, "The Lord your God goes with you; He will never leave you nor forsake you" (Deuteronomy 31:6).

JOURNAL: _____

_____

_____

FRIDAY: Read II Chronicles 32:1-23. Meditate on God's Word and listen to what He has to say to you. Using the text as a guide, spend time in praise, confession and thanksgiving.

Pray for your president, to look to the Lord when he is afraid and trust in His power as he leads our country: Heavenly Father, I pray that I would be faithful to lift our president up to You for strength, for wisdom, for protection, and for courage as he leads our nation. I am sure he is confronted daily with very difficult and frightening situations to handle. When his body has no rest, but is harassed at every turn – "conflicts on the outside, fears within" (II Corinthians 7:5), I pray that he would look to You for guidance in making decisions and so receive Your peace that passes all understanding. Just as King Hezekiah took all the precautions he could, I pray that our president would have the foresight he needs to fortify and reinforce our land today. Please place godly men and women in his inner circle so that when he consults with his officials and military staff, he would receive sound counsel in line with Your will for our country. May he know You, Lord Jesus, as his personal Lord and Savior, and may he be able to boldly say, "but with us is the Lord our God to help us and to fight our battles" (II Chronicles 32:8).

JOURNAL: _____

_____

_____

SATURDAY: A Day of Application

Read Deuteronomy 20:1-4.

Do you struggle with fears?

_____

What are the "horses and chariots" in your life that seem insurmountable and are keeping you in bondage to your fear?

_____

Find rest in the fact that the Lord promises to be with you! "Do not be fainthearted or afraid; do not be terrified or give way to panic before them. For the Lord your God is the One who goes with you to fight for you against your enemies to give you victory" (Deuteronomy 20:3b-4). Give these fears to the Lord and thank Him for His very sure promise of victory over them:

_____

SUNDAY: A Day of Praise

Read Psalm 46:1-11.

Praise God that He is your refuge! He is an ever present help when you are afraid.

"Therefore we will not fear, though the earth give way and the mountains fall into the heart of the sea" (Psalm 46:2).

"Be still, and know that I am God" (Psalm 46:10).

WRITE OUT YOUR PRAYER OF PRAISE HERE:

_____

_____

_____

CHECK YOURSELF! WRITE YOUR MEMORY VERSE HERE:

_____

_____

WEEK FORTY-EIGHT
Good Works

"Do not withhold good from those who deserve it, when it is in your power to act. Do not say to your neighbor, 'Come back later; I'll give it tomorrow' – when you now have it with you"
(Proverbs 3:27-28).

DIAPERS FOR FLANNEL SHEETS

How many times have I been too busy, too selfish, or just plain too uncaring to do a good deed for someone else? It is easy to think, "I have so much on my plate today, there is no possible way I can do something for someone else!" Or, "Someone else should take care of that need... it's really not my place. After all, I don't really know them that well." Or, "I was the one who helped last time...let someone else take a turn for a change!"

Almost daily, we are all presented with opportunities to "do good" for others. It might be an act of service, like cooking a meal for a sick family. It might be a gift of time, like volunteering to help out at church or school. Or it might just be an act of love, like a kind word to someone who is having a difficult day. The Bible says, "Let us not become weary in doing good, for at the proper time we will reap a harvest if we do not give up. Therefore, as we have opportunity, let us do good to all people, especially to those who belong to the family of believers" (Galatians 6:9-10). "As we have opportunity"...and the opportunities usually abound!

I have discovered that when I choose to "do good," God sometimes has a blessing in store for me as well. I might receive a card, or a hug, or a heartfelt thanks. But a recent encounter really had me thanking God for His goodness to bless me when I followed through on His command

342

to help another person. I had received an email asking for a donation of diapers for a single mother in need at my children's school. I remember thinking, "I don't even know this lady! Why would I be sent this message?" I planned to just ignore the request, but later that day when I was at the store, the email came back to my mind. As I began again to rationalize away my responsibility to help, God spoke Proverbs 3:27-28 clearly to my heart: "Do not withhold good from those who deserve it, when it is in your power to act. Do not say to your neighbor, 'Come back later; I'll give it tomorrow' – when you now have it with you." It was in the power of my hand to give, and I felt like God wanted me to give, so I placed a $20 package of diapers in my cart next to the $20 set of flannel sheets for which I had come. When I got to the checkout stand and the cashier told me how much I owed, it was only $24.02 for both items. I told her she must have made a mistake – that was not enough money. She showed me that the flannel sheets were a seasonal item and had been marked 90% off! The $20 sheets were now only $1.99! God had asked me to "do good," and He had blessed me in return.

Sometimes the Lord gives us a tangible blessing in exchange for our willingness to help others, but other times such acts go seemingly unnoticed. Either way, we can rest assured that God is pleased when we act in obedience to His directive to "do good". I love to hear His voice whisper to my spirit, "Well done, good and faithful servant" (Matthew 25:21). And that is possibly the best blessing of all.

Memory Verse:
"Do not withhold good from those who deserve it, when it is in your power to act. Do not say to your neighbor, 'Come back later; I'll give it tomorrow' – when you now have it with you"
(Proverbs 3:27-28).

MONDAY: Read Acts 10:24-38. Meditate on God's Word and listen to what He has to say to you. Using the text as a guide, spend time in praise, confession and thanksgiving.

Pray for yourself, asking God the Father to help you model His Son's example of doing good: Oh Father, thank you for giving us the perfect example in Jesus Christ of One Who "went around doing good" (Acts 10:38). Forgive me when I act selfishly, choosing to ignore the needs of those around me, while rationalizing that someone else should be responsible for that duty. Help me to resist such sin and obey Your command to "turn from evil and do good" (Psalm 34:14). Please be with me, just as You were with Jesus, filling me up with the power and presence of Your Holy Spirit, so that I might be poured out in service for You. I want to be like Your disciple Tabitha, "who was always doing good and helping the poor" (Acts 9:36). Open my eyes to see the many opportunities I have in my life to help someone in need. May I never be known for my selfishness, but rather earn a reputation for "good deeds, such as bringing up children, showing hospitality, washing the feet of the saints, helping those in trouble and devoting [my]self to all kinds of good deeds" (I Timothy 5:10).

JOURNAL: _____

_____

_____

TUESDAY: Read James 2:14-24. Meditate on God's Word and listen to what He has to say to you. Using the text as a guide, spend time in praise, confession and thanksgiving.

Pray for your husband, that he would desire to do good deeds, living out his faith by his actions: Lord Jesus, Your Word says that we prove our faith in You by our actions. Just as Abraham's "faith and actions were working together, and his faith was made complete by what he did" (James 2:22), so should our faith and actions work together. So I lift my husband up to You, praying that he would be a man "ready to do whatever is good" (Titus 3:1). If he sees a brother or sister without clothes and daily food, may he be willing to step in and provide as You direct. If he has an opportunity to give of his time, may he find joy in living out his faith in this way. If You ask him to do something very difficult, may he respond in obedience as Abraham did. Then, it will be "credited to him as righteousness," and he will be called Your friend (James 2:23). May I never begrudge the time or resources he feels led to give but support him to act as You direct. In all things may my husband be rich in good deeds, generous and willing to share. In this way he will lay up treasure for himself as a firm foundation for the coming age (I Timothy 6:18-19).

JOURNAL: _____

_____

_____

WEDNESDAY: Read Luke 6:27-36. Meditate on God's Word and listen to what He has to say to you. Using the text as a guide, spend time in praise, confession and thanksgiving.

Pray for your household, that you would obey God's command to do good, even to your enemies: Lord Jesus, I understand Your directive and really do desire to do good to those around me. But in all honesty I must admit that my flesh rises up against Your teachings in this passage. You tell us to bless those who curse us, pray for those who mistreat us, and turn the cheek when someone strikes us (Luke 6:28-29). Such ideas seem backward, crazy even, and the world around us laughs at such behavior. But Your Word points out that it is easy to love and do good to those who love us... so "what credit is that to you?" Even 'sinners' can do that (Luke 6:32)! You ask us to do the harder thing: to love our "enemies, do good to them, and lend to them without expecting to get anything back" (Luke 6:35). So please help us to do what You command. May my husband and I teach our children by example that we are to do to others as we would have them do to us (Luke 6:31), regardless of how they treat us. And when we do, our "reward will be great, and [we] will be sons of the Most High, because He is kind to the ungrateful and the wicked" (Luke 6:35).

JOURNAL: ____

____

____

THURSDAY: Read Ephesians 2:1-10. Meditate on God's Word and listen to what He has to say to you. Using the text as a guide, spend time in praise, confession and thanksgiving.

Pray for your children, to understand that salvation is through grace alone, but to realize their responsibility of doing good works: Father, thank you, thank you, thank you, that it is by GRACE that we are "saved, through faith – and this not from ourselves, it is the gift of God – not by works, so that no one can boast" (Ephesians 2:8-9). May I never be guilty of leading my children to believe that their works are what save them....they could never do enough to earn salvation and neither could I! Only by confessing their sins and placing their faith in You can they be guaranteed an eternity in heaven. Rather, may I show them that good works flow out of salvation – that a desire to do good to others results from a knowledge of all You have done for us. The eyes of my children are on me, so may I "set them an example by doing what is good" (Titus 2:7) at every turn. As they grow in their knowledge of You, may they understand that they are "God's workmanship, created in Christ Jesus to do good works, which God prepared in advance for [them] to do" (Ephesians 2:10). Instill in my children the desire to do good to others, thereby proving their love for You.

JOURNAL: ____

____

____

FRIDAY: Read Titus 3:1-15. Meditate on God's Word and listen to what He has to say to you. Using the text as a guide, spend time in praise, confession and thanksgiving.

Pray for your church, to take seriously the responsibility of helping those in need in your congregation and your community: Lord Jesus, thank You for Your kindness and love in saving us, not because of righteous things we have done, but because of Your mercy (Titus 3:5). Now in response to such great love, as those who have trusted in God, may we be careful to devote ourselves to doing what is good (Titus 3:8). May my church have a reputation in our city for doing everything we can to help others and seeing that they have everything they need (Titus 3:13). I pray that our church members would "consider how we may spur one another on toward love and good deeds" (Hebrews 10:24), so that it may be said we are doing more now than we did at first (Revelation 2:19). May each good deed have a domino effect throughout our entire congregation, motivating person after person to serve You by serving others. And may we "live such good lives among the pagans that, though they accuse [us] of doing wrong, they may see [our] good deeds and glorify God on the day He visits us" (I Peter 2:12).

JOURNAL: _____

_____

_____

SATURDAY: A Day of Application

Read Colossians 3:15-17.

Our good works are meant to point others to Jesus and bring glory to God. Are you guilty of "withholding good" when it is in your power to act? What are some of your excuses?

_____

_____

Pray and ask the Lord to forgive you if you are guilty in this area:

_____

Ask God to show you how you can glorify Him by "doing good" to someone this week.

Suggestions: Take care of a financial need for another person; Do yard work for a neighbor/single mom; Take a meal/groceries to someone in your church with a new baby; Volunteer at a homeless shelter; Babysit a friend's children for the afternoon.

Write down what you plan to do and then check it off when you have done it!

_____

_____

SUNDAY: A Day of Praise

Read Psalm 86:5-10.

Praise God that He is Good - virtuous, excellent, upright; God is essentially, absolutely and consummately good. His deeds are marvelous! (V.10)

WRITE OUT YOUR PRAYER OF PRAISE HERE:

_____

_____

CHECK YOURSELF! WRITE YOUR MEMORY VERSE HERE:

_____

_____

Being Prepared to Witness

"But in your hearts set apart Christ as Lord. Always be prepared to give an answer to everyone who asks you to give the reason for the hope that you have. But do this with gentleness and respect"
(I Peter 3:15).

ARE YOU PREPARED?

As a mom, I always want to be prepared to handle the needs of my family. I like to have band-aids, safety pins and a few extra dollars tucked away in my purse for anything unexpected that might come up while we are away from home. On Saturday nights I try to have all the church clothes laid out before bed, so that Sunday mornings go smoothly. If we decide on the spur of the moment that we need some chocolate chip cookies, I want to have all the ingredients on hand to whip up a batch. My mother taught me to have a well-stocked pantry in order to prepare meals for my family and even the last-minute dinner guest. I guess I do go a little overboard at times when my husband looks in the packed refrigerator and asks if I left anything on the shelves at the grocery store! By the way, can you really have too much toilet paper?

But when I am not prepared, I always feel a little disappointed in myself. "Why didn't I think ahead? I should have remembered to do that," I tell myself. And while these are just little things, things that won't be remembered even next month, there is one really big thing that we all need to be prepared to do. I Peter 3:15 says, "But in your hearts set apart Christ as Lord. Always be prepared to give an answer to everyone who asks you to give the reason for the hope that you have. But do this with gentleness and respect." God's Word tells me that I must be prepared to testify about my Lord and the hope I have in Him.

When I first understood this verse, God impressed on me the need to sit down and write out my own personal testimony. For several weeks I worked on this, describing what my life was like before I met Christ, my actual salvation experience, and how my life was different now that Jesus was my Lord and Savior. What a walk I took down memory lane as I recalled my many mistakes and my Lord's abundant grace! I marveled at the way God had lovingly taught me, as a father teaches and disciplines His children. I saw His divine hand on my life, putting people in place to train and encourage me. The process was not quick or easy, but later on when my Sunday School teacher asked me to share my testimony in class, I was already prepared to do it! The next thing God challenged me to do was to be prepared to share the Gospel along with my testimony. This included knowing and memorizing Scripture, such as verses from the book of Romans* that I could use to show others their separation from God and need for a Savior. It didn't take long for God to reveal very clearly that He wanted me to witness to a good friend. Even in all my nervousness, it was a joy to share with her the hope I have in Christ Jesus and see her give her life to Christ as well.

There are many things in life for which we should be prepared...let's not fail to be prepared in the most important thing. If someone were to "ask you to give an answer for the hope you have", would you be ready to give an account?

* Romans 3:23, Romans 5:8, Romans 6:23, Romans 10:9-10, Romans 10:13

Memory Verse:
"Always be prepared to give an answer to everyone who asks you to give the reason for the hope that you have" (I Peter 3:15).

MONDAY: Read John 4:27-42. Meditate on His Word and listen to what He has to say to you. Using the text as a guide, spend time in praise, confession and thanksgiving.

Pray for yourself, committing to be prepared to be a witness for Christ before others: Oh Father, sometimes it feels like my heart will almost burst with the knowledge of all You have done in me and for me. You have made such a wonderful difference in my life, giving me new desires, new attitudes, new priorities, and a new purpose. Your Word sums it up perfectly: "If anyone is in Christ, he is a new creation; the old has gone, the new has come" (II Corinthians 5:17)! Please help me not to feel overwhelmed by the idea of witnessing...it starts simply by telling others what You have done in my life! Rather, may I be so overwhelmed by Your love for me that I would be unable to stop myself from speaking to others about You. May I be like the Samaritan woman, urging the people to come and meet You for themselves. How I would love for others to believe in You because of my testimony (John 4:39). Open my eyes to see the fields ripe for harvest (John 4:35-36) and "enable Your servant to speak Your Word with great boldness" (Acts 4:29). May I take seriously Your command to "always be prepared" to show others the Way to eternal life.

JOURNAL: _____

_____

_____

TUESDAY: Read John 1:1-14, 29-34. Meditate on His Word and listen to what He has to say to you. Using the text as a guide, spend time in praise, confession and thanksgiving.

Pray for your husband, to fearlessly testify about the Lord: I praise You, Lord Jesus, as the Living Word, the One and Only, the Lamb of God, the True Light that shines in darkness! Thank you for the difference You make in our lives. As John the Baptist experienced You for himself, he was able to declare, "I have seen and I testify that this is the Son of God" (John 1:34). In like manner I pray that my husband will experience You personally and be a witness who testifies concerning the light of Jesus Christ so that through him others might believe (John 1:7).

May he be so aware of Your Presence, so grateful for Your blessings on his life, that he must speak of Your goodness to those around him. Please give my husband opportunities to share Your love with his co-workers, clients, and others he deals with on a daily basis. Whenever he opens his mouth, give him Your Words so that he "will fearlessly make known the mystery of the gospel" (Ephesians 6:19). Then, he will shine like a star in the universe as he holds out the word of life (Philippians 2:15-16) to those around him.

JOURNAL: _____

_____

_____

WEDNESDAY: Read Acts 18:1-13. Meditate on His Word and listen to what He has to say to you. Using the text as a guide, spend time in praise, confession and thanksgiving.

Pray for your family, to use your home as a tool for serving others and sharing the Gospel at every opportunity: Father God, I cannot thank You enough for my family and my home. Like Crispus, may my husband and I with our entire household believe in the Lord (Acts 18:8) and be saved. And like Paul, may we too try to persuade others to worship God (Acts 18:13). Give us the desire to first show others the love of Christ by helping with their physical needs; then, we will be able to take the next step by sharing how Christ can meet their spiritual needs. Help us not to be afraid, but keep on speaking (Acts 18:9) even when our message is not well received. Anytime a visitor comes to our home, I pray that You would open a door for our message, so that we may proclaim the mystery of Christ. How I pray that we would proclaim it clearly, as we should! May we be wise in the way we act toward outsiders, making the most of every opportunity. And let our conversation be always full of grace, seasoned with salt, so that we may know how to answer everyone (Colossians 4:3-6).

JOURNAL: _____

_____

_____

—◦◦◦—

THURSDAY: Read I Thessalonians 2:1-13. Meditate on His Word and listen to what He has to say to you. Using the text as a guide, spend time in praise, confession and thanksgiving.

Pray for your children, to have a burden to share Christ in the face of opposition: Oh Father, I love my children so much! How I want them to grow up to know You, to love You wholeheartedly and to be witnesses for You. But I know all too well that it is not always easy to share the Gospel with others. Quite the contrary, Your servants have suffered and endured insult and opposition for being faithful to do so. As my husband and I teach our children to testify about Christ, may we remind them that it is always better to please You rather than man (I Thessalonians 2:4b). Thank You that we can trust the Word of God, which is at work in our children who believe (I Thessalonians 2:13). As they spend more and more time in Your Word, give them a burden to see the lost come to You. I pray that my children would boldly declare: "I am not ashamed of the Gospel, because it is the power of God for the salvation of everyone who believes" (Romans 1:16). May my husband and I be ever faithful to bend the knee in prayer for our children, all the while encouraging, comforting and urging them to live lives worthy of You (I Thessalonians 2:12).

JOURNAL: _____

_____

—◦◦◦—

FRIDAY: Read II Timothy 4:1-8. Meditate on His Word and listen to what He has to say to you. Using the text as a guide, spend time in praise, confession and thanksgiving.

Pray for your pastor, to be a faithful ambassador for Christ: I lift my pastor up to You, Father God, thanking You for his leadership and service to my church. With the burden of so many things pressing on him, I ask that You help him stay focused on what is most important. Help him to be faithful at our church to "preach the Word; be prepared in season and out of season; correct, rebuke and encourage – with great patience and careful instruction" (II Timothy 4:2). When he grows weary and tired in his work, remind him of the great importance of his calling...he is therefore Christ's ambassador, as though God were making His appeal through him (II Corinthians 5:20). Please help my pastor to keep his head "in all situations, endure hardship, do the work of an evangelist," and discharge all the duties of his ministry (II Timothy 4:5). May he be able to stand before You one day and declare, "I have fought the good fight, I have finished the race, I have kept the faith" (II Timothy 4:7).

JOURNAL: _____

_____

_____

SATURDAY: A Day of Application

Read Romans 10:13-15.

We have learned this week that God tells us to be prepared to witness about our new life in Christ and share the Good News with others. "How can they believe in the One of whom they have not heard?" (Romans 10:14). Ask God to show you who you can witness to this week. Write his/her name here:

_____

Pray that you would "not be ashamed to testify about our Lord" (II Timothy 1:8), knowing that Jesus said, "Whoever acknowledges Me before men, the Son of Man will also acknowledge him before the angels of God" (Luke 12:8). Pray that God would give you both a burden and a boldness to share with this person:

_____

If you are not ready to "give an account of the hope that is within you," today is the day to get prepared! Spend some time writing out your own personal testimony. Things to think about would include:

I. Your salvation experience
- What your life was like before you met Jesus
- How/when you realized you needed Jesus
- How you committed your life to Jesus
- How you are different now that Jesus is Your Lord
II. Your personal experiences with the Lord
- What has God taught you through times of waiting or doubt, through failure or disappointment, through answered prayer and blessing, through illness or healing, through criticism or discipline, through other believers?
- In what way is God dealing with you right now?
- For what issues has God given you a passion to speak out or a desire to encourage others?
III. How to experience salvation through Jesus Christ
- Refer to the lesson on "Salvation" in Week 21 for a simple outline for sharing the Gospel
- For more detailed information on salvation and witnessing, visit these websites:
1) Campus Crusade for Christ at www.campuscrusade.org. - "Four Spiritual Laws"
2) Evangelism Explosion International at info@eeinternational.org. – "You Can Share the Gospel"

Your Testimony (use extra paper as needed):

_____

_____

_____

_____

_____

_____

_____

_____

Well done, good and faithful servant! Now that you are ready, pray that you would "be active in sharing your faith, so that you will have a full understanding of every good thing we have in Christ" (Philemon 1:6).

SUNDAY: A Day of Praise

Read John 14:1-6.

Praise Jesus as the Way, the Truth and the Life! Praise Him that He is preparing a place for you in heaven at this very moment!

WRITE OUT YOUR PRAYER OF PRAISE HERE:

_____

_____

_____

CHECK YOURSELF! WRITE YOUR MEMORY VERSE HERE:

_____

_____

Accepting Correction and Discipline

"No discipline seems pleasant at the time, but painful. Later on, however, it produces a harvest of righteousness and peace for those who have been trained by it" (Hebrews 12:11).

OUT OF LOVE, FOR OUR GOOD

I've been putting off this lesson on correction and discipline for months. I've wrestled with it, I've considered leaving it out, and I've prayed repeatedly that God would show me how to handle it. The pure and simple fact of the matter is this: no one likes to be disciplined. No one enjoys being corrected or told that they are doing something wrong. Especially me! But while I have been hesitant to write on this topic and would really rather not, the Lord has "corrected me" and impressed on my heart that it is too important of an issue to neglect.

The book of Hebrews, chapter 12, sheds much light on this delicate topic, beginning with God's motivation in discipline. "My son, do not make light of the Lord's discipline, and do not lose heart when He rebukes you, because the Lord disciplines those He loves, and He punishes everyone He accepts as a son" (Hebrews 12:5-6). When God disciplines us, dear friends, it is always out of LOVE! In addition, "Our fathers disciplined us for a little while as they thought best; but God disciplines us for our good, that we may share in His holiness" (Hebrews 12:10). God always has our best interest at heart, and everything He does in our lives is for our GOOD! Just as the loving parent is motivated to discipline her child for running out in the street, not wanting the child to come to harm, so God disciplines us <u>out of love for our good</u>!

Now that being said, I agree that discipline is not fun! "No discipline seems pleasant at the time, but painful. Later on, however, it produces a harvest of righteousness and peace for those who have been trained by it" (Hebrews 12:11). An athlete must submit himself to physical discipline in order to develop endurance, perseverance and strength. Only through rigorous and often painful training can he improve his performance and produce better results. In the same way, God uses discipline in our lives to "train us up" into the godly men and women He longs for us to be. He wants our lives to bear the fruit of righteousness and peace in ever-increasing amounts. So when He sees ungodly attitudes and worldly behaviors in our lives, He rebukes and disciplines us so that we can correct them.

Sometimes God corrects His children as they read His Word. "All Scripture is God-breathed and is useful for teaching, rebuking, correcting and training in righteousness" (II Timothy 3:16). Sometimes God corrects His children through His Holy Spirit. "You gave Your good Spirit to instruct them" (Nehemiah 9:20). Sometimes God uses other believers to speak truth into our lives that we desperately need to hear. "By Your Spirit You admonished them through Your prophets" (Nehemiah 9:30). And when He does, we have a choice to make. Will we react in anger or indignation? Will we respond by pouting and feeling sorry for ourselves? Will we stubbornly refuse His correction, thereby inviting His discipline on our lives? Or will we humbly receive His correction and allow ourselves to be trained by it? The choice is ours.

God always works "out of love, for our good." We would do well to remember it.

Memory Verse:

"No discipline seems pleasant at the time, but painful. Later on, however, it produces a harvest of righteousness and peace for those who have been trained by it"
(Hebrews 12:11).

MONDAY: Read Hebrews 12:5-11. Meditate on God's Word and listen to what He has to say to you. Using the text as a guide, spend time in praise, confession and thanksgiving.

Pray for yourself, to accept correction and discipline from the Lord: Almighty God, I praise You as the loving Father that You are! Please forgive me when I resist Your hand of correction in my life. When You point out sin or disobedience I pray that I would be willing to listen! May I not make light of Your discipline – laughing it off as unimportant – or lose heart when You rebuke me – going off in a corner to pout. Rather, may I see it as it really is…as proof that I am Your child and that You love me (Hebrews 12:5-6). Lord, this reminds me how important it is that I be in Your Word every day so that You can correct me quickly when I go astray. Use Your Holy Spirit to bring conviction where needed and send godly men and women who will speak the truth to me in love. The Bible says, "He who heeds discipline shows the way to life, but whoever ignores correction leads others astray" (Proverbs 10:17). Open my eyes to see that when I ignore your correction in my life it doesn't just affect me. Help me yield to Your training so that my life will produce a harvest of righteousness and peace!

JOURNAL: _____

_____

_____

———❖———

TUESDAY: Read Psalm 94:8-15. Meditate on God's Word and listen to what He has to say to you. Using the text as a guide, spend time in praise, confession and thanksgiving.

Pray for your husband, to accept God's authority and humbly receive His correction: Father, this passage reminds us that as the One who gave us ears and formed our eyes, You hear and see everything that goes on in our lives. On top of that You know everything, including our very thoughts. We fool ourselves when we think we can escape Your notice and do whatever we want without consequence. So I pray for my husband, asking You to give him a fresh awareness of Your omniscience and his responsibility to live under Your authority. "The fear of the Lord is the beginning of knowledge, but fools despise wisdom and discipline" (Proverbs 1:7). Give my husband a humility that makes him hungry for Your Word and willing to yield to Your correction in his life. Bind back the enemy who would deceive him with prideful indignation to continue down a wayward path. "Blessed is the man you discipline, O Lord, the man you teach from your law" (Psalm 94:12). May he see Your hand of discipline on his life for what it really is…Your loving means of protecting him, teaching him, and conforming him into the image of Christ.

JOURNAL: _____

_____

_____

WEDNESDAY: Read I Samuel 2:12-17, 22-25, 27-34; 3:11-14. Meditate on God's Word and listen to what He has to say to you. Using the text as a guide, spend time in praise, confession and thanksgiving.

Pray for yourself and your husband as parents, to administer discipline to your children as God directs: Oh Father what a tragic story! I'm sure that Eli loved his sons, but he made the mistake of failing to discipline them. When Eli heard about their sin he confronted them, but the Bible says, "His sons, however, did not listen to their father's rebuke" (I Samuel 2:25). Instead of following through with discipline, Eli "failed to restrain them" (I Samuel 3:13). His sons continued in their sinful behavior, and as a result, they both died. Dear God, how I pray that my husband and I would never make the same mistake as Eli! Your Word says, "He who spares the rod hates his son, but he who loves him is careful to discipline him" (Proverbs 13:24). We love our children so much that we must discipline them. Please convict us if we are guilty of shirking this responsibility. When our children disobey and need correction, remind us to rebuke them patiently but firmly. If they ignore our rebuke, it is time to lovingly administer discipline. I pray that Your Holy Spirit would be our guide so that we would never discipline too much or too little. May we receive peace and delight (never disgrace!) because we have disciplined our children as You commanded (Proverbs 29:15, 17).

JOURNAL: _____

_____

_____

———≡○○○≡———

THURSDAY: Read Proverbs 13:1, 10, 13, 18. Meditate on God's Word and listen to what He has to say to you. Using the text as a guide, spend time in praise, confession and thanksgiving.

Pray for your children to heed instruction, accept correction and respond to discipline: Lord Jesus, as much as we need wisdom to correctly discipline our children, they need wisdom to listen to us! "A wise son heeds his father's instruction, but a mocker does not listen to rebuke" (Proverbs 13:1). Please convict my children if they mock us behind our backs or show disrespect for our authority in any way. Help them to understand that our words of correction are for their benefit...we don't want to have to discipline them! But when they stubbornly continue down the wrong path, then our discipline is for their good. Your Word says, "He who ignores discipline comes to poverty and shame, but whoever heeds correction is honored" (Proverbs 13:18). Give my children teachable hearts and eyes to see that there is blessing and honor in accepting correction. But even if they harden their hearts and turn away from us when discipline is required, may we stand firm out of love for them. We put our hope in Your Word: "Train a child in the way he should go, and when he is old he will not turn from it" (Proverbs 22:6).

JOURNAL: _____

_____

_____

———≡○○○≡———

FRIDAY: Read Revelation 3:14-19. Meditate on God's Word and listen to what He has to say to you. Using the text as a guide, spend time in praise, confession and thanksgiving.

Pray for your church, to be receptive to the Lord's correction: Lord Jesus, this church in Laodicea was full of lukewarm Christians guilty of indifference, idleness, self-sufficiency and half-hearted service for You. As a result, You declared, "So, because you are lukewarm...I am about to spit you out of My mouth" (Revelation 3:16). But no sooner had You severely corrected them than You spoke these words out of a heart of compassion and concern: "Those whom I love I rebuke and discipline. So be earnest, and repent" (Revelation 3:19). Lord, thank You that You only correct Your children because You love us. And when we are willing to repent, You always welcome us back. "Therefore, this is what the Lord says: "If you repent, I will restore you" (Jeremiah 15:19). So I pray for my church, asking You to show us any way that we have become complacent. If we have become blind or callous to the needs of those around us, rebuke us. If we have made other people or things more important than You, correct us. And when You do, I pray we would bow the knee in repentance out of hearts that love You.

JOURNAL: _____

_____

_____

SATURDAY: A Day of Application

Proverbs 5:12 says: "You will say, "How I hated discipline! How my heart spurned correction!" Is this quote true of you? Do you hate discipline and spurn correction?

_____

Proverbs 3:11-12 says: "My son, do not despise the Lord's discipline and do not resent His rebuke, because the Lord disciplines those He loves, as a father the son he delights in." If you are angry/resentful/hard-hearted toward God because He has corrected you, ask Him to forgive you. Then thank Him that He only disciplines you out of love:

_____

Proverbs 1:23 says: "If you had responded to my rebuke, I would have poured out My heart to you and made my thoughts known to you." Pray and ask the Lord to give you the wisdom to receive His words of correction so that you can grow closer to Him! Write out your prayer here:

_____

_____

SUNDAY: A Day of Praise

Read Psalm 89:30-33.

Praise the Lord for His great mercy and grace! "I will punish their sin...but I will not take My love from him, nor will I ever betray My faithfulness" (Psalm 89:32-33).

WRITE OUT YOUR PRAYER OF PRAISE HERE:

_____

_____

_____

CHECK YOURSELF! WRITE YOUR MEMORY VERSE HERE:

_____

_____

Seeking God's Blessing

"The Lord bless you and keep you; the Lord make His face shine upon you and be gracious to you; the Lord turn His face toward you and give you peace" (Numbers 6:24-26).

BLESSING, ABUNDANT BLESSING

There is an old Irish blessing that says:

"May the road rise up to meet you, may the wind be ever at your back.
May the sun shine warm upon your face and the rain
fall softly on your fields.
And until we meet again, may God hold you
in the hollow of His hand."

What a beautiful picture the words of this blessing conjure up in my mind! I see visions of people living in ease and comfort, in prosperity and protection. I see images of good health, success, and happiness at every turn. I see the very blessings I hope and pray that God will grant in the lives of those I love! I frequently do pray that God would bless my home and keep us safe. I fervently pray that God would bless the work of my husband's hands, that He would bless him with a satisfying job, and that I would be a blessing to him as his wife. I earnestly pray that God would bless my children with godly friendships, bless them in their future marriages, and bless them with good grades or good jobs. We want blessings in our lives!

And do you know what? As much as we long to be blessed, God wants to bless us as well! Not just with earthly blessings, but with spiritual blessings, drawing His children into deeper intimacy with Christ. Numbers 6:24-26 records for us the blessing that the Lord gave Moses to speak over the Israelites during their journey to the Promised Land: "The Lord bless you and keep you; the Lord make His face shine upon you and be gracious to you; the Lord turn His face toward you and give you peace." There have been many times that I have prayed these words over another person, hoping that God would truly bless their lives. But the *Life Application Study Bible* gives further insight into the idea of blessing spoken of in this passage: *"A blessing was one way of asking for God's divine favor to rest upon others. This ancient blessing in these verses helps us understand what a blessing was supposed to do. Its five parts conveyed hope that God would (1) "bless and keep them"- meaning to favor and protect them; (2) "make His face shine upon them" - meaning to be pleased with them; (3) "be gracious to them" - meaning to be merciful and compassionate to them; (4) "turn His face toward them"- meaning to give His approval of them; (5) "give them peace." When you ask God to bless others or yourself, you are asking Him to do these five things."*[9]

I just love this deeper meaning behind asking God's blessing on someone. Not only asking God to bless them with "things," but that He would bless them with His favor, His approval, His pleasure, and His peace. Have you ever stopped to consider that God's approval is a blessing to be asked for? Or that His pleasure in how you live your life is a blessing to be desired? Oh that God would favor my children, blessing them with His attentive care and protection! How I pray that my husband's actions would be pleasing to the Lord, causing His face to shine with delight. May God be merciful and compassionate toward my family, so that when we fall into sin, His grace would cover every offense. My heart's desire is that God would turn His face toward me in approval instead of looking away in shame. And that no matter what crosses our paths today, that His peace would abound. Blessing, abundant blessing!

Memory Verse:
"The Lord bless you and keep you; the Lord make His face shine upon you and be gracious to you; the Lord turn His face toward you and give you peace"
(Numbers 6:24-26).

MONDAY: Read Psalm 115:1-18. Meditate on God's Word and listen to what He has to say to you. Using the text as a guide, spend time in praise, confession and thanksgiving.

Pray for yourself, that you would be rightly related to God and aware of all of His blessings on your life: Oh Father, I praise You as the Living God, not a dead god made by human hands. You are alive, and You think about me and You care for me! I thank You that Your Word says, "He will bless those who fear the Lord – small and great alike" (Psalm 115:13). May I honor You, may I please You, may I prove by my actions that I fear You, so that I will not miss out on any of the blessings You have planned for me! Thank you, Father, for the tremendous gifts You have placed in my life... my family, my health, Your provision, Your protection...were I to count all of my blessings, they would be too many to declare! I know that every single one comes from Your hand and for that, I give You praise. Indeed, I am blessed! On difficult days may I cling to Your Promise that says, "The Lord remembers us and will bless us" (Psalm 115:12). Please help me to keep my eyes on You and trust in You – You are my help and shield (Psalm 115:11).
JOURNAL: _____

_____

_____

———————

TUESDAY: Read Ephesians 3:14-20. Meditate on God's Word and listen to what He has to say to you. Using the text as a guide, spend time in praise, confession and thanksgiving.

Pray for your husband, that God would bless him beyond his greatest expectations: Oh Lord Jesus, thank you for blessing me with my dear husband. How I long for Your blessings on his life...that he would be happy in our home, satisfied in his work, and fulfilled in his life. I pray that out of Your glorious riches You would strengthen my husband with power through Your Spirit, so that Christ may dwell in his heart through faith. I pray that he, "being rooted and established in love, may have power...to grasp how wide and long and high and deep is the love of Christ, and to know this love that surpasses knowledge" (Ephesians 3:16-19). As my husband seeks You first and Your righteousness, may You bless him with the desire of his heart and make all his plans succeed (Psalm 20:4). When difficult things come into his life, would You "turn the curse into a blessing" for him, because You love him (Deuteronomy 23:5). Please Lord, do immeasurably more for my husband than all I can ask or even imagine according to Your power that is at work within him (Ephesians 3:20).

JOURNAL: _____

_____

_____

WEDNESDAY: Read Psalm 128:1-6. Meditate on God's Word and listen to what He has to say to you. Using the text as a guide, spend time in praise, confession and thanksgiving.

Pray for your marriage and for those in your household, asking God for His abundant blessings: Father, how neat to learn that this psalm has been called the "marriage prayer" because it was often sung at Israelite weddings! I truly thank You for my marriage, and I long for each one of the blessings listed in this passage of Scripture. When I look at my children around the dinner table each night, remind me that they are a heritage and a reward from You. "Like arrows in the hands of a warrior are sons born in one's youth. Blessed is the man whose quiver is full of them" (Psalm 127:3-5). So thank You for rewarding us! Help us Father to fear You, to walk in Your ways, and to honor You as the true Head of our home. May my husband and I love each other more every day, and may we always extend unconditional love to our children. I want to be the wife who brings my husband "good, not harm, all the days of her life" (Proverbs 31:12). Please continue to bless our marriage and our household year after year, and allow us to see the prosperity of our land and live to see our children's children (Psalm 128:5-6).

JOURNAL: _____

_____

_____

THURSDAY: Read Isaiah 44:1-5. Meditate on God's Word and listen to what He has to say to you. Using the text as a guide, spend time in praise, confession and thanksgiving.

Pray for your children, to be Spirit-filled and blessed by God: Father, I recognize that my children belong to You. You have entrusted them to me and my husband to raise up for Your kingdom, but they are Yours. It is You who has made them and formed them in the womb (Isaiah 44:2). Thank you for the privilege of being their mother. And while I love them and want only the best for them, it's wonderful to know that You want even better! Your Word says, "If you, then, though you are evil, know how to give good gifts to your children, how much more will Your Father in heaven give good gifts to those who ask" (Matthew 7:11). So I come asking You to pour out Your Spirit on my offspring and Your blessing on my descendants (Isaiah 44:3). I pray that they would grow up healthy and strong, like grass in a meadow and trees by flowing streams. May they be full of the joy that comes only from You, experience Your unconditional love, and be at peace with You and others. And I pray that each of them would live their lives for You, declaring "I belong to the Lord" (Isaiah 44:5).

JOURNAL: _____

_____

_____

FRIDAY: Read Psalm 33:12-22. Meditate on God's Word and listen to what He has to say to you. Using the text as a guide, spend time in praise, confession and thanksgiving.

Pray for your country, to put your hope in God and receive His blessings: Lord, Your Word says, "Blessed is the nation whose God is the Lord" (Psalm 33:12). And there is no denying the fact that we are blessed! Blessed to live in freedom, in prosperity, and in ease, while so many others live in bondage, in poverty and in fear for their lives. May we never take your blessings for granted! Even more than material blessings, Father, I pray for Your spiritual blessings of pleasure and approval on this land. This earth is not the end....You are preparing a Paradise for Your children that is full of blessings we cannot even imagine! Oh may we not miss out on Your very best blessings of all because we were too focused on this earth and worldly pleasures. As You look down from heaven and see us living out our lives on earth, I pray that You would be pleased in everything we do. May we not trust in our own strength, or even in our armies, for they cannot save (Psalm 33:16-17). Rather, we must trust in You: "We wait in hope for the Lord; He is our help and our shield" (Psalm 33:20).

JOURNAL: _____

_____

_____

SATURDAY: A Day of Application

Read Jeremiah 17:5-10.

"I the Lord search the heart and examine the mind, to reward a man according to his conduct, according to what his deeds deserve" (Jeremiah 17:10). Ask God to search your heart and examine your mind. Is your conduct worthy of His reward?

_____

What things do you need to change in order to receive the blessings of God's pleasure and approval on your life?

_____

Pray and ask the Lord to help you trust in Him, so that you will be like the well-watered tree that never fails to bear fruit:

_____

SUNDAY: A Day of Praise

Read Philippians 4:19 & Ephesians 3:20.

Praise God that He is Jehovah Jireh – "the Lord will provide" – this name tells us God is willing and able to meet every need of His people.

WRITE OUT YOUR PRAYER OF PRAISE HERE:

_____

_____

_____

CHECK YOURSELF! WRITE YOUR MEMORY VERSE HERE:

_____

_____

Continuing in Him

"But as for you, continue in what you have
learned and have become convinced of"
(II Timothy 3:14).

PUT IT INTO PRACTICE

Nothing motivates me to get organized, rearrange a room, or launch into a redecorating project like watching one of those home and garden shows on television. In just a short 30-minute segment, those people can dramatically transform a house or backyard and make me think I can do it too! Now, while I know that my husband and I cannot knock out walls, replace carpeting, and tile an entire kitchen in just three days like they manage to pull off on TV, a lot of times I will see a segment that is actually doable... especially the ones on organization. The episodes on organizing kitchens and home offices are particularly intriguing to me, where "stuff" just naturally accumulates, multiplies and takes over. Those organization gurus show you how to set up systems for keeping it all in order: bills, kitchen utensils, toys, paperwork, jewelry, pots and pans, you name it! By the end of the show I am motivated and ready to get started on an organization project of my own, determined to cut the clutter and straighten up. With all those great ideas filling my head, I not only know what to do, but also how to do it!

But here is the problem…just knowing how to get organized, or even just doing it once, is not enough. It is a continual, on-going, day-to-day process. I can have volumes of organizing tips for every room in the house, but my home will never actually be organized unless I put all that great information into practice. And it definitely won't stay organized unless I determine to continue in what I have learned. It angers me when I have spent hours organizing an area, only to find it cluttered again because I have lapsed into old habits and failed to put things away correctly. In order for those organizing tips to make any lasting difference, I must implement what I have learned and then stick with it.

In just the same way, dear sister, we must be very intentional in our devotion to the Lord. We must determine to spend time with Him, every day. We must consistently practice what we have learned about spiritual discipline if it is to have any lasting value for us. The very fact that you are reading these words means that you have stayed with this devotional book for the entire year. And for that, I am honored! It is my hope that time alone with the Lord has become a permanent part of your daily routine. It is my prayer that you have enjoyed frequent times of praise, confession and thanksgiving to Him. I am anxious to know just how many of these verses of Scripture you were faithful to "hide in your heart" and how many times the Lord has spoken them back to you. By using the pre-written prayers in this book I hope you have learned how to pray God's Word back to Him and have made prayer an utmost priority. I am certain God has changed you as you have been obedient to apply His Word to every part of your life.

But just because you are at the end of this book, it does not mean you are finished. "But as for you, continue in what you have learned and have become convinced of" (II Timothy 3:14). As you have become convinced of the wonderful privilege and necessity of spending time with God in prayer, now it is your turn to put into practice some of the things you have learned. The prayers for this final lesson will be of your own making. I have provided the Scripture passages, but it is up to you to formulate the prayers. Choose verses that speak to you and pray these verses back to the Lord. You can do it. I promise.

"And now, dear children, continue in Him, so that when He appears we may be confident and unashamed before Him at His coming" (I John 2:28).

———— ⊶⊷ ————

Memory Verse:
"But as for you, continue in what you have learned and have become convinced of" (II Timothy 3:14).

———— ⊶⊷ ————

MONDAY: Read Matthew 7:24-27. Meditate on God's Word and listen to what He has to say to you. Using the text as a guide, spend time in praise, confession and thanksgiving.

Pray for yourself to be a wise woman, who hears the words of God and puts them into practice: (also use Ezekiel 33:31)

_____

_____

_____

_____

_____

_____

TUESDAY: Read Hebrews 11:23-27. Meditate on God's Word and listen to what He has to say to you. Using the text as a guide, spend time in praise, confession and thanksgiving.

Pray for your husband, to persevere in his faith till the end, always looking ahead to his reward: (also use II Chronicles 15:7)

_____

_____

_____

_____

_____

_____

WEDNESDAY: Read Colossians 2:6-13. Meditate on God's Word and listen to what He has to say to you. Using the text as a guide, spend time in praise, confession and thanksgiving.

Pray for those in your household, to continue following Christ and not be led astray: (use Philippians 3:14 also)

_____

_____

_____

_____

_____

_____

THURSDAY: Read James 1:22-25. Meditate on God's Word and listen to what He has to say to you. Using the text as a guide, spend time in praise, confession and thanksgiving.

Pray for your children, to not merely listen to God's Word but to do what it says: (also use Philippians 4:9)

_____

_____

_____

_____

_____

_____

FRIDAY: Read Revelation 2:1-7. Meditate on God's Word and listen to what He has to say to you. Using the text as a guide, spend time in praise, confession and thanksgiving.

Pray for your church, to learn from the church in Ephesus - to be known for hard work and perseverance till the end; to not forsake your "first love": (also use James 1:4)

_____

_____

_____

_____

_____

_____

SATURDAY: A Day of Application

Read I Kings 8:23-24.

Spend some time thanking the Lord that He keeps His promises... especially His promise of unconditional love! Write out your prayer of thanksgiving here:

_____

_____

Verse 23 says that God keeps His covenant of love with those who continue wholeheartedly in His way.

Write out your prayer of commitment to "continue wholeheartedly" in His way all the days of your life:

_____

_____

_____

_____

SUNDAY: A Day of Praise

Read John 17:25-26.

Praise the Lord Jesus who makes the Father known to us! Thank Him for this awesome privilege – that we really can <u>know</u> God!

WRITE OUT YOUR PRAYER OF PRAISE HERE:

_____

_____

_____

CHECK YOURSELF! WRITE YOUR MEMORY VERSE HERE:

_____

_____

A Final Word

As I have searched through Scripture to pray over each of these devotionals, I have discovered something I call the "overlap principle" in God's Word. Each biblical virtue is not mutually exclusive of the others...they are intertwined and overlap. For example, when praying for a greater love for others, an emerging pattern of kindness and compassion naturally follows. As we intercede for lost loved ones, the desire to be a bold witness is born. As we ask God to cultivate patience in our lives, He uncovers fleshly tendencies like pride and selfishness that need to be dealt with first. As we seek to obey God in every area of our lives, He reveals a lack of submission and the desire to be in control. Do you see what I mean? It was often difficult to stay focused on just one topic because each biblical virtue has close ties to so many others.

But isn't that the way it <u>should</u> be? When Christ comes into someone's heart, He should be given the freedom to infiltrate every single part of that person's life! As the believer permits Him access to one area, another area in need of attention is revealed. And as we pursue Him with intention, not content with just a little of God but determined to know Him more, He allows us to find Him in ways we never thought possible!

As we finish this journey together, it is my prayer that we would both be willing to continue to open our lives up to God, daily allowing Him to conform us more and more into the image of His Son. And when that long-awaited day finally arrives, "He will transform our lowly bodies so that they will be like His glorious body" (Philippians 3:21). Come quickly, Lord Jesus, come!

Notes

1 Taken from *Streams in the Desert* by Mrs. Chas. E. Cowman. Copyright © 1945 by The Oriental Missionary Society. Use by permission of Zondervan. www.zondervan.com

2 Reprinted by permission. "*Jesus Calling*, Sarah Young, 2004, Thomas Nelson Inc. Nashville, Tennessee. All rights reserved."

3 Taken from *The Five Silent Years of Corrie Ten Boom* by Pamela Rosewell. Copyright © 1986 by The Zondervan Corporation. Use by permission of Zondervan. www.zondervan.com

4 J.M. Barrie, *Peter Pan and Wendy* (UK: Hodder & Stoughton, 1911; US: Charles Scribner's Sons, 1911)

5 For more information about *Moms in Prayer* or to find a group in your area, please visit their website: www.MomsInPrayer.org

6 Spice for Living ®
PO Box 25575
Scottsdale, AZ 85255
480-419-7379
website: spice4living.com
email: spiceforliving@cox.net
GREAT GIFTS, FUNDRAISER, GIVEAWAYS, ETC.

7 Taken from *Life Application Study Bible*, NIV, Zondervan (footnote on Proverbs 31:10-31) Copyright © 1978 by The Zondervan Corporation. Use by permission of Zondervan. www.zondervan.com

8 Taken from *My Utmost for His Highest* by Oswald Chambers, © 1935 by Dodd Mead & Co., renewed © 1963 by the Oswald Chambers Publications Assn., Ltd. Used by permission of Discovery House Publishers, Grand Rapids MI 49501. All rights reserved.

9 Taken from Life *Application Study Bible*, NIV, Zondervan (footnote on Numbers 6:24-26) Copyright © 1978 by The Zondervan Corporation. Use by permission of Zondervan. www.zondervan.com

Made in the USA
Lexington, KY
28 March 2013